Environmental Governance of Invasive Species

The consequences of the introduction and spread of invasive alien species in non-native ecosystems is an area of growing interest for international policymakers and regulators. Globalisation has increased the rate and magnitude of biological invasions, resulting in huge environmental, economic and social costs. Until recently, the effectiveness of international efforts to provide a coordinated response to the threat of alien invasions has been limited. This book considers the existing Multilateral Environmental Agreements and looks at the potential role of regional environmental governance, particularly in consideration of the adoption of the European Parliament and Council regulation 1143/2014 on the management and control of invasive species, to provide an effective response to this global threat.

Donato Gualtieri is a Post-Doctoral Fellow in EU Administrative Law at the Department of Management, University of Turin (Italy).

Routledge Research in International Environmental Law

www.routledge.com/Routledge-Research-in-International-Environmental-Law/book-series/INTENVLAW

Common Pools of Genetic Resources
Equity and Innovation in International Biodiversity Law
Edited by Evanson Chege Kamau and Gerd Winter

International Climate Change Law and Policy
Cultural Legitimacy in Adaption and Mitigation
Edited by Thoko Kaime

International Liability Regime for Biodiversity Damage
The Nagoya-Kuala Lumpur Supplementary Protocol
Edited by Akiho Shibata

The Precautionary Principle in Marine Environmental Law
With Special Reference to High Risk Vessels
Bénédicte Sage-Fuller

International Environmental Law and Distributive Justice
The Equitable Distribution of CDM Projects under the Kyoto Protocol
Tomilola Akanle Eni-Ibukun

Environmental Governance in Europe and Asia
A Comparative Study of Institutional and Legislative Frameworks
Jona Razzaque

Climate Change, Forests and REDD
Lessons for Institutional Design
Edited by Joyeeta Gupta, Nicolien van der Grijp and Onno Kuik

International Environmental Law and the Conservation of Coral Reefs
Edward J. Goodwin

Environmental Governance of Invasive Species
An EU Perspective
Donato Gualtieri

Environmental Governance of Invasive Species

An EU Perspective

Donato Gualtieri

Routledge
Taylor & Francis Group
LONDON AND NEW YORK

First published 2018
by Routledge

2 Park Square, Milton Park, Abingdon, Oxfordshire OX14 4RN
52 Vanderbilt Avenue, New York, NY 10017

Routledge is an imprint of the Taylor & Francis Group, an informa business

First issued in paperback 2019

British Library Cataloguing-in-Publication Data
A catalogue record for this book is available from the British Library

Library of Congress Cataloging-in-Publication Data
A catalog record for this book has been requested

ISBN: 978-1-138-29299-4 (hbk)
ISBN: 978-0-367-88674-5 (pbk)

Typeset in ITC Galliard
by Apex CoVantage, LLC

In loving memory of my father, Romualdo Gualtieri.
A man who gave body and soul to the words “dignity” and “courage”.
To my mother, for her silent example. To my wife, for her relentless support.

Contents

Acknowledgements

This book never would have seen the light of day without the continuous feedback and precious advice from my supervisor at the University of Pavia, Professor Giulia Rossolillo, the linguistic editing by Dr Stephen Phillips, and the relentless work and dedication by the amazing staff at Routledge and Apex CoVantage (Rob Gibson, Siobhán Poole, Hannah Lovelock, Katherine Wetzel and Renata Corbani).

My deepest gratitude to the Coordinator of the Doctoral School, Professor Cristina Campiglio, for having given me the chance to freely follow my path and aspirations, as well as to Professor Piercarlo Rossi and Professor Carola Ricci for the support offered to my work as a post-doc researcher.

Thanks to all the colleagues, professors and experts who honoured me with insightful remarks and critical comments both in Pavia and in a number of different conferences around the world, and particularly to my fellow members in the World Commission on Environmental Law at the IUCN.

Finally, a grateful thought to John and Anne Jacobs – dear friends and "adjunct" parents during my period as a Visiting Doctoral Student at the University of Waikato – as well as to my in-laws, Margherita and Giorgio, and to all my friends for supporting me when I was without my family.

Tables

Acronyms and abbreviations

Adv Ecol Res	*Advances in Ecological Research*
Afr Aff	*African Affairs*
Agr Ecosyst Environ	*Agriculture, Ecosystem and Environment*
AJPSIR	*African Journal of Political Science and International Relations*
Am J Sociol	*American Journal of Sociology*
Ardeola	
ASEAN	Association of the South East Asian Nations
Biol Control	*Biological Control*
BioScience	*BioScience*
Biol Inv	*Biological Invasions*
Boston College Int Comp Law Rev	*Boston College International and Comparative Law Review*
CBD	Convention on Biological Diversity
CEC	Commission on Environmental Cooperation
CFSP	Common Foreign and Security Policy
CITES	Convention on International Trade of Endangered Species of Wild Flora and Fauna
CJEC	Court of Justice of the European Communities
CJEU	Court of Justice of the European Union
CMS	Convention on the Conservation of Migratory Species of Wild Animals
Conserv Lett	*Conservation Letters*
COP	Conference of Parties
COREPER	Committee of Permanent Representatives
Crop Prot	*Crop Protection*
CFREU	Charter of Fundamental Rights of the European Union

DAISIE	Delivering Alien Invasive Species Inventory for Europe
Diversity Distrib	Diversity and Distributions
DPSIR	Driving forces-Pressure-State-Impact-Response
EAC	East African Community
EAEC	European Atomic Energy Community
EAP	Environmental Action Programme
EC	European Community
EDG	Directorate General for Environment
Ecol Appl	*Ecological Applications*
Ecol Econ	*Ecological Economics*
Ecol Law Q	*Ecology Law Quarterly*
Ecology	*Ecology*
ECSC	European Carbon and Steel Community
EEA	European Environmental Agency
EEC	European Economic Community
EEEL Rev	*European Energy and Environmental Law Review*
EESC	European Economic and Social Committee
EFSA	European Food Safety Authority
EFSA Journal	*European Food Safety Authority Journal*
ELR	*Erasmus Law Review*
ENVI	Committee on Environment, Public Health and Food Safety of the European Parliament
Environ Manage	*Environmental Management*
Envtl L & Pol'y J	*Environs: Environmental Law and Policy Journal*
ESEU	*Environmental Sciences Europe*
EU	European Union
FAO	Food and Agriculture Organisation
Front Ecol Environ	*Frontiers in Ecology and the Environment*
Geo Int'l Envtl L Rev	*Georgetown International Environmental Law Review*
Geo L J	*Georgetown Law Journal*
GIGA Working Papers	German Institute of Global and Area Studies Working Papers
GISP	Global Invasive Species Programme
Global Environ Polit	*Global Environmental Politics*
Hist J	*Historical Journal*
ICJ	International Court of Justice

IISD	*International Institute for Sustainable Development*
ILC	International Law Commission of the United Nations
IEEP	Institute for European Environmental Policy
IMPEL	European Network for the Implementation and Enforcement of Environmental Law
Int Aff	*International Affairs*
IPPC	International Plant Protection Convention
ISPM	International Standards on Phytosanitary Measures
ISSG	Invasive Species Specialist Group
IUCN	International Union for the Conservation of Nature
J Appl Ecol	*Journal of Applied Ecology*
J Bacteriol	*Journal of Bacteriology*
J Common Mark Stud	*Journal of Common Market Studies*
J Econ Entomol	*Journal of Economic Entomology*
JED	*Journal of Environment and Development*
J Plant Pathol	*Journal of Plant Pathology*
LIFE	*L'Instrumment Financier pour l'Environnement*
Local Env	*Local Environment*
Mamm Rev	*Mammal Review*
Millennium J Int Stud	*Millennium, Journal of International Studies*
NAFTA	North American Free Trade Agreement
NGO	Non-Governmental Organisation
Norweg J Agr Sci	*Norwegian Journal of Agricultural Sciences*
NYIL	*Netherlands Yearbook of International Law*
OECD	Organisation for Economic Cooperation and Development
PJCCM	Police and Judicial Cooperation in Criminal Matters
PPP	Polluter Pays Principle
OQDS	Olive Quick Decline Syndrome
SEA	Single European Act
TEC	Treaty establishing the European Community

TEEC	Treaty establishing the European Economic Community
TEU	Treaty on the European Union
TFEU	Treaty on the Functioning of the European Union
UNCED	United Nations Commission on Environment and Development
UNEP	United Nations Environmental Programme
U Pa J Int'l L	*University of Pennsylvania Journal of International Law*
Utrecht L Rev	*Utrecht Law Review*
Yale Law J	*Yale Law Journal*
YEEL	*Yearbook of European Environmental Law*
World Today	*The World Today*
WFD	Water Framework Directive
WWF	World Wide Fund for Nature
ZUR	*Zeitschrift für Umweltrecht*

Introduction

On 29 September 2014, representatives of the 28 Member States of the European Union – gathered in the 334th meeting of the Council in its General Affairs composition – approved the proposal for a regulation on the management and control of the impact and spread of invasive alien species, as amended by the European Parliament in its plenary session of 16 April 2014.

Following publication in the *Official Journal of the European Union* (OJEU), the regulation entered into force on 1 January 2015.

The scarce level of interest paid by both the public opinion and the mass media to the regulatory intervention by European institutions and Member States appears questionable when taking into account the increasing presence of non-native species within the European territory: among the over 12,000 living organisms which have been found to be alien to the European environment, 10–15% have in fact reproduced and spread to an extent that has caused environmental, economic and social damage. As such, invasive alien species are the second cause of biodiversity loss and species extinction; moreover, they can be vectors of diseases or directly cause health problems, damage infrastructures and recreational facilities, hamper forestry activities and cause agricultural losses. The annual cost of prevention, control and eradication within the borders of the European Union is estimated by the European Environmental Agency (EEA) to be €12 billion.

Nevertheless, there are reasons for which the silence accompanying the approval of the regulation is far from surprising: invasive alien species often operate at a micro-level within host ecosystems, and the consequences of biological invasions on everyday life can be measured – in the greatest majority of cases – in decades. Nor has the occurrence of the event been characterised by a disrupting discontinuity with respect to the past.

Indeed, the difficult relationship that exists between human beings and invasive species is not an exclusive feature of modern times. As early as 73 A.D. Pliny the Elder in his *Naturalis Historia* reported on the severe problems experienced by Roman troops in controlling and eventually eradicating an invasion of rabbits in the Balearic Islands. Throughout the centuries, then, the phenomenon has unceasingly shaped the biological, economic and social scenario. A particularly significant episode in European history testifying to the adverse effects of the introduction of non-native living organisms has been the "potato famine" in the 19th century. The famine was caused by the *Phytophthora infestans* – a fungus native to Mexico which reached Ireland through a shipment of potatoes from the United States, and it produced economic and social consequences in terms of emigration, as well as changes to agricultural methods.

This was a paradigmatic case in which a biological invasion has been facilitated – and, to a certain extent – determined by human agency. In fact, since the 19th century the Industrial Revolution has increased the transoceanic and transcontinental movement of people and goods, thus giving exotic species unparalleled opportunities to overcome those natural barriers which for millennia have impeded the spread of living organisms beyond their natural range of dispersal. Besides the quantitative aspect, the dramatic growth in the seriousness of social, health and economic consequences has added a highly innovative profile to the phenomenon. Indeed, the observation of the hazardous effects of biological invasions has progressively led national and international policy-makers to take a regulatory intervention into consideration and, subsequently, to enact legal responses.

Having its focus on the international side of the normative production, this work strives to fill a gap in the relevant literature. Mirrored by a substantial absence at the regulatory level, a great number of the studies on the regulatory tools on invasive alien species deal either with the national or universal plan, thus downplaying the potential role of regional organisations. In this respect, regulation 1143/2014 – though likely to remain for a long time the only attempt at solving the issue at the regional level, in consideration of the peculiarities of the European integration process – has the potential to pave the way for future developments in other areas of the world.

The first two chapters of this study set the theoretical background by clarifying the object of the research, presenting the global legal and regulatory framework with its many gaps, overlaps and inconsistencies and, finally, trying to find an alternative in regional environmental governance. The second part of the dissertation, in turn, analyses the environmental side of European law, with a particular focus on the protection of biological diversity and on regulation 1143/2014.

The study begins by clarifying the object of the research by providing a comprehensive definition of "invasive alien species", combining both ecological and legal elements. Subsequently, the first chapter examines the centrality of biological invasions in the contemporary scientific, academic and regulatory panorama by applying the DPSIR model – an analytical tool elaborated by the European Environmental Agency (EEA) – in order to highlight invasive species' pressures on the state of the environment. Having determined the impact of biological invasions, the chapter concludes by taking a closer look at the human-led responses, focused on the so-called three-tier approach (prevention, control and eradication of invasive species) recommended at the international level by the Sixth Conference of Parties to the Convention on Biological Diversity held in The Hague in 2002.

The accent posed on the role of international organisations in formulating a response to invasive alien species is, in this sense, an ideal bridge to the second chapter, which looks at the abundant production of international legal instruments aimed at halting biological invasions. This regulatory scenario can be interpreted as a result of pressures increasingly coming from environmentalist groups on the one hand, and of the specialisation of the *ius gentium* in a multiplex unity of sectorial *leges specialis* on the other. If observed under the lenses of effectiveness, however, such a hypertrophic normative production has favoured a fragmented approach to the question without ensuring a greater level of environmental protection. The chapter seeks to address the causes of this overall failure by referring to a bi-dimensional matrix of ineffectiveness. At a more superficial level, the existence of gaps, overlaps and inconsistencies is a powerful driver of operational inefficiency. As for the root causes, transboundary phenomena – such as biological invasions – cannot be easily framed within the current Westphalian system of international relations, inextricably linking legal production, judicial enforcement and territoriality. The envisaged alternative is to decouple the ultimate regulative authority from territorial sovereignty as a way to attain environmental protection against invasive alien species at the regional level through the agency of multilateral, independent institutions.

In this sense, regional environmental governance offers a greater chance to succeed as it provides a more homogeneous polity and a shared system of values, principles and norms. After having set the theoretical and historical foundations of regionalism, the chapter presents this type of international organisation as a paramount actor in environmental governance. Such a perspective is reinforced under the neoregionalist interpretative paradigm, capable of combining the geographical and functional notions of territory. In conclusion, the second chapter sketches out – with practical examples – the five successive steps of environmental regionalisation in a continuum going from cooperation to integration.

On the theoretical basis laid out on the first two chapters, the third chapter describes the European Union as the only contemporary example of a regional organisation pursuing factual and comprehensive integration, or – to use the words of Weiler – as "one of the most remarkable political metamorphoses of modern times" (Weiler, 1991). Such unique features are particularly prominent if considered from the environmental standpoint. In recent decades, in fact, European institutions have been gradually vested with competences and regulatory powers as ecological concerns were transformed into policy priorities through a process called "spill over". After the identification of the temporal coordinates determining the development of a European-wide environmental policy – from the initial abstention to the signing of the European Single Act (1987) and until the approval of the Treaty of Lisbon (2007) – the chapter analyses its general principles and objectives, together with the exact balance of competences within the European institutions and between those supranational bodies and Member States. It is observed that thanks to the primacy of Union law and the binding value of its legal acts the European regional framework provides a strong institutional apparatus and a new legal order. In conclusion, the chapter introduces a specific analysis of the action of the Union in the field of the protection of biodiversity in general, and of biological invasions in particular. Specifically, after having presented the situation of biological invasions in the European territory and the rationale for EU interventions, the work looks at the "exogenous factors" which have progressively introduced the question of invasive alien species within community law, as well as to the "endogenous" reflexes of such a regulatory pressure, with particular regard to the cornerstones of the European policy against biological invasions until the approval of the dedicated regulation: the *Birds* directive (1979) and the *Habitats* directive (1992). Besides that, the analysis of other significant acts – which are, however, confined to regulatory niches related to individual species or ecosystems – reveals the existence of many gaps and paves the way to a more comprehensive legal tool aimed at addressing the phenomenon of biological invasions as a whole. In this sense, the fourth and final chapter illustrates the contents of the proposal made by the Commission and the legislative *iter* followed by the *sui generis* Union's bicameral system – formed by the European Parliament and by the Council – towards the adoption of regulation 1143/2014. The final paragraph of the chapter evaluates the strengths and weaknesses of the act, together with threats and opportunities deriving from such a regulatory intervention by the European Union.

Bibliography

Weiler, J.H.H. (1991), The transformation of Europe in *Yale Law J* 100: 2403–2483.

1 Background information on biological invasions

SUMMARY: 1.1. Introduction – 1.2. Preliminary clarifications: definitions and key terms – 1.3. Analysing biological invasions under the lenses of the DPSIR model (a. At the roots of biological invasions: pressures exerted by driving forces; b. Impacts of invasive alien species on the state of natural and human environment; c. The role of policy-makers in response to biological invasions) – 1.4. Is there a role for supranational environmental regulation?

1.1 Introduction

Centuries-old olive trees dried up with rotting leaves, trunks flaked off, in a region which has shaped its landscape, history, cultural identity and economic welfare around a symbiotic relationship with those plants. *Olea europaea* covers 60% of the entire territory of the Salento peninsula in the southern region of Apulia (Italy), and ensures an average annual production of 3,000,000 quintals of olives (30% of the national total) and 500,000 quintals of olive oil (80% of the national total).

According to studies by the European Commission and the European Food Safety Authority (European Commission, 2015; EFSA, 2015a; EFSA, 2015b), the bacterium *Xylella fastidiosa*, in its subspieces *pauca*, has, since 2013, infected around 10% of the 11 million autochthonous olive trees with the so-called Olive Quick Decline Syndrome (OQDS)[1] In the short span of three years 1,600 plants have already been eradicated in order to contain the impact of the disease to a limited area, and there exists a climate of escalating tension between the European Commission, national authorities and local environmental NGOs and farmers associations.[2]

The pathogen proliferates in the lymph-conducting vessels of leaves and causes the obstruction of xylematic veins, ultimately blocking the plant's nutrition and leading to a series of alterations. Younger plants (around 50–60 years of age) suffer from withering and desiccation of scattered shoots and small branches; in centenarian trees consequences are far more serious, as the symptoms extend to the rest of the canopy and ultimately lead to structural collapses (Cariddi et al., 2014).

Native to Costa Rica (where a ST53 twin-strain has caused diseases in oleanders, mango and macadamia nuts), this particular strain of *Xylella fastidiosa* has been introduced to Europe through trade in ornamental plants: the most likely hypothesis postulates that the bacterium has entered Europe via the port of Rotterdam, the main continental access point for different varieties of plants native to Central and South America. It is possible that the pathogen infiltrated some coffee plants, healthy carriers of the bacterium where its presence is totally asymptomatic, and then reached Salento as a "hitchhiker" of the Meadow froghopper (*Philaenus spumarius*), an insect already identified as a vector of many *Xylella*-related diseases, such as Pierce's disease in many Californian vineyards (Purcell, 1980).[3] Once introduced, *Xylella fastidiosa* found a particularly suitable environment for its reproduction and establishment, as emphasised by the report issued by the EFSA in January 2015 (EFSA, 2015a). Climatic and biological factors have particularly facilitated the uncontrolled spread of the bacterium: from the first standpoint, it is very likely that the pathogen thrived in a region where the summer climate is torrid while winters are generally mild and humid (Hoodle, 2004) As for the biologic factor, no competing species (i.e. other microbes) are as yet known to displace *Xylella fastidiosa*, while its natural enemies (i.e. specific bacteriophages) are geographically contained to North America (Summer et al., 2010; Ahern et al., 2014), or can only attack the vector with limited effects in terms of control (Waloff, 1980; Ceresa-Gastaldo and Chiappini, 1994; Eilenberg et al., 2001). Still, the EFSA report gives a solid rationale for considering this case of biological invasions as a priority matter for the European Union (EU), with particular reference to its environmental and socio-economic impact:

> the overall potential consequences . . . in the European continent are rated as major considering the severe losses on olive in the Apulian outbreak. . . . In commercial crops, when conditions are suitable for symptom expression and efficient vectors are present, yield losses and damage would be high and imply costly control measures. The disease also has a negative social impact since it is not readily controllable in smallholdings and family gardens. . . . In addition to those elements, the use of insecticide may have environmental impacts.
>
> (EFSA, 2015a)

Given these considerations, this extreme southeastern offshoot of Italy is currently both a privileged viewpoint and one of the most recent cases of biological invasion, a phenomenon generally characterised by "a species' acquiring a competitive advantage following the disappearance of natural obstacles to its proliferation, which allows it to spread rapidly and to conquer novel areas within recipient ecosystems in which it becomes a dominant population" (Valery et al., 2008).

This chapter primarily aims at providing an exhaustive yet synthetic overview of the main aspects of biological invasions. In this sense, a first necessary step is the exact determination of what invasive alien species are: an enquiry on the biological and legal meaning of relevant terms helps to piece together a univocal and coherent bio-legal definition. Subsequently, the use of the DPSIR (Driving forces-Pressure-State-Impact-Response) model – a causal framework elaborated by the European Environmental Agency (EEA) in the 1990s – shows how biological invasions find their primary cause in the progressively expanding role of human agency, conceived as a multi-level combination of driving forces which exerts pressures on nature. A closer look at policy responses to biological invasions emphasises the role of a three-tier approach focused on prevention, control and eradication of invasive species and the need for a multilateral response capable of transcending national borders in order to achieve a multi-level regulation, the effectiveness of which will be analysed in greater detail in the next chapter.

1.2 Preliminary clarifications: definitions and key terms

Broadening the picture with respect to the case of *Xylella fastidiosa*, the occurrence of a biological invasion is far from exceptional. The phenomenon regards – to a greater or lesser extent – all taxonomic groups and biological realms in almost every region of the world. Virtually no ecosystem can be considered safe from the vast array of threats invasive alien species pose, not only to the environment but also to human health and socio-economic well-being. Such threats often exceed national borders and capacities. It is thus not difficult to understand why a domain once reserved for natural scientists has gradually become a central issue in national and international law and policy-making.

Before analysing the legal and political framework in greater detail it seems useful to provide some background information on biological invasions, beginning with the identification of key terms and the formulation of a comprehensive definition of the expression "invasive alien species". Indeed, many definitions have been stratified over the decades thanks to the relentless interest of conservationists and biologists on the matter. Nevertheless, this semantic abundance has been at the source of many ambiguities and misconceptions at a time when such a delicate and multi-faceted issue has become an object of regulatory intervention. Ambiguities are also related to the different outcomes of natural and legal research: the first, in fact, is more oriented to investigate the causes of a phenomenon; the latter, in turn, is particularly focused on the effects and possible remedies of a fact. In this sense, it would be useful to streamline and condense in standard, coherent, comprehensive *bio-legal* definitions the complex ecological processes which lie underneath biological invasions.

A preliminary clarification as regards the definition of what a "species" is can be found in the Guidelines for the Prevention of Biodiversity Loss caused by Invasive Alien Species, developed in 2000 by the International Union for the Conservation of Nature (IUCN). The Guidelines offer a comprehensive explanation which satisfies both scientific precision and legal certainty, as they are defined as "subspecies and lower taxa, as well as any part, gametes, seeds, eggs or propagule of such species that might survive and subsequently reproduce" (SSC-ISSG, 2000). In fact, the process of biological invasion – and its related damages – can be caused not only by species, but also by lower taxonomic units. Once identified as the object of the research, it is of paramount importance to understand the meaning of the adjectives "alien" and "invasive". Even though the commonly accepted expression is "invasive alien species", a species becomes "alien" at first and "invasive" later.

The term "alien" has been officially introduced at the international level through Article 8(h) of the Convention on Biological Diversity (CBD), obliging each Contracting Party to prevent "as far as possible and as appropriate . . . the introduction of, control or eradicate those alien species which threaten ecosystems, habitats or species". Furthermore, the Guiding Principles for the Prevention, Introduction and Mitigation of Impacts of Invasive Alien Species, developed by the Subsidiary Body on Scientific, Technical and Technological Advice in the framework of the Convention on Biological Diversity in 2000, use the word "alien" as encompassing a series of expressions (such as "non-native", "exotic", "foreign", "new") employed to identify species found outside their "normal distribution". In 2002, in turn, Decision VI/23 of the Conference of Parties to the CBD changed the definition to "species occurring outside its natural past or present distribution". This concept is both temporal and spatial, as it includes the past and present range of distribution of a species, on the one hand, and its dispersal potential, on the other. However, such an apparently precise definition risks being "poorly-suited" to regulatory purposes for two main reasons (Shine et al., 2000). On the one hand, the concept of "natural distribution" better corresponds to ecological than political boundaries. This constitutes a source of difficult employability of the concept in legal reasoning, as law-making follows jurisdictional – i.e. artificial – boundaries rather than natural ones. On the other hand, there are many cases in which it is not possible to determine if species are native to a certain area, have arrived there through their own natural dispersal abilities, or have been pushed beyond those limits in the near or remote past thanks to human assistance. A possible solution to such an insidious dilemma is to focus the analysis on the role played by human agency in the relevant process of introduction of a given species in a particular ecosystem. For many centuries, in fact, the spread of non-native organisms inside a host region has been a totally natural phenomenon, whose dimensions were limited by entirely ecological factors. Many species had, in fact, very reduced dispersal abilities and could not travel for long distances; at the same time, rivers, mountains and oceans provided insurmountable barriers to the diffusion of living organisms beyond their usual ranges. Similarly, the pathways of introduction were entirely natural: ocean currents, winds, earth movements and continental shifts (Shine, 2008). In brief, introductions respected millennial mechanisms called to protect the environmental balance, and changes occurred at an utterly gradual speed (Shine, 2008). The phenomenon of biological invasions became global with the so-called "Age of Discoveries", which lasted from the early 15th century to the end of the 17th century. The dislocation of alien species over long distances and beyond natural borders was, indeed, a logical complement of transoceanic trade and of the settlement of overseas colonies by many of the European powers. After the discovery of the American continent, the process of species dispersal accelerated, acquiring uncontrolled and sometimes dangerous characteristics: the so-called Columbian Exchange – defined by the environmental historian Alfred W. Crosby as a phenomenon of ecological imperialism (Crosby, 1986) – allowed many Eurasian species to invade the New World, often with devastating impacts. With the differentiation of global routes of exchange in recent decades, a quantitatively higher and geographically wider volume of human beings and manufactured goods started to spread, while at the same time the increase in the efficacy and use of rapid means of transport made distances shorter and borders more porous. New pathways of introduction have been set up, and the flow of the introductions ceased to be unidirectional. As an example, one of the most active global pathways currently is the "Pacific hallway" between Asia and North America.

Human agency thus plays a primary role in defining the *magna divisio* between "native" and "alien" species, provided that the adjective "native" is intended here in biological terms to indicate a species evolved in a particular habitat, or grown elsewhere but autonomously arrived in a region. At the same time, however, the intervention of humans is not a sufficient condition to turn an "alien" into an "invasive" species, intended as a population of introduced individuals which succeed in colonising their host environment by establishing a significant population capable of resisting the initial threat of extinction and, subsequently, to maintain itself without further human intervention through a process of assimilation, or naturalisation, to their new bioregion. However, this course of events is extremely unlikely: the overall rate of successful introductions – meaning the total percentage of introduced species which succeed in becoming established – is actually quite low, as much as the possibility that established species may become capable of spreading and becoming invasive (Keller et al., 2011).

In the late 1980s, Di Castri estimated that only 10% of alien species could survive introductions in new habitats, and that the likelihood of a surviving species successfully out-competing native populations and thriving in the new location could be estimated at around 20–30%. In absolute terms, then, the actual possibilities of a successful biological invasion were considered to be less than 3% (Di Castri, 1989). In 1996, Williamson and Fitter proposed the "tens rule", holding that only 10% of alien species survive introductions to new habitats, with a 10% likelihood that a surviving species could succeed in out-competing native populations and thrive in the new location (Williamson and Fitter, 1996). Since then, scholarship has gradually agreed on two main facts: on the one hand, such a figure was absolutely underestimated; on the other, it is very difficult to have a single percentage on invasions, since each species has a peculiar degree of invasiveness. Later studies on vertebrate invasions in Europe and North America conducted in 2005 by Jeschke and Strayer suggested that the overall rate of successful introduction and spread might be comprised in a wide confidence interval from 5% to 75% for each of the steps of the process (Jeschke and Strayer, 2005). Overall, and from a rigorous biological standpoint, only a fraction of "alien" species is entitled to be called "invasive" as a result of the combination of four factors: a high reproduction rate, which allows invasive species to rapidly colonise their new habitat; the ability to tolerate a wide range of environmental conditions; a generalist attitude towards alimentation, in a way to take advantage of a variety of resources; the lack of natural predators in the new environment; and/or the presence of an ecological niche that the species is able to fill.

Once a species is classified as "invasive", it is also important to determine the stage of the invasion: according to Colautti and McIsaac this classification is deeply influenced by the distribution and abundance of the non-native species, considered as individual populations and not at a more aggregate level. In this sense, there are five stages in an invasion process, from stage 0, where propagules are still present in the native area of a potential invader, to stage 5, when invasive species are widespread and dominant in a host environment. Each stage is reached as soon as the non-native species has overcome a barrier to its introduction and diffusion (Colautti and McIsaac, 2004). A more detailed categorisation defines three subsequent phases in the invasion process: a "lag phase", which starts with the arrival of a numerically irrelevant number of non-native species in a new habitat and ends with the elimination or naturalisation of the species; the "expansion phase", characterised by an increase in the abundance and geographical distribution of the species in the host environment; and a "persistence phase", in which the invasive species succeeds in occupying all favourable habitats (Boudouresque et al., 2005).

Finally, an important element in the definition of the content of the expression "invasive" is the degree of dangerousness of the species. The already mentioned CBD Guiding Principles define the concept of invasiveness with reference to the possible damages to the biological diversity of the host ecosystem. In particular, " 'invasive alien species' means an alien species whose introduction and/or spread threatens biological diversity" (CBD, 2002). Evidently, the parties to the CBD decided to keep the focus on the detrimental effects of biological invasions on the environment and ignored their socio-economic consequences. Conversely, Executive Order 31112 signed by the then President of the United States Bill Clinton in 1999 defined "invasive species" as those "alien species whose introduction does or is likely to cause economic or environmental harm or harm to human health".[4] Actually, both aspects deserve attention in defining the "invasiveness" of a species, while the determination of the environmental or economic threshold of the damage has to be necessarily postponed to a "case-by-case" appraisal.

To draw a conclusion, a possible coherent and comprehensive bio-legal definition would describe invasive alien species as those "species *or* lower taxonomic units that have been voluntarily or unintentionally introduced in an ecosystem beyond their range of natural dispersal thanks to human agency, have succeeded in colonising their host environment through a process of assimilation or naturalisation, are capable of maintaining themselves without further human assistance, and cause or are likely to cause significant socio-economic or environmental harm".

1.3 Analysing biological invasions under the lenses of the DPSIR model

Biological invasions are at the same time the result of increased human agency throughout the centuries and the pre-condition for imbalances likely to affect the planet both at the local and global levels. If considered, in this sense, as a by-product of the interaction between the ecologic, social and economic dimensions, it is possible to examine biological invasions through the lenses of the DPSIR (Driving forces-Pressure-State-Impact-Response) model elaborated by the European Environmental Agency in 1999 as a slightly extended version of the PSR (Pressure-State-Response) model already used by the OECD. Under this scheme, a series of driving forces exert pressures on the environment and consequently have an impact not only on nature, but also on human health and wealth, so that a societal response is needed (Agu, 2007). The DPSIR model is thus a fundamental tool in identifying the causes and consequences of biological invasions on the one hand, and in determining the most adequate responses on the other.

a At the roots of biological invasions: pressures exerted by driving forces

The term "driving forces" – when used in relation to biological invasions – implies all those social, economic or institutional triggers operating at different yet interconnected levels for the introduction, release, spread and establishment of invasive alien species (LeMaitre et al., 2002; Spangerberg, 2007). This multi-level approach is fully justified when considering that driving forces operate in different areas, either exercising a "primary" direct pressure on the environment, permanently modifying the structural aspects of the social organisation related to the human-environment relationship (the so-called "secondary driving forces"), or influencing those societal behaviours which have a direct repercussion on nature through the so-called "tertiary driving forces" (Rodriguez-Labajos et al., 2009).

In particular, it is possible to identify as primary driving forces all those anthropogenic activities affecting the way natural resources are exploited and local ecosystems are managed. It is clear that human beings have deeply modified the surrounding environment on the basis of their needs (Di Castri, 1989), thus favouring migrations and invasions of alien species. The direct influence of human agency on nature has followed a gradual evolution: at first, it took the forms of forest clearing and primeval agriculture; later on, it was characterised by migrations and nomadism, inshore coastal traffic, settlement of colonies and the intensification of agriculture. Finally, it encompassed offshore traffic and trade, the build-up of large empires with the consequent expansion of communication and transporting systems, long-ranging wars and military expansion. Since the 15th century the geographical extent and the depth of human-related biological invasions has amplified dramatically against a much more restricted temporal background: in six centuries – and even more so during the current "era of globalisation" or "Third Phase" (Hulme, 2009)[5] – trends that began in the previous centuries continued to develop while new driving forces, such as long-distance trade and the construction of market-oriented economies, emerged.

International trade is a paradigmatic case of "secondary driving force": in fact, intercontinental and transoceanic commerce has deeply and continuously modified the societal structure and the relationships between humans and nature (McNeely, 2001; Meyerson and Mooney, 2007; Pyšek et al., 2010). In fact, if on the one hand the increasing global connectedness has undoubtedly favoured the possibility to share information and knowledge (McNeely et al., 2001), on the other it has implied severe costs as

> it has broken down the natural barriers of oceans, mountains, rivers and deserts which for millennia provided the isolation essential for unique species and ecosystems to evolve. In just a few hundred years these barriers have been rendered ineffective by major global forces that combined to help alien species travel vast distances to new habitats and become alien invasive species.
>
> (SSC-ISSG, 2000)

Beginning with the Industrial Revolution, and with a greater emphasis after the Second World War, global merchandise trade underwent a substantial, unprecedented acceleration, the effects of which were transferred to the ecological domain with a very small temporal lag: in the last 25 years, in fact, the highest rates of introductions occurred, suggesting an unparalleled step-change in the process (SSC-ISSG, 2000). A study in which global invasive species databases were used to regress biological invasions data per-country on a suite of economic and social variables found a direct proportion between the number of non-native species in a country and its openness to international trade. As an example, both China and the United States are importers/exporters of substantial quantities of goods, and they are among the major sources and recipients of invasive alien species (Lodge et al., 2006). Alongside primary and secondary driving forces, which directly or indirectly exert pressures on the environment, the so-called "tertiary driving forces" take into account ideologies and lifestyles, emerging social interests, new platforms of communication and changes of perspectives on environmental protection which are a distinctive part of modern societies and have a prominent role in factually facilitating or theoretically supporting the introduction of non-native species in a particular environment.

b Impacts of invasive alien species on the state of natural and human environment

As for the consequences, i.e. the impact produced by the pressure of driving forces, the experts of the Global Invasive Species Programme (GISP) emphasised how "the scope of species invasions is global, and the cost is enormous, both in environmental and economic terms" (McNeely et al., 2001). Indeed, biological invasions threaten, either directly or indirectly, human health and/or wealth, they affect the structure and functioning of ecosystems, and they disturb the maintenance or restoration of native biological diversity. For these reasons, invasive alien species are one of the first most rapidly growing – and most difficult to reverse – threats to food security, human and animal health and biodiversity (Millennium Ecosystem Assessment, 2005).

The impact of invasive alien species on biodiversity and ecological processes is immense, insidious and usually irreversible. It is immense because it does not exclude any type of ecosystems; it is insidious as not every effect of the invasion is evident from the beginning and many invasions increase in severity over time through the quantitative growth of the invasive population (Shine et al., 2008); and the impact is usually irreversible as a consequence of the two-faceted influence of biological invasions on natural dynamics. In the short term, invasive alien species out-compete native wildlife through competitive exclusion, niche displacement, hybridisation and ultimately extinction, while in the long term they alter ecosystem processes in a way that changes the rules of existence for all species, as biological invaders influence productivity, decomposition, hydrology, geomorphology, nutrient cycles and disturbance of ecological processes.

Furthermore, the introduction of non-native species has significant consequences on human activities. Together with threats to biological diversity and ecologic processes, biological invasions have high economic costs. Even if it is not possible to have reliable and aggregated estimates at the global level, an assessment based on data from the United States, the United Kingdom, Australia, South Africa, India and Brazil concluded that invasions of non-native species caused over $314 billion in damage per year in those six countries, with a projection of more than $1.4 trillion per year at the global level (Pimentel et al., 2001). Those expenses include direct as well as indirect costs. Examples of primary direct costs are the spoiling or loss of agricultural and breeding productivity; the impossibility of using the crops or livestock for human consumption; the increase in the price of commodities; the decrease in internal demand and export earnings; relevant impacts on fisheries and aquaculture; the adoption of measures of prevention and management; increased monitoring, testing, diagnostic and treatment costs deriving from human health issues associated with introduced pathogens and toxic species; and loss of tourism revenue. Indirect costs include the degradation of ecosystems services; loss of human productivity due to time and resources allocated for dealing with invasive alien species; further imbalances between developed and developing nations, as the latter have narrower margins for dealing with additional costs; and damage to infrastructure due to ecosystem changes, as the consequences of biological invasions can facilitate fires, floods and landslides. Other relevant indirect costs are related to non-market values: losses in cultural, recreational, aesthetic and spiritual benefits can, in fact, threaten the survival of a community and its traditional knowledge, customs and practices.

Finally, invasive alien species may pose risks to human health, either directly or as vectors of specific diseases. From this latter point of view, paradigmatic examples are the cyclic diffusion of the influenza virus, which becomes pandemic for humans after periodic exchange of genes between the viruses of wild and domestic animals, or the introduction of the smallpox virus by

European conquistadores in the 15th and 16th centuries in North and Central America. Alternatively, invasive species can be a source of more direct problems for human health: an example is the Asian tiger mosquito (*Aedes albapictus*), whose larvae have been introduced in Italy via the United States in 1990 through the intercontinental trade of used tyres. This insect, which can feed on most mammals and birds, is a known vector of yellow fever, *chikungunya* and dengue fever. In addition, biological invasions may also worsen the situation of already fragile health systems. In Africa and most parts of Asia the bacterium that causes cholera (*Vibrio cholerae*) is an invasive alien species which thrives in both marine and freshwater habitats (including lagoons, estuaries, lakes and wetlands) and persists in shellfish and plankton in coastal areas. The bacterium has been imported through live food trade and has become endemic or epidemic in many areas where sanitation is poor and a prompt and effective medical response still does not exist.

c The role of policy-makers in response to biological invasions

Even if biological invasions are "low probability events with a high potential cost" (SSC-ISSG, 2000), the irreversibility of their consequences in terms of ecosystem alteration and biodiversity loss, combined with the uncertainty which surrounds the extent of the damages that they may cause from an economic point of view, emphasises the need for a differentiated and multifaceted response. As far as the identity of the most adequate responder is concerned, the nature of biological invasions and their impact on public goods such as ecosystems and individual health suggests the delegation of control of responses to public authorities. In fact even if economic effects are all but negligible, it seems impossible to entrust the market with the response to biological invasions without risking the under-supply of control and management aspects (ISSG, 2012).

Once it is clarified that control measures are to be discussed and adopted at the public level, it is possible to give them the more accurate name of "policies". In general, policies aimed at contrasting biological invasions are articulated in a three-tier approach in which the effectiveness of the response decreases in a *continuum* ranging from prevention to early detection and eradication, up to the *extrema ratio* of management and/or adaptation. Such an approach has been explicitly supported by the CBD Guiding Principles for the Prevention, Introduction and Mitigation of Impacts of Invasive Alien Species, as Principle 2 calls for a "three-stage hierarchical approach" (SSC-ISSG, 2000).

Wittemberg and Cock have acutely pointed out that "an ounce of prevention is worth a pound of cure" (Wittemberg and Cock, 2005). Such an approach constitutes the first and most cost-effective line of defence against biological invasions, as it tries to impede the introduction of a non-native species in a new environment in such a way as to precede its establishment and avoid the consequent economic and environmental costs of eradication and/or management. Many countries have established means of preventing the import of invasive species through the development of particular procedures of interception, inspection and treatment on imported commodities and early warning mechanisms. Albeit desirable and cost-effective in the long run, the preventive approach has the downside of immediately showing its high installation and maintenance costs to a public opinion which has a poor appreciation of the magnitude of the problem, particularly considering the temporal lag often separating introductions from invasions.

Even though prevention is the best remedy to biological invasions, it is also true that it is not always possible or effective, and in some cases invasive species successfully colonise a host environment. At that point, the next best possible policy response in terms of technical feasibility is the early detection of the threat in order to implement an eradication campaign. Such a mitigation strategy is the last chance to contain the invasion until its numbers are small, or its extension confined to a limited area. Nonetheless, it should be the result of a careful evaluation of its feasibility, as its costs are often significant and its impact on the receiving environment is far from subtle. Indeed, all the mechanisms which have been tested – biological control (which implies the targeted inoculation or mass release of specific living organisms in the host environment in order to contain or even eliminate the exotic species), mechanic control (which strives to put physical barriers to the advance of the invasion, such as fences, traps, row covers, even handpicking) and chemical control (achieved through the application of often dangerous herbicides and pesticides) – have proved to produce both positive and negative consequences. In fact, each of those mechanisms fails to provide at least one of the relevant and necessary characteristics of cost-effectiveness, efficiency and minimum impact on host ecosystem and native species.

If eradication campaigns fail, the possibility of completely eliminating the targeted invasive alien species is no longer an option (Mack et al., 2000). The only remaining measure which can actively impact on the pervasiveness of the invasion is containment, the ultimate aim of which is the geographical isolation and numerical reduction of the presence of the invasive species to an insubstantial and isolated threshold of individuals. However, some species become so widespread, and their control over the host environment so pervasive, that eradication and containment measures become more costly than the attempt to reduce the severity of the impacts on other species or on the ecosystem as a whole. In such a case, it is necessary to operate a shift from the control of invasive species to the protection of the receiving ecosystems in order to increase the resilience and reproduction capacities of native species. Such an approach, known as habitat management, tries to reduce the numbers and impact of invasive species *a contrario*, i.e. by increasing the presence of native populations.

1.4 Is there a role for supranational environmental regulation?

The three-stage response to biological invasions cannot be fully operative if not supported by a sound, effective, functioning and multi-layered normative environment.

In particular, the definition of an appropriate regulatory response to the threats posed by invasive alien species represents one of the biggest challenges for the international community in the 21st century, as it requires multilateral cooperation in a number of different fields, such as identification, assessment, control and management.

Supranational legal reactions towards the uncontrolled diffusion of invasive alien species have progressed at a fairly slow pace, but underwent a swift acceleration in the last two decades. Until the 1990s a "regulatory paralysis" frustrated any policy action against biological invasions: the causes of inaction did not originate from a substantial uncertainty over the magnitude of the consequences of an uncontrolled introduction of exotic species; rather, the presence of economic activities which derived considerable benefits from such a practice – mainly in the agricultural and farming sector – worked as a driver of procrastination, impeding even an embryonic re-thinking of the balance between the pursue of legitimate socio-economic activities and an appropriate safeguard of the environment (Shine et al., 2005).

In relation to economic considerations, Keller and Perrings have argued that two factors have hampered efforts to halt the international spread of environmental invaders (Keller and Perrings, 2011). On the one hand, nations generally act defensively to control the introduction of invasive species through border control rather than committing themselves to more comprehensive action including stricter vigilance on exported goods; on the other, the control of invasive alien species is a "weakest-link" public good, as the overall global risk of biological invasions is closely linked to the nation operating the least effective programmes to control species transport and introduction. Far from justifying protectionist or isolationist regulatory efforts, these remarks clearly show how each nation's possibilities to succeed in fighting the introduction and uncontrolled spread of non-native species are inextricably linked to its neighbours' actions and, therefore, how international cooperation becomes an aim of paramount importance. This is all the more so if considering the normative background which characterises contemporary international law, in which the classical dynamics of coexistence have been substituted by the progressive institutionalisation of multilateral cooperation between actors in an ever-increasing number of fields, including the environmental sphere.

International environmental law is intended here as the ultimate result of the evolutionary process, which began at the end of the Second World War and intensified following the foundational United Nations Conference on the Human Environment, convened in Stockholm on 5 June 1972, and has led ecological themes to leave the gregarious role of side problems and become a priority, first locally and then on the global stage. This transformation can be explained if looking at the deflagrating impact of two parallel evolutions: as for the content, an unequalled role has been played by the affirmation of the ethical and legal category of environmentalism; as for the context, it is almost impossible to explain contemporary international environmental regulation without making reference to the process of fragmentation of the *ius gentium*.

The simultaneous presence of those factors has caused changes of unprecedented depth and magnitude in the way ecological concerns are addressed and regulated, particularly at the supranational level. On the one hand, environmentalism disrupted the old paradigm of domination to embrace a fully ecologically backed approach in which the preservation of nature and wildlife would become a primary goal *per se*, without being forcefully subjected to socio-economic evaluations or *realpolitik* considerations; on the other hand, the progressive fragmentation of the international legal order into a multiple unity of *leges speciali* caused environmental questions to become a supranational priority insofar as more specific and sectorial issues were taken into consideration by the international community. The pressure of environmental activism and the diversification of the *ius gentium* into a multiple unity of more or less "self-contained" regimes have caused the transit of ecological concerns from the periphery to the centre of the international legal debate (Van Hasselt, 2012).[6] Progressively, the raising in scale of environmental challenges and the increasing in depth of the specialisation of the autonomous branches of international law has led to a tightening of the focus on particular problems within the environmental domain. This process took the form of a progressive shift from a general debate on the desirability of legal regulations *for* the environment to a specialised and multi-sectorial range of solutions aimed at granting protection *within* the environment.

Following those considerations, the next chapter will analyse the multilateral framework set up in recent decades against biological invasions and assess its key strengths and main weaknesses in order to propose alternative normative solutions.

Notes

1 Although an unconfirmed record of *Xylella fastidiosa* in Kosovo was published in 1996 and its presence was already rumoured to exist in the Salento peninsula since 2008, it was only in October 2013 that Italian authorities notified both to the European Union and the European Plant Protection Organization (EPPO) of its first detection in the southern province of Lecce.

2 In February 2014 the European Commission adopted implementing decision 2014/87/EU, prohibiting the movement of plants for planting purposes from the province of Lecce. This decision was later amended in May 2015 by implementing decision 2015/789/EU, detailing preventive measures to be taken by Member States in order to contrast the introduction into the Union of *Xylella fastidiosa*, detect its presence in a timely manner, take all possible eradication or – where impossible – management actions and contain the spread of the disease with the introduction of a buffer zone of 10 km around the province of Lecce. In December 2015, implementing decision 2015/2417/EU updated emergency measures to reflect the evolving situation in Italy and in light of the detection of *Xylella fastidiosa* in Corsica and Cote d'Azur (France). Meanwhile, the European Union started an infraction procedure against Italy, whose national authorities were not fully respecting the obligation to eradicate *Xylella fastidiosa* by delaying the cutting down of all trees in an area of 100m around the infected plants. In May 2016, implementing decision 2016/764/EU further amended decision 2015/789 in order to ensure effective protection of the rest of the Union territory by enlarging the containment area. In June 2016, the European Court of Justice in the Joined

Cases C-78 and C-79/16 (*Giovanni Pesce et al. v. Presidenza del Consiglio dei Ministri et al.*) confirmed the validity of implementing decision 2015/789 calling for trees to be cut down in order to halt the advance of the disease and added that the Commission's intervention was "appropriate and necessary to prevent the spread of the bacterium" if read in light of the proportionality and precautionary principles as laid out in Council Directive 2000/29. As Italian authorities continued to delay containment measures, in July 2016 the European Commission sent a second letter of infraction, opening the path to an infringement procedure.

3 According to Purcell, all the xylem fluid feeders should be considered to be potential vectors, but only the *Philaenus spumarius* is present in Europe.

4 *U.S. Executive Order 13112(1999) establishing the National Invasive Species Council* in *Federal Register*, Vol. 64, No. 25, February 8, 1999, Presidential Documents. An executive order is a legally binding order issued by the president of the United States of America directing federal agencies in their execution of existing laws.

5 The "third phase" is the immediate follower of the period which started with the Industrial Revolution (the "second phase"), and traces its origins back to the first round of introductions, which took place since the 16th century.

6 The first author to use the expression "self-contained regimes", in turn, was Bruno Simma while examining the possibility for specialized regimes to exist in isolation from general international law: B. SIMMA (1985), *Self-contained regimes* in *NYIL*, 16.

Bibliography

Agu, G. (2007), *DPSIR typology matrix*, European Environmental Agency, Copenhagen, Denmark.

Ahern, S.J., Das, M., Bhowmick, T.S., Young, R. and Gonzalez, C.F. (2014), Characterization of novel virulent broad-host-range phages of Xylella fastidiosa and Xanthomonas in *J Bacteriol* 196: 459–471.

Boudouresque, C., Ruitton, S. and Verlaque, M. (2005), Large-scale disturbances, regime shift and recovery in littoral systems subject to biological invasions in V. Velikova and N. Chipev (eds.), *UNESCO-Roste/BAS workshop on regime shifts*, 14–16 June 2005, Varna, Bulgaria, 85–101.

Cariddi, C., Saponari, M., Boscia, D., De Stradis, A., Loconsole, G., Nigro, F., Porcelli, F., Potere, O. and Martelli, G.P. (2014), Isolation of a Xylella fastidiosa strain infecting olive and oleander in Apulia, Italy in *J Plant Pathol* 96(3): 1–5.

CBD (2002), *Guiding Principles for the implementation of Article 8(h)*, Decision VI/23 of the 6th Conference of Parties to the Convention on Biological Diversity, The Hague, 7-19 April 2002.

Ceresa-Gastaldo, L. and Chiappini, E. (1994), Observations on the coccon of Oligosita krygeri Girault (Hymenoptera: Trichogrammatidae) oophagous parasitoid of Cicadella viridis (Homoptera: Cicadellidae) in *Norweg J Agr Sci* 16(Supplement): 131–140.

Colautti, R.J. and MacIsaac, H.J. (2004), A neutral terminology to define 'invasive' species in *Diversity Distrib* 10: 135–141.

Crosby, A.W. (1986), *Ecological imperialism: The expansion of Europe 900–1900* (2nd ed. 2004), Cambridge University Press, Cambridge.

Di Castri, F. (1989), History of biological invasions with special emphasis on the old world in J.A. Drake, J.J. Mooney, F. Di Castri et al. (eds.), *Biological invasions: A global perspective*, Wiley-Blackwell, Chichester.

EFSA. (2015b), Response to scientific and technical information provided by an NGO on Xylella fastidiosa in *EFSA Journal* 13(4): 4082, 13.

EFSA Panel on Plant Health. (2015a), Scientific opinion on the risks to plant health posed by Xylella fastidiosa in the EU territory, with the identification and evaluation of risk reduction options in *EFSA Journal* 13(1): 3989, 262.

Eilenberg, J., Hajek, A. and Lomer, C. (2001), Suggestions for unifying the terminology in biological control in *Biol Control* 46: 387–400.

European Commission. (2015), Questions and answers on Xylella fastidiosa, 17 July, available at http://europa.eu/rapid/press-release_MEMO-15-5346_en.htm.

Hoodle, S. (2004), The potential adventive geographic range of glassy-winged sharpshooter, Homolodisca coagulata and the grape pathogen Xylella fastidiosa: Implications for California and other grape growing regions of the world in *Crop Prot* 23: 691–696.

Hulme, P.E. (2009), Trade, transport and trouble: Managing invasive species pathways in an era of globalization in *J Appl Ecol* 46: 10–18.

ISSG. (2012), IUCN and BirdLife. in *Red List of Threatened Species* (update).

Jeschke, J.M. and Strayer, D.L. (2005), Invasion success of vertebrates in Europe and North America in *Proceedings of the National Academy of Sciences of the U.S.A* 102(20): 7198–7202.

Keller, K.P., Geist, J., Jeschke, J.M. and Kühn, I. (2011), Invasive species in Europe: Ecology, status, and policy in *ESEU* 23: 23.

Keller, R.P., and Perrings, C. (2011), International policy options for reducing environmental impact of invasive species in *BioScience* 61(12): 1005–1012.

Le Maitre, D., Reyers, B. and King, N. (2002), *National core set of environmental indicators. Phase 3: Selection of indicators: Biodiversity and natural heritage*, National Department of Environmental Affairs and Tourism, Special Report 3(3), Pretoria.

Lodge, D.M., Williams, S., MacIsaac, H.J., Hayes, K.R., Leung, B., Reichard, S., Mack, R.N., Moyle, P.B., Smith, M., Andow, D.A., Carlton, J.T. and McMichael, A. (2006), Biological invasions: Recommendations for US policy and management in *Ecological Applications* 16: 2035–2054.

Mack, R.N., Simberloff, D., Lonsdale, W.M., Evans, H., Clout, M. and Bazzaz, F.A. (2000), Biotic invasions: Causes, epidemiology, global consequences, and control in *Ecol Appl* 10: 689–710.

Mcneely, A. (2001), *The great reshuffling: Human dimensions on invasive alien species*, IUCN, Gland, Switzerland and Cambridge.

McNeely, J.A., Mooney, H.A., Neville, L.E., Schei, P. and Waage, J.K. (eds., 2001), *A global strategy on invasive species*, IUCN Secretariat, Gland, Switzerland.

Meyerson, L. and Mooney, H.A. (2007), Invasive alien species in an era of globalization in *Front Ecol Environ* 5: 199–208.

Millennium ecosystem assessment. (2005), *Ecosystems and human well-being: Synthesis.* Island Press, Washington, DC.

Pimentel, D., McNair, S., Janecka, J., Wightman, J., Simmond, C., O'Connell, C., Wong, E., Russel, L., Zern, J., Aquino, T. and Tsomondo, T. (2001), Economic and environmental threats of alien plant, animals, and microbe invasions in *Agr, Ecosyst Environ* 84: 1–20.

Purcell, A.H. (1980), Almond leaf scorch: Leafhopper and spittlebug vectors in *J Econ Entomol* 73(6): 834–838.

Pyšek, P., Vojtèch, J., Hulme, P.E., Khün, I., Wild, J., Arianoutsou, M., Bacher, S., Chiron, F., Didžiulis, V., Essl, F., Genovesi, P., Gherardi, F., Hejda, M., Salit, K., Lambdon, P.W., Desprez-Lostau, M.L., Nentwig, W., Pergl, J., Poboljšaj, K., Rabitsch, W., Roques, A., Roy, D.B., Shirley, S., Solarz, W., Vilà, M. and Winter,

M. (2010), Disentangling the role of environmental and human pressures on biological invasions across Europe in *Proceedings of National Academy of Sciences of the U.S.A* 107(27): 12157–12162.

Rodriguez-Labajos, B., Binimelis, R. and Monterosso, I. (2009), Multi-level driving forces of biological invasions in *Ecol Econ* 69(1): 63–75.

Shine, C. (2008), *A toolkit for developing legal and institutional frameworks for invasive alien species*, Global Invasive Species Programme (GISP), Nairobi, 7.

Shine, C., Williams, N. and Burhenne-Guilmin, F. (2005), Legal and institutional frameworks for invasive alien species in H.A. Mooney, R.N. Mack, J.A. McNeely, L.E. Neville, P. Schei and J.K. Waage (eds.), *Invasive alien species: A new synthesis*, Island Press, Washington, DC.

Shine, C., Williams, N. and Gündling, L. (2000), *A guide to designing legal and institutional frameworks on invasive alien species*, IUCN, Gland, Switzerland, Cambridge and Bonn.

Shine, C., Kettunen, M., Genovesi, P., Gollasch, S., Pagad, S. & Starfinger, U. 2008. *Technical support to EU strategy on invasive species (IAS) – Policy options to control the negative impacts of IAS on biodiversity in Europe and the EU (Final report for the European Commission)*. Institute for European Environmental Policy (IEEP), Brussels, Belgium).

Simma, B. (1985), Self-contained regimes in *NYIL*, 16: 111–136.

Spangerberg, J.H. (2007), Biodiversity pressures and the driving forces behind in *Ecological Economics* 61(1): 146–158.

Species Survival Commission, Invasive Species Specialist Group. (SSG-ISSC, 2000), *IUCN guidelines for the prevention of biodiversity loss caused by alien invasive species*, IUCN, Gland, Switzerland.

Summer, E.J., Enderle, C.J., Ahern, S.J., Gill, J.J., Torres, C.P., Appel, D.N., Black, M.C., Young, R. and Gonzalez, C.F. (2010), Genomic and biological analysis of phage Xfas53 and related prophages of Xylella fastidiosa in *J Bacteriol* 192: 179–190.

Valery, L., Lefeuvre, J.C. and Simberloff, D. (2008), In search of a real definition of the biological invasion phenomenon itself in *Biol Inv* 10: 1345–1351.

Van Hasselt, H. (2012), Managing the fragmentation of international environmental law: Forests at the intersection of climate change and biodiversity regimes in *New York University Journal of International Law and Politics* 44(1205): 1207–1274.

Waloff, N. (1980), Studies on grassland leafhoppers (Auchenorrhyncha, Homoptera) and their natural enemies in *Adv Ecol Res* 11: 81–215.

Williamson, M. and Fitter, A. (1996), The varying success of invaders in *Ecology* 77(6): 1661–1666.

Wittemberg, R. and Cock, M.J.W. (2005), Best practices for the prevention and management of invasive alien species in H.A. Mooney, R.N. Mack, J.A. McNeely, L.E. Neville, P. Schei and J.K. Waage (eds.), *Invasive alien species: A new synthesis*, Island Press, Washington, DC.

2 Gaps in the global legal framework and the regional alternative

SUMMARY: 2.1. Introduction – 2.2. The locus standi *of biological invasions in international environmental law (a. A general overview of the normative and institutional context; b. General principles of international environmental law and their coordinative role; c. Relevant treaty law provisions: a history of evolution) – 2.3. A deluding assessment of the global normative framework (a. Immediate causes of ineffectiveness: gaps, overlaps and inconsistencies; b. Structural causes of ineffectiveness: environmentalism v. state-centrism) – 2.4. Regionalism as a theoretical and legal phenomenon (a. What's in a name? Conceptualizing and contextualizing "region" and "regionalism"; b. Legal interpretations of the regionalist phenomenon) – 2.5. Introducing environmental concerns into the neoregionalist paradigm – 2.6. Regional environmental governance in practice – 2.7. Final remarks: an* ex ante *justification for analysing the European Union*

2.1 Introduction

The first aim of the chapter is to look at the way contemporary international environmental law, intended as the product of two converging forces – the emergence of the environmentalist *weltanschaung* on the one hand, and the specialisation of the once granitic *ius gentium* in a plurality of progressively sectorialised *leges specialis* on the other – has tried to give a response to transboundary phenomena such as biological invasions.

In this sense, the second section presents the *locus standi* of biological invasions within the broader picture of international environmental law, with particular respect to the role of general principles – such as the prevention, precaution and polluter pays – and to the main treaty provisions contained in relevant international conventions and soft law agreements. In trying to assess the overall effectiveness of the global response to the uncontrolled introduction and diffusion of non-native species in host ecosystems, the third section not only emphasises the existence of many gaps, overlaps and inconsistencies at all levels (from the definition of key terms to taxonomic coverage and enforcement), but also questions the compatibility of environmental law with the state-centric approach which is typical of the Westphalian international order.

Proposing a decoupling between territory and sovereignty, so that the first has not to be merely seen as a complement or "sphere of exercise" of the latter, the fourth section postulates a shift from the global to the regional level as the most adequate level of regulation in the field of cross-border environmental issues in general, and of biological invasions in particular. To do this, the section sheds some light on the theoretical, historical and legal foundations of the phenomenon, particularly focusing on the concepts of "region" and "regionalism". The section also looks at the role of the Cold War as an engine of modern regionalisation and at the influence of globalisation in shaping *new regionalism*, seen as a school of thought that identifies in regional cooperation not only a tendency in international relations but also a regulatory option capable of reconciling geographical and functional notions of region around a nucleus of shared norms, values and interests. The abstract presentation is followed by a comprehensive review of concretely existing examples of regionalism in the environmental sphere: the fifth section delineates five successive steps of environmental regionalisation, thus drawing a teleological division between regions of environmental cooperation and regions of environmental integration. The difference between those two categories will be based on the existence of an environmental focus and on the pervasiveness of the legal framework. Following this *magna divisio*, the chapter emphasises how the European Union is, at the moment, the only regional actor that exceeds the simple cooperative dimension, thus providing the basis for its subsequent analysis.

2.2 The *locus standi* of biological invasions in international environmental law

The international regulatory framework set up to give a multilateral response to biological invasions perfectly illustrates the concept of "global environmental law", which has recently been introduced to define a field of study which strives to examine the interactions between globalisation and environmental concerns in order to draw an "emerging set of independent and convergent legal principles" (Yang and Percival, 2009). Such an ambitious aim is pursued through a shift in approach from the individuation of the most appropriate jurisdiction to the identification of the most suitable response to pressing problems, so as to focus attention on empirically grounded questions such as the coordination of a multiplicity of actors and norms (Boyd, 2010).

a A general overview of the normative and institutional context

Using "global environmental law" as an interpretative tool, it is thus possible to consider the current legal framework on biological invasions as the result of a process of "double unbundling" at the subjective and substantial level. On the one hand, the cross-border nature of the issue complicates the usually plain state-centric approach of international regulation, and poses the question of how states – and their apparatus – participate in the global normative process together with other actors (such as international organisations, individuals and non-governmental organisations). On the other hand, the usually strict and rigid division *ratione materiae* of international agreements is forced to give way to a multi-faceted regime composed of a vast array of conventions with overlapping mandates: this latter characteristic is confirmed when looking at the ever-increasing number of bilateral and multilateral environmental agreements registered since 1972 and in which the United Nations (UN) system has had a primary role of promotion (Brown Weiss, 1993). Among these international instruments, more than 50 deal with some aspect of the introduction, control, management and/or eradication of alien species (Shine, 2005). Beyond the expansion of the treaty system, another distinctive feature of the international legal order – contributing to the creation of a "diffuse" corpus of norms finding a unitary *raison d'être* in their ultimate aim to give an effective response to the increasing flow of invasive alien species – is the multiplication of non-binding but functionally indispensable tools such as codes of conduct and guidelines, which have proven to be fundamental in clarifying and detailing the provisions contained in hard law instruments.

b General principles of international environmental law and their coordinative role

In this scenario marked by complexity, diversification and pluralism, an absolute need for coordination among different regulatory frameworks emerges. Provisions contained in different legal regimes need, in this sense, a synergetic approach able to minimise the conflicts and maximise the benefits in the presence of overlapping mandates.[1] In order to achieve this apparently ambitious aim, a central role can be played by those common principles which, in force of their generality, can work as bridges between seemingly disconnected normative islands: the precautionary, prevention and "polluter pays" principles are in this sense the cornerstones on the basis of which environmental regulation can find unity.

Precaution or, to be more precise, the precautionary principle ensures that a substance or activity posing a threat to the environment is prevented from deploying its adverse effects, even if there is no conclusive scientific proof linking that particular substance or activity to actual environmental damages (Cameron and Abouchar, 1991). This principle has a distinctively pragmatic role, as its goal is to guide policy- and law-makers to take into full consideration the harmful effects of an activity before taking any step for its implementation. In relation to the risks connected to the introduction of non-native species, the precautionary principle postulates that the lack of scientific certainty shall not be used as a reason to postpone measures to avoid or minimise a threat of significant reduction or loss of biological diversity (McNeely, 2001), or a menace to the socio-economic wellbeing of a community.

In turn, the principle of prevention has found a particularly receptive and fertile soil in environmental protection provisions: the preventive principle, in fact, has been at the basis of many contemporary instruments of international environmental law (Sands et al., 2012). If precaution has been described as a *guiding* principle, prevention has a rather *abstaining* allure, as its main content is a *de non facere* obligation pending upon States. As such, however, it risks being confused with the duty of States to avoid transboundary environmental harm (Handl, 1991; Guruswamy and Hendricks, 1997; Paradell-Trius, 2000). Although a fundamental tenet of international environmental law, to the point that it is universally considered to be a customary norm (Birnie and Boyle, 2002), this obligation differs from the preventive principle for their respective objects: in fact, whereas the duty to avoid transboundary harm takes its *ratio* and *opinio iuris* in the dogma of State sovereignty, the preventive principle seeks to protect the environment as an autonomous end and does not see its application limited to cross-border damages (Trouwborst, 2009). In relation to biological invasions, this principle tries to shift the focus from remedial measures (such as control and eradication) to preventive efforts (e.g. border controls or controls by exporter countries).

Finally, the "polluter pays" principle requires that the cost of pollution shall be borne by those who cause damage to the environment.[2] Derived from an intuition of early 20th-century economist Pigou, who introduced the idea that pollution should be addressed as a negative externality, the principle has leaped from the strictly economic debate to the environmental regulation domain (Pigou, 1920). Indeed, at present the "polluter pays" principle is supported by relevant international organisations (such as the OECD and the EU) and is mentioned in Principle 16 of the 1992 Rio Declaration and in the Kyoto Protocol, where parties share the obligation to pay the cost of reducing polluting emissions on the basis of common but differentiated responsibilities. Furthermore, the principle has already been applied in many judicial cases (such as the *Exxon Valdez* case in 1989).[3] In relation to biological invasions, the "polluter pays" principle would imply that the natural or legal person(s) responsible for causing the introduction of an alien invasive species – within or outside national borders – should bear the cost of control and remedial measures (McNeely, 2001).

From such a brief assessment, the role played by these rather general principles in giving unity to an otherwise utterly complex and divided normative framework clearly emerges and permits the transition to the presentation of those concrete legal tools elaborated in recent decades to face the challenge posed by invasive alien species.

c Relevant treaty law provisions: a history of evolution

The first treaty provisions tangentially dealing with biological invasions largely relied on multilateral agreements aimed at controlling the introduction and spread of pests and diseases and/or at protecting animal and plant health by means of quarantine systems, with a fundamentally economic-driven attitude which left very little room for environmental concerns (Shine, 2005).

Already developed as a regulatory tool since the 14th century in Europe to stop the spread of diseases and pestilences (Schepin and Yemarkov, 1991), quarantine regimes began to exceed the national dimension in the 19th century. The increase in trade which followed the end of the Napoleonic wars emphasised a fragmented regulatory reality and the inconsistent standards imposed on merchants by different countries while at the same time significantly favouring the potential movement of viruses and bacteria beyond national borders. The need for a reform began a debate culminating in a series of International Sanitary Conferences, during which states negotiated shared solutions on the matter (Huber, 2006). Nevertheless, the agreements issued by those conferences proved to be largely modest in their achievements, and it was only after the Second World War that the question was challenged in a rather innovative and more comprehensive way. A first example, in this sense, comes from the International Plant Protection Convention (IPPC).[4] This multilateral agreement had a twofold aim: on the one hand, it adopted a preventive approach aimed at limiting the spread of pests of plants and/or plant products between countries; on the other, it encouraged countries to adopt appropriate measures for the effective control of pests within their borders. Originally, the IPPC had no other link with the phenomenon of biological invasions if not the provision in Article 2 of an embryonic definition of pest as "any species, strain, or biotype of plant, animal, or pathogenic agent injurious to plants or plant products". Obviously, this link subsisted as long as the pest was a non-indigenous species, strain or biotype, and, even in case of persistence of such a connection, the *ratio* of the provisions contained in the IPPC was far from being entirely environmentally oriented. Rather, the commitment to prevent and manage the introduction of pests was only nominally equal for cultivated and wild plants: in fact, the protection of native flora never took the form of an autonomous goal, and invasive pests were not conceived as a threat to biological diversity or to the environment in general, as the implementation regarded almost exclusively those plants having an agricultural value and/or those able to meet an economic demand. Nevertheless, the IPPC contained *in nuce* the seeds of the customary duty of international cooperation on environmental issues through a system of reports and exchange of information coordinated by the Food and Agriculture Organisation (FAO). More recent innovations regard the way in which the IPPC may be applied to pests that affect unmanaged ecosystems or to those damaging non-economic interests (Shine, 2005): the most powerful tool, in this sense, is the implementation of the International Standards on Phytosanitary Measures (ISPM). These technical instruments, developed since the 1990s by the IPPC Secretariat in accordance with the provisions contained in the Agreement on Sanitary and Phytosanitary Measures (SPS Agreement) negotiated in the World Trade Organisation framework, have contributed to a more environmentally oriented approach during the last decade, to the point that one of the latest regulations – the ISPM15 – is dedicated to the prevention of international transport and spread of diseases or insects that could negatively affect plants or ecosystems by means of precise standards on the heat-treatment of all wood packaging materials. Overall, the dynamic and practical approach of this Convention has allowed a functional adaptation to new emerging concerns and has contributed to building a more cooperative relationship between states. This increasing collaborative attitude proved to be fundamental in giving to the environmentalist claims a non-chaotic response when the issue of conservation emerged at the international level in the 1970s.

During that "environmental decade", the international community adopted three multilateral treaties, the importance of which has been paramount in the development of environmental regulation on the global stage: the Convention on Wetlands of International Importance, especially as Waterfowl Habitat (Ramsar Treaty, 1971); the Convention on International Trade in Endangered Species of Wild Fauna and Flora (CITES, 1973); and the Convention on the Conservation of Migratory Species of Wild Animals (CMS, 1979). Even if none of these agreements was primarily directed to give a response to biological invasions, it is noteworthy to mention that in the following decades the progressive emergence of the threats and challenges posed by the uncontrolled spread of invasive alien species has led to a partial revision of their provisions.

The Ramsar Convention was signed in 1971 with the aim to conserve – and wisely use (the expression "sustainable development" still did not enter into the environmental law vocabulary) – wetlands in order to stem the progressive encroachment on, and loss of, wildlife in those delicate ecosystems. In 1999, the Conference of Parties held in San José (Costa Rica) formally recognised the link with invasive alien species by adopting a resolution which explicitly identified biological invasions as a threat to the ecological character and to terrestrial and marine wetland species. Like any soft law instrument, the resolution urges parties, where necessary, to adopt legislation or programmes aimed at preventing the introduction of new and environmentally dangerous alien species into their jurisdictions and at building adequate capacities for the identification of these species, including those tested for agricultural and horticultural use.

Two years after the negotiation of the Ramsar Convention – and with the remarkable interlude of the Convention Concerning the Protection of World Natural and Cultural Heritage (the World Heritage Convention), adopted in Paris by the General Conference of UNESCO in 1972 – a new multilateral treaty aimed at protecting endangered plants and animals threatened with extinction from uncontrolled international trade was signed in 1973: the CITES offers a multi-layered protection to wildlife, according different degrees of protection to more than 35,000 specimens of animals and plants: species are in fact divided in three appendices, depending on the extent of the threat of extinction and on the tightness of the controls on trade (from Appendix 1, which comprises plants and animals immediately threatened with extinction and whose trade is illegal, to Appendix 3, including wildlife which is endangered on a local basis). Even if the focus on trade has been made clear by the title of the Convention, a rising awareness among parties about the limitations in the structure and philosophy of the CITES has progressively led to the consideration of topics such as habitat loss and ecosystem conservation (Hutton and Dickson, 2000). The connection with biological invasions has been almost immediate, and has taken the form of resolution 13.10, approved during the 13th Conference of Parties held in Bangkok in 2004. This resolution particularly addresses the issue of flora and fauna introduced in non-native habitats as a result of international trade and recommends parties to "consider the problems of invasive species when developing national legislation and regulations", "consult with the Management Authority of a proposed country of import . . . when considering exports of potentially invasive species", and "consider the opportunities for synergy between CITES and the Convention on Biological Diversity (CBD)".

The CMS (also known as the Bonn Convention), signed in 1979 under the aegis of the United Nations Environmental Programme (UNEP), symbolically closes the "conservation decade". The ultimate aim of the Convention under Article 2 is to conserve terrestrial, marine and avian migratory species throughout their natural range. Similarly to the CITES, the degree of protection varies according to the extent of the risk of extinction, and the commitment of states can imply conservative or restorative actions, mitigation and control of the endangering factors, cooperation and sharing of information. Furthermore, the CMS operates as an "umbrella convention": in fact, both binding and non-binding agreements can be signed under its framework in order to give more targeted protection to individual species or to promote closer cooperation among some of the parties. As far as biological invasions are concerned, the Bonn Convention identifies in non-native species a factor that may endanger migratory wildlife, requiring parties to take prevention and management measures through explicit provisions contained in the treaty: Article III.4 of the CMS, in fact, specifically states that

> Parties that are Range States of a migratory species listed in Appendix I shall endeavor . . . to the extent feasible and appropriate, to prevent, reduce or control factors that are endangering or are likely to further endanger the species, including strictly controlling the introduction of, or controlling or eliminating, already introduced exotic species.

Furthermore, Article V.5 provides that agreements adding to Annex II should provide for – but should not be limited to

> conservation and, where required and feasible, restoration of the habitats of importance in maintaining a favorable conservation status, and protection of such habitats from disturbances, including strict control of the introduction of, or control of already introduced, exotic species detrimental to the migratory species.

The conservation decade had a powerful impact on the perception of environmental challenges at the global level. However, the intensity of the impact was not followed by a coherent and continuative commitment by the international community. Indeed, during the 1980s the *realpolitik* of the Cold War drove the efforts of states away from environmental concerns. Nevertheless, that decade witnessed an increased awareness of the damages that human-related activities caused to species and ecosystems, fuelled by unprecedented rates of wildlife extinction.

As a response to these growing concerns, in 1988 the United Nations Environment Programme (UNEP) convened a Working Group of Experts on Biological Diversity to explore the need of an international agreement aimed at addressing the problem of biodiversity loss as a consequence of species extinction. After six months of meetings, in May 1989 the ad hoc group of experts opened the way to a Working Group of Technical and Legal Experts charged with the task of preparing an international legal instrument for the conservation and sustainable use of biological diversity. In 1991, this technical body became an Intergovernmental Negotiating Committee, whose work culminated on 22 May 1992 with the adoption of the Convention on Biological Diversity during a conference convened in Nairobi (Kenya). Opened for signature on the occasion of the 1992 Earth Summit held in Rio de Janeiro (Brazil), the Convention can count today on an almost universal participation, and its legally binding status obliges parties to work towards the three main goals of the agreement: the conservation of biological diversity, the sustainable use of its components, and the fair and equitable sharing of benefits arising from the use of genetic resources.

As far as alien species are concerned, Article 8(h) of the Convention requires each contracting party to prevent the introduction of alien species capable of threatening ecosystems, habitats or species and, in case of unsuccessful prevention, to control and/or eradicate those who succeed in establishing themselves in a host environment. During the negotiations strenuous efforts were made to achieve the inclusion of stronger provisions on non-indigenous species (Jenkins, 1996), particularly through the establishment of a scientific authority styled after the one provided for in the CITES and the creation of a list of high-priority species threatening biodiversity. Nonetheless, the final version of the treaty watered down these proposals, and Article 8(h) was approved in its quite general form, as it does not specify how parties should implement its requirements (SCBD, 2001). However, a teleological reading of other provisions of the CBD provides meaningful relations with crucial issues such as national and integrated strategic and cross-sectorial planning (Art. 6); regulation or management of potentially damaging processes and categories of activities (Art. 8 *sub* l); involvement of local populations and the private sector (Art. 10); incentives and environmental impact assessment (Art. 11); and transboundary notification and emergency planning (Art. 14).

As the combination of these different provisions clearly shows, biological invasions are regulated as a cross-cutting issue, and as such they have been recognised by the Fourth Conference of Parties (CoP4) held in 1998 in Bratislava (Slovakia). Since then, each CoP has taken into account the phenomenon of invasive alien species: the decision taken during the Sixth Conference of Parties (CoP6), held in 2002 in the Hague (Netherlands), is in this sense particularly important, as it contains a set of Guiding Principles adopted in order to assist national governments in implementing the provisions contained in Article 8(h). Though non-binding *per se*, these principles are important as a first attempt to give substance to a supranational, coordinated and specific action in the field of biological invasions. This instrument recognises as a valid policy option the so-called three-tier approach and reiterates the hierarchical scale which sees prevention as the most cost-effective and environmentally desirable choice. However, if an alien species has been introduced, early detection and rapid response are deemed as absolutely necessary, and eradication is considered as a particularly effective measure. If eradication is not feasible, containment and long-term management should be implemented as a remedial measure of last resort.

Even though the Guiding Principles have opened the way to a more operative application of Article 8(h) of the Convention, a major critical remark can be made as regards the lack of full legal value of this document and, at a more general level, of all those international instruments which look at biological invasions as a matter of global concern. With the notable exception of the CMS, in fact, the integration of such a delicate issue inside conservation treaties has occurred with remarkable delay, and mainly through soft law instruments, such as resolutions and decisions. On the one hand, the prevalence of the *droit mou* in the international response to the spread of non-native species and to its consequences is certainly an expression of states' unwillingness to make any stricter commitment. On the other, it would nonetheless be a symptom of a certain short-sightedness to totally deprive these instruments of any significance, as their non-binding nature does not immediately imply that they are totally deprived of legal importance at the global or national levels. From the international standpoint, in fact, they contribute to the progressive development of a normative approach to the question of biological invasions; at the national level, then, they can become useful tools as far as the implementation of relevant conventions is concerned.

Rather than focusing on the consequences of the lack of binding instruments on the poor enforcement of international norms dealing with biological invasions, the next paragraph will present and explain the ineffectiveness of the system as a result of two concurring factors: on the one hand, the plethoric corpus of insufficiently connected multilateral norms which originates gaps, overlaps and inconsistencies; on the other, the difficulties in accommodating the fight against biological invasions – and international environmental law in general – within the current state-centric international system.

2.3 A deluding assessment of the global normative framework

The contemporary international legal order is characterised by more than 3,000 bilateral and multilateral agreements, 50 of which directly or indirectly deal with the question of invasive alien species. This "treaty congestion" is a reflection of the proliferation of dedicated international instruments which have challenged the theme with a piecemeal, emergency logic. The idea of fragmentation – which has been dismissed at the beginning of this chapter by referring to the concepts of "specialisation" and "sectorialisation" – thus risks reappearing in terms of "operational inefficiency" in a more shallow fashion if compared to the most recurrently identified threats of "regimes incompatibility".

Considering the significant abundance of treaties dealing with the question of biological invasions – each of which addresses the issue from a particular perspective or angle – the existence of gaps, overlaps and inconsistencies is not surprising. Nevertheless, those "regulatory failures" are just the first and most evident reason for the ineffectiveness of the global regime. At a more profound level, a thorough reflection on the theoretical foundations of international law reveals that gaps and inconsistencies are actually effects of a more rooted dysfunction: as an eminently trans-territorial phenomenon overhauling state borders and capacities, biological invasions stand in a rather dialectic relationship with the state-centric system developed since the times of the Peace of Westphalia (1648), such that the response to the transboundary impacts of invasive alien species can be accommodated within contemporary international law only at the price of a certain degree of ineffectiveness (Biermann and Dingwerth, 2004).

a Immediate causes of ineffectiveness: gaps, overlaps and inconsistencies

In relation to the first observation, lack of comprehensiveness, duplication of mandates and inconsistency of the legal framework operate both at the same time and at the most diverse levels: definition of terms, contents, preventive and/or remedial measures, and consequences of transboundary damages.

As far as terminology is concerned, a "semantic gap" has an impact on the use of relevant terms. This driver of inefficiency is further exacerbated by the lack of a common glossary of relevant scientific concepts. In a total vacuum of agreed definitions this produces legal uncertainty. This lack of clarity has led, over the decades, to a flourishing of the terms used to describe non-native species in an often pejorative escalation deriving from the perception of the damages inflicted to the host environment and of the impacts on human health and/or wealth. The first attempt to have a comprehensive international document dealing with biological invasion (the Agenda 21) uses different terms in an almost undifferentiated way, as it makes reference to invasive alien species as "exotic", "pests" and "foreign". The farming and conservation sectors have over time produced a great number of terms to describe the phenomenon of biological invasions. In the farming sector, international conventions use terms like "pests", "weed" and "disease"; in the conservation context the preferred terms are "exotic" and "alien", and binomials such as "indigenous/non-indigenous" or "native/non-native" are often used. The gaps, overlaps and inconsistencies in terminology are the most evident demonstration of the difficulties that the international community is facing in regulating the responses to biological invasions at the global level: inefficiencies in the use of terminology are, in fact, a powerful means of hampering cross-sectorial planning and coordination on the one hand, and undermining compliance on the other.

Secondly, many multilateral treaties are characterised by a piecemeal approach, particularly under three crucial perspectives: taxonomic, ecosystems and pathways/vectors coverage. A case-by-case approach is justified when designing measures related to ecosystems in consideration of the high variability with which different habitats are hit by biological invasions and of the particular vulnerability of isolated ecosystems, as long as it does not lead to overlaps of mandate between different treaties.[5] Nevertheless, the patchy attitude with which taxonomic coverage and modalities of introduction are faced by the current global regulatory framework remains to be explained. Gaps in the taxonomic coverage regard the prevalence international norms accord to higher taxa of alien animals and plants, while coverage below the species level is a quite rare feature, often confined to regional or sub-regional agreements on specific threats posed by single species.[6] It is neither rare nor surprising, however, that this underestimation of lower taxa is the result of the emphasis governments have chosen to place on certain taxonomic groups: in the present international regulatory environment, political and economic considerations emerge – and in some cases pass over – ecological concerns. Indeed, it regularly occurs that crops, forestry plants, farmed fish, animals and garden plants are not regarded as invasive species as long as they thrive where humans planned that they had to grow (Low, 1999), despite the fact that those activities usually result in the impoverishment of local biological diversity. At a more substantial level, the increasing movement of goods and peoples for trade and tourism purposes has contributed to the regulatory ineffectiveness through a series of gaps, overlaps and inconsistencies. The frontline of regulation, from this standpoint, is the quarantine system. Abstractly conceived to cover all pathways, the quarantine system has been deeply influenced by continuously varying practices which have determined changes in scope and priorities depending on economic and political choices. In addition, and further complicating the scenario, resource constraints in many developing countries are a significant driver of inefficiency and inconsistency, together with transports associated with humanitarian and military programmes, as they can provide a gap through which invasive species can be introduced and begin to establish themselves. At a more specific level, as far as transport of invasive alien species is concerned there are no applicable and binding international standards, and even where soft law instruments exist (such as in the case of the 1997 International Maritime Organization's guidelines on ballast water and sediments) they cover only a minimum part of the vectors.

The logical consequence of this piecemeal approach to the issue of biological invasion is the establishment of invasive species in the host environment. A general agreement among regulators identifies preventive measures as a priority tool, by virtue of their ecological and economic effectiveness, while eradication at the earliest possible stage is considered to be the second best, followed by control and containment as residual options. As far as prevention is concerned, regulatory options are characterised by gaps in terms of coordination and implementation: indeed, the variegated set of norms developed by a series of multilateral instances tends to be completely deprived of operational coherency on the one hand, and of concrete indicators and criteria for practical implementation on the other (SCBD, 2001). From the first point of view, the absence of international coordination among inconsistent agreements originates overlapping and, often, contrasting provisions, with a range of approaches varying from strong prohibition to generic instructions.[7] Secondly, and beyond any consideration on the degree of strength of the regulatory framework, common traits of most parts of the attempts to prevent introductions are the total absence of indicators on where prohibitions or restrictions should be imposed, which procedures are to be established for cooperation with the countries of origin of the alien species that may impact on biodiversity, and which criteria should be evaluated to promote consistent decision-making. By contrast, there are some generic words which are redundantly repeated as a call to arms against biological "threats" and "serious harms". In this quite disappointing panorama, there is however room for some exceptions, which nevertheless derive from situations that are too specific to give reasonable perspectives for future improvements at the global level. In fact, the prescription of permit-based systems of control for voluntary or involuntary introductions concern regional instruments (such as the 1998 Madrid Protocol to the Antarctic Treaty, which requires a permit for the introduction of any animal or plant not native to the region), or agreements whose main focus exceeds ecological concerns on invasive species to embrace more economically related matters, such as the sanitary and phytosanitary measures aimed at protecting the health of commercially valuable plants or animals.

However, if some indications exist in relation to preventive measures, most international instruments are weak, if not eloquently silent, on the question of eradication and control, particularly on delicate questions such as the way in which environmental risk analysis should be conducted. Exceptions are provided at the global level by the Ramsar Convention, the Convention on Migratory Species and the Convention on Biological Diversity, and at the regional level by the Convention for the Conservation of the Biodiversity and the Protection of Wilderness Areas in Central America (also known as the Managua Convention, which mandates the adoption of mechanisms to control or eradicate all exotic species which threaten ecosystems, habitats and wild species), and the Convention on the Conservation of European Wildlife and Natural Habitats (also known as the Bern Convention, which introduces an explicit distinction between "eradication" and "control" while at the same time issuing targeted recommendations on the eradication or control of named alien species).

Finally, effective rules in relation to transboundary damages to the environment as a consequence of the introduction of invasive species are lacking, or where they exist, are incomplete or inconsistent. To avoid transboundary damages, states planning to undertake or authorise activities that may have measurable effects on the environment of another state should inform and consult with that state in order to support coordinated approaches in accordance with a relevant, well-established principle of customary international environmental law.[8] However, the majority of the multilateral environmental agreements dealing with biological invasions do not elaborate on this provision of customary law and do not specify state responsibilities towards neighbouring countries regarding alien species, thus opening a serious gap, as prevention and control obligations are not underpinned by a deterring element. The situation does not get any better if considering the traditional counterpart of liability, that is redress (i.e. the availability of remedies for victims of environmental damage): at present, no multilateral environmental agreement possesses provisions capable of addressing this dimension, at least if the focus is closely kept on invasive species. Certainly, these gaps are at the same time the cause and the effect of the weaknesses which characterise dispute resolution, as most of the legal frameworks set up to respond to biological invasions are totally deprived of such types of institutions, and intergovernmental negotiation is seen as the only possible alternative.

b Structural causes of ineffectiveness: environmentalism v. state-centrism

If gaps, overlaps and inconsistencies at the most diverse level are the *prima facie* deluding aspect in the evaluation of the global fight against biological invasions, there are causes working at a less superficial, yet important, level. The normative framework set up against biological invasions, as a part of international environmental law, stands in a rather dialectic relationship with the state-centric system and its supporting legal structures based on the contraposition between "subjects" (states) and "objects" (environment and, ultimately, territory) of the regulatory effort. This dichotomy has, in fact, proved to be at the basis of the current ineffectiveness, as the environmentalist logic – which tends to focus on the territorial aspect rather than on the ultimate political or legal authority – can be problematically framed within the traditional Westphalian state-centric system (Biermann and Dingwerth, 2004).

This remark appears all the more well-founded if looking at the poor results of many global treaties dealing with transboundary environmental issues, and to the even scarcer outcomes of intergovernmental conferences which have often raised great expectations. As a matter of fact, the quantitative explosion of environmental treaties dealing with the widest possible range of ecological issues has had as one of its main consequences the multiplication of secretariats and intergovernmental conferences of parties, and the flourishing of commitments for governments in their domestic arena. Furthermore, this expansion has not been combined with a decisive move towards better coordination, and differences in the cultural, economic and social spheres among states have led to an increasing "conventional fatigue" (Chasek, 1997) in dealing with overlapping, contradictory and often unrelated agreements. Moreover, the rush to the convention has been followed by an unceasingly expanding number of meetings convened on a vast array of environmentally related issues, further complicating the picture and exacerbating the impression of a general ineffectiveness of the incremental global approach (Vandeever, 2003). Furthermore, the time-consuming negotiations, the weak outcomes (often reached on a least common denominator), the chronic absence of a capacity to monitor countries compliance, and the lack of enforcement measures are all good reasons to retain at least as a hypothesis the search for a valid alternative.

In this sense, the presence of still strong and active state actors – far from promoting some kind of imaginary post-Westphalian scenario – suggests a more realistic conceptual re-construction, capable of separating sovereignty and territory (Sassen, 2007). In such a way, the territorial element would lose its mainly "cartographic" features by finally detaching its legal value of possession "integrally related to the state" from its actual, environmental significance of a reality "not inherently tied to the state" (Biggs, 1999). Shifting the view of territory from a basis for the exercise of jurisdiction to a – maybe more abstract but also less politicised – new concept of "space for governability", new paths emerge in order to challenge pressing and non-deferrable emergencies such as the environmental, social and economic consequences of biological invasions without, however, confining regulatory powers within fixed borders or national containers (Cooper, 2001).

This spatial and political configuration might support the cooperation of actors at the sub- or supranational level with a direct interest in the effective safeguard of a given ecosystem. In this sense, there are a number of reasons militating in favour of a regionalist approach to the regulation of biological invasions. Indeed, recent experiences in the field of regional cooperation – even if not forcefully limited to environmental protection – have provided outstanding examples confirming that a more homogenous society of states can be a more suitable space of governance, in which the lack of universality is compensated by a more compelling regulatory framework, particularly if looking at "success stories" relating to the development of regional organisations aimed at protecting and promoting human rights through a fully judicial system composed of binding norms and courts vested with real statutory and enforcement powers. As far as environment is concerned, it is possible to lay down a two-sided hypothesis on the reasons for the "collective action advantage" of the regional over the universal level. On the one hand, internal cooperation: regional environmental agreements have a better chance to succeed because of greater similarity of interests, norms, perceptions and values (Conca, 2012). On the other, external scepticism: national governments are starting to see regional cooperation as a more promising and effective way to achieve progress in environmental issues if compared to the limited results of the ongoing global efforts (Halle, 2012). Following the pattern designed from these two determinants, regionalism would preserve a transnational approach, with the added value of greater cultural homogeneity and more effective responsiveness to pressing issues.

2.4 Regionalism as a theoretical and legal phenomenon: general concepts

Before analysing in greater detail how regional environmental governance could become a viable alternative in order to obtain a more effective and comprehensive safeguard of the ecosystems against the threats posed by non-native species, it seems particularly useful to shed some light on the theoretical and legal foundations of regionalism itself, seen as a specific type of political aggregation in the broader category of "international organisations".

a What's in a name? Conceptualising and contextualising "region" and "regionalism"

The notion of region derives from the Latin lemma *regio*, which could indicate at the same time an administrative zone or a broad area characterised by similar geographical features. For its intrinsic ambiguity, the notion can also have a "geographical" meaning, emphasising physical and strategic elements, and a "functional" reading, highlighting the role of regions as spaces of economic, socio-cultural and environmental governance. Actually, regional organisations can be identified as the combination of these two elements: they are indeed social constructs, in which geographical, political, economic, strategic and cultural concerns are fundamental "drivers of agglutination" for a number of actors bound together by trends, values, practices and – in some cases – binding norms (Fawcett, 2014). Regional organisations can thus be defined as supranational aggregations characterised by a common sense of identity and purpose, combined with the creation and implementation of institutions expressing a particular identity and shaping collective action within a geographically and/or functionally defined region (Evans, 2005).

From the historical point of view, the modern idea of regionalism is a by-product of the 20th century and has developed its main features in opposition to the so-called "malevolent regionalism" (Teló, 2007), the name conventionally given to the attempt made between the 1930s and 1940s by Germany in Europe and Japan in the Asia/Pacific to impose *manu militari*, their political and economic hegemony over surrounding regions. If such a pathological antecedent was marked by domination, brutality and unilateralism, international lawyers have found as cornerstones of modern regionalism the legal origin of the agreement, the free consent of the parties, and the mutual nature of the obligations. Emerging at the end of the Second World War, regionalism has been influenced by the dynamics of confrontation between the US and the USSR and by the immediate rupture of the post-war international system built around the twin pillars of national sovereignty and multilateral institutions (Hurrell, 2007). While the contraposition between the champions of the two blocks in which the international society was polarising escalated, the United Nations faced growing constraints, and regional ties started to be conceived not only as complementary but also as alternative routes to universal cooperation, at first in the military field through the establishment of security alliances, and later in the economic and trade spheres (e.g. NATO and EEC against Warsaw Pact and COMECON). During the process of decolonisation, regionalisation started to be seen as an "independence movement" aimed at detaching "southern" questions of development from "northern" issues of security and trade (Grunwald et al., 1972). Finally, in the final decades of the 20th century, the end of the Cold War – and the simultaneous acceleration of globalisation – led regionalism to face an epochal transition, focused on the adaptation to the complexity of the new political, economic and security scenario. The emerging "plural" and "decentralised" international society provided incentives for a quantitative increase in the number of regional organisations, seen not as "resurgent spheres of influence but as a complement to healthy internationalism" (Boutros-Ghali 1992), together with qualitative modifications in terms of expanded membership, agency, capacities and tasks (Fawcett and Hurrell, 1995).

In this new paradigm, known as neoregionalism, states keep their role as principal actors in international affairs, but on a totally different stage marked by a substantial reconfiguration of political and spatial models of governance. This innovative vision has another, fundamental, consequence: if regionalism was in its origin a product of state attempts to reaffirm their boundaries into territorially exclusive groups, new regionalism draws further reasons of existence from the independent interplay of sub- and transnational economic, environmental and cultural actors (Gochhayat, 2014). In other words, regional organisations work as "clearing houses" in those sectors in which states cannot play as autonomously as before, thus facilitating political aggregations around emerging demands and pressing needs (Crouch and Streeck, 1997).

This remark permits a transition from the theory of international relations to the legal and regulatory perspectives that can be linked to the neoregionalist approach. In order to enquire on "environmental regionalism" as a possible alternative to the ineffectiveness of the universal regulatory reaction to biological invasions it seems useful to understand if – and how – regional regimes can qualify as legal entities, and not only as economic, social, strategic and political actors.

b Legal interpretations of the regionalist phenomenon

In the international legal debate, the combination of decolonisation, globalisation and fragmentation of international law have contributed in raising the issue of regionalism from the mere policy level to a more concrete debate, to the extent that the International Law Commission of the United Nations (ILC) has dedicated to the "varying uses of the expression regionalism as part of legal and political rhetoric" a section of its study on the fragmentation of the international legal order (Koskenniemi, 2006). In particular, the Commission has found three distinct meanings of regionalism in international law.

The first category of interpretations considers regionalism in its broader sense as a set of approaches and methods for examining international law. In particular, it looks at regionalism as a way to make reference to specific orientations of legal thought and culture. An important example of this idea of regionalism can be found in Article 8 of the Statute of the International Law Commission itself, which requires that its composition should represent "the main forms of civilisation and of the principal legal systems of the world". Another important reflection of this notion of regionalism is the criterion of the "equitable geographic distribution" informing the composition of the greater part of the UN bodies.

A second possible reading identifies in regionalism a privileged forum for international law-making because of the relative homogeneity of the interests and values of concerned actors, favouring a more efficient and/or equitable implementation of the norms together with a greater legitimacy of the regulation. This reading – which has met fierce opposition by scholars interpreting regionalism as an instrument of hegemony (Schmitt, 1950; Grewe, 2000)[9] – is deeply rooted in the sociological theory of international law and postulates that states progressively become part of larger normative units as a result of expanding circles of "solidarity" fuelled by cultural affinities, economic linkages and perception of common threats (Scelles, 1948; Bull, 1977).

A third reading of regionalism under an international law perspective can be designed as "exceptionalist". In this sense, regional arrangements would not only create geographically restricted customs and rules, but also limit or preempt the legal force of universal international law in such a region in favour of a rule or principle with an autonomous sphere of validity. Furthermore, regional rules would also impose their binding value on those states and subjects of international law in the region not wishing to accept them. Such claims of an "independent" and "exclusive" application of a regional norm have been brought to the International Court of Justice in 1950 in the *Asylum* case (*Colombia v. Perù*), related to the emergence of a separate body of "Latin American" law on the matter of diplomatic asylum. Even if in this particular case the Court did not specifically address the possible existence of separate regional legal orders – existence which is, by the way, accepted as far as considered as a regional custom – there is in state practice very little support for an extremist reading of such an interpretation.

In sum, these three theoretical readings of the phenomenon of regionalism can be distributed along a continuum which goes from the mere recognition of the cultural and historical contribution given by regional traditions to universal international law to the claim of independence of regional norms and principles by the general *ius gentium*. If the first reading seems too reductionist, since different regional legal traditions have originated local treaty and customary norms, it is nevertheless important to emphasise how the "exceptionalist" reading pushes the legal reasoning too far, giving to regionally developed principles an excessive autonomy and claiming a total disconnection from universal international law. If these conflicting tendencies are not representative of the current state of the art in international law, the second option is an adequate middle ground: on the one hand, it does not reduce regionalism to the role of cultural influence; on the other, it does not exaggerate its actual value beyond the real intentions of the states. According to this school of thought, regional organisations can be seen as *fora convenientes* where states can find more homogenous views and implement more effective solutions for shared problems and pressing concerns.

The sociological theory of international law combined with the geo-functionalist notion of region and with the neoregionalist theoretical paradigm thus offers, under the environmental perspective, a powerful alternative to the ascertained ineffectiveness of the global regulatory framework. If the geo-functionalist nature of regional organisations is the ideal ground in order to approach a dynamic reality marked by the interrelation between human actions and the surrounding environment, the neoregionalist approach to international relations is particularly helpful in conveying the role of non-state actors in ecological concerns. The sociological theory of international law, then, adds to these eminently political observations an authoritative legal component as regional organisations can prove to be fundamental spaces for law-making in a transnational issue such as the response to biological invasions. The next section will present the result of this combination of relevant factors as "environmental regionalism", thus representing a key passage in beginning the *pars construens* of this work.

2.5 Introducing environmental concerns into the *neoregionalist* paradigm

Along the centuries, environment has become an enabler of state authority and/or national identity. Rivers, mountains and seas have worked for centuries as "natural borders", defining the limits of nation-states' territorial sovereignty. Throughout human history wars have been fought for the conquest of secure boundaries coinciding with natural barriers, while the absence of landmarks has sometimes determined the extinction of entire state entities. Whatever may be the case, the Westphalian international order has always seen environment as an element of separation, rather than as a driver of trans-boundary cooperation. This is one of the reasons explaining the late appearance of environmental regionalism in the socio-political and legal debate.

Based on the idea that ecological concerns have gained enough strength to influence regionalism as an ideology – and regionalisation as a process (Bälsiger, 2011) – environmental regionalism is rooted in the increasing awareness about cross-border environmental issues, such as ozone depletion, climate change, and water and air pollution (Dodds, 1998), and in the disappointment which has accompanied the "conventional rush" at the universal level. It implies that adequate policies should be coordinated and implemented at the regional level as a response to the failure of the global approach, with the ultimate aim of realising a type of polity in which "political dynamics should correspond to ecological areas" (Church, 2010).

This ambitious aim has, as a first necessary step, to provide a definition of the rather undetermined notion of "ecological area". Over the past decades, many terms have been proposed to identify the ecological scale in which regional policy should be conducted: terms like "ecoregion", "bioregion", "georegion" and "biogeographical province" have thus been suggested, and their meaning has been deeply influenced by the adoption of an ecological, geographical or political perspective. Actually, all these expressions can be used as synonyms, even if the most common reference in academic and scientific debates is to "ecoregions".

Firstly, crafting a definition of "ecoregion" is not a perfect science. Many disciplines can, in fact, rightfully claim their own right in determining which combination of common traits is necessary to qualify a particular area as an environmentally homogeneous spatial entity. As an example, biologists can suggest that an ecoregion would be defined by "recurring pattern of ecosystems associated with characteristic combinations of soil and landform that characterise that region" (Brunckhorst, 2000). Still, geographers can add up to that definition and identify ecological regions as those "areas within which there is spatial coincidence in characteristics of geographical phenomena (such as geology, vegetation, climate, hydrology, flora and fauna) associated with differences in the quality, health, and integrity of ecosystems" (Ormenik, 2004). At the same time, the definition of what an ecoregion is varies in time and in space, as ecosystems gradually change and are modified in such ways that it becomes difficult to identify exact dividing boundaries.

Notwithstanding this high variability, a fairly consensual definition of ecoregion has been achieved, thus marking a neat difference with respect to the uncertainty that still characterises the general concept of region. According to this perspective, the ecosystem approach has worked as a powerful catalyst for an interdisciplinary, agreed concept. According to this notion, "ecoregions" are "large areas of relatively uniform climate that harbour a characteristic set of species and ecological communities" (Udvardy, 1975). This definition has also worked as a basis for the World Wide Fund for Nature (WWF) in its effort to outline a science-based, comprehensive map of the most biologically distinct ecoregions in the world. According to the WWF, an ecoregion is "a large area of land or water that contains a geographically distinct assemblage of natural communities that share a large majority of their species and ecological dynamics; share similar environmental conditions; and interact ecologically in ways that are critical for their long-term persistence" (WWF, 2000).

Once the spatial element is identified, there are many possible ways in which political and regulatory dynamics could be rescaled beyond national borders. There are, in fact, cases in which ecoregions and environmental agreements insist over the same territory. At the same time, environmental concerns can also lead to the formation of functional regions (Bälsiger et al., 2012). In other circumstances, environmentally defined regions do not correspond with the boundaries of functional regions.

The challenge for international relations and international law is to find ways to overcome the hiatus that often separates the ecological identity of a region – defined according to its natural elements or internal structure (Paasi, 2003) – on the one hand, and the institutional framework in which environmental issues are addressed and dealt with on the other. In this sense, environmental regionalism is the result of the simultaneous process of the "emancipation" of ecological concerns from mere territorial considerations, and of a "contamination" of the legal definition of regionalism with geographic elements. There are considerations supporting this remark, both in theory and from a governance standpoint.

A first set of argumentation has a theoretical nature, as it consists of a thorough enquiry on two key concepts: boundary creation and functional sectorialisation. Pressing and transboundary ecological challenges are increasingly working as agents of territorial reconfiguration, as they shift the borders of the political body beyond the national dimension towards the nearest possible level to the source of the ecological concern. The description of an ecoregion as a geographic cluster identified by environmental elements acquires a more political sense through the inclusion of societal factors. This passage is crucial to realise the shift towards a prescriptive notion of regionalism as a normative option aimed at dealing in a more effective way with ecological concerns through a "cooperative" form of post-territorial and multi-level governance (Hurrell, 1995). Differently from the similar dynamic which led to the formation of the modern nation-state on the basis of security-driven dynamics, however, regional arrangements cannot be established by the desire of a ruler to preempt previously independent entities from their faculty of territorial organisation. Rather, this delegation of sovereignty is the product of "negotiated and agreed partnership institutions" (Veggeland, 2004) which set up fora for multilateral dialogue in issues where the national state is faced by overwhelming challenges. Precisely in this latter feature lies the solution to the alleged incompatibility between boundary marking and functional sectorialisation, as the territorial element of ecological regions is tempered by a solidarity link between political units, which gives origin to "functional constellations" (Bälsiger, 2011). The issue of boundary marking is thus inextricably intertwined with functional sectorialisation, since it constitutes one of its founding moments (Rokkan, 1999).

Secondly, the compatibility of these two different interpretations in a unique *weltanschauung* is explained by considerations relating to environmental governance. Particularly, natural regions and environmental regionalisation are two inextricable aspects of ecological regulation: the first deals with problem setting, while the latter regards problem solving. In other words, it is human intervention that marks the transition of ecoregions from entities existing *per se* to objects of governance. Even if boundaries do not forcefully coincide, it is still possible for regional organisations to work in a functional way to protect ecoregions within their territorial assets, in a situation of heterarchy, that is "*a* plurality of overlapping elements lacking a clear ranking and having varying degrees of connectivity" (Crumley, 1995). This can happen because regional cooperation implies "concentric circles of political nature . . ., compromised by numerous crosscutting allegiances, connection, and modes of collaboration" (Connolly, 2000) and constitutes "multiple overlapping networks of interaction that crystallize around different sites of power, producing patterns of activity which do not correspond in any straightforward way to territorial boundaries" (Held, 1999). Applying this reasoning to the European integration, Schmitter suggests that "instead of a single Europe with recognized and contiguous boundaries, there would be many Europes: a trading Europe, an energy Europe, an environmental Europe, a social welfare Europe, even a defence Europe" (Schmitter, 2000). The application of the neoregionalist interpretative paradigm can thus easily reconcile this apparently unsolvable contraposition between the ecological and functional definitions of region. Within these extremes lies the construction of environmental regionalism, the practical embodiments of which will be presented in the next paragraph.

2.6 Regional environmental governance in practice

What in abstract terms can be referred to as regional environmental governance underpins in concrete a plurality of situations. Taking into account this pluralist reality, it is possible to categorise environmental regional experiences according to a three-dimensional taxonomy: the first dimension – or political dimension – deals with membership, which is understood as the expression from legitimate state authorities of the will to be bound by an international instrument. In recent decades, many agreements have been signed by states at the bilateral and multilateral levels in order to manage transboundary issues, such as air or water pollution, protection of migratory birds, and fragile ecosystems management (Chester, 2006). The second dimension relates to the spatial ambit, in which environmental problems are addressed by members to a given agreement. To these two dimensions, it is possible to add a third relational aspect: contiguity. The membership of an environmental agreement is contiguous if the territories of the members meet at their respective borders. Similarly, membership is non-contiguous if there are no shared borders. As far as the spatial ambit is concerned, contiguity refers to the perfect correspondence between the object of the agreement and a definite territory.

The introduction of these three variables is of paramount importance, since it contributes not only to isolating the regional gene, but also to understanding the dynamics of regional environmental cooperation. The combination of those dimensions generates four types of international agreements and identifies three ideal types of environmental regional organisation.

Following the evidence shown in the table, there are three main forms of regional organisations in the environmental domain: the core-regional, in which membership and the spatial ambit fully coincide; the ambit-regional, composed of non-contiguous states; and the membership-regional, in which contiguous states achieve an agreement on a non-contiguous spatial ambit. Bearing this distinction in mind, it is undoubtedly easier to find practical examples for each of these broadly defined categories. In this sense, a great help comes from the Ecolex, a database on environmental law operated jointly by the Food and Agriculture Organization (FAO), the United Nations Environment Programme (UNEP) and the World Conservation Union (IUCN).

Table 2.1 Basic types of international environmental agreements (with examples)

		Membership	*(Territorial jurisdiction)*
		Contiguous	*Non-contiguous*
Spatial ambit	**Contiguous**	Core-regional (Agreement on the Cooperation for the Sustainable Development of the Mekong River Basin, 1995)	Ambit-regional (Convention on the Conservation and Management of Highly Migratory Fish Stocks in the Western and Central Pacific Ocean, 2000)
	Non-contiguous	Membership-regional (Nordic Mutual Emergency Assistance agreement in connection with Radiation Accidents, 1963)	Non-regional

Author's elaboration based on Bälsiger et al., 2012

As far as core-regional agreements are concerned, an example of very strong core-regional cooperation with a territorial application that is coextensive to the jurisdiction of all concerned member states is the Agreement on the Cooperation for the Sustainable Development of the Mekong River Basin, signed by Cambodia, Lao PDR, Thailand and Vietnam in 1995. It is also possible that contiguous members would sign an agreement regarding a restricted, yet contiguous, spatial ambit. In relation to membership-regional agreements, the main category is represented by agreements aimed at establishing cooperation between contiguous states in a determinate field which is non-specific in terms of spatial application, or which imposes obligation on the members within their borders. In this sense, the relation between the spatial ambit and membership cannot be explained in terms of co-extensiveness. It is, in turn, the concept of adjacency which can better express this type of relation. The cases of the Nordic Mutual Emergency Assistance agreement in connection with Radiation Accidents (1963) and the European Commission for the control of Foot-and-Mouth disease (1954) are paradigmatic cases.

Finally, ambit-regional organisations usually include states from non-contiguous parts of the world that establish a cooperation aimed at protecting a specific, restricted spatial ambit. An example is, in that sense, the Convention on the Conservation and Management of Highly Migratory Fish Stocks in the Western and Central Pacific Ocean (2000): this agreement is, in fact, opened not only to the coastal states of the Western and Central Pacific, but also to those which have fishing interests in that region.

Nevertheless, it is crucial to remark on how geographical diversity is just a component – perhaps, the most evident – of a far more complex scenario: regional environmental governance is, in fact, shaped by a variety of social, political and legal entities addressing ecological concerns (Debarbieux, 2012). Under this perspective, the debate needs to be translated from a mere categorisation of *what* a region ontologically is to a more epistemological plan, and particularly to the identification of *how* regional environmental governance is institutionalised and translated into practice. In this sense, the study of environmental regionalism fluctuates between two extremes: regional scope and scope of regionality.

Both of these theoretical concepts exert pressure on one of the extremes of the abovementioned alleged conflict between geographical and functional regions. On the one hand, the regional scope looks at the ways in which regional entities are built around pre-existing ecological regions or environmental concerns; on the other, the enquiry on the scope of regionality is focused on the evolution of an existing political, regulatory, or legal framework in an environmentally oriented sense. If the first school of thought seems inextricably linked to a geographical conception of region, thus sacrificing the functional dimension, the second stream is particularly linked to a dynamic interpretation of what environmental regulation is. In fact, even if *prima facie* the quest for an environmental scope in already existing regional organisations seems to be a methodological constraint aimed at using old parameters to judge new phenomena, it is nevertheless true that those aggregations are capable of overhauling the mere form of cross-border cooperation among state entities.

This new argumentation can be ingrained into the practice of regional environmental governance. In particular, it is possible to enquire into the degree of pervasiveness of a regional environmental organisation into national legislation and regulations. The adoption of this parameter helps in identifying and distinguishing "environmental regional cooperation" from "environmental regional integration", and in distributing concrete experiences in a continuum which varies from very weak to very strong regionalisation of environmental concerns.

Those theoretical assumptions can be operationalised through a process of five consecutive steps towards regionalisation: information-sharing, consultation, cooperation, harmonisation, and finally, total integration (VanNijnatten, 2011).

Generally speaking, information-sharing is the basis of any international agreement – bilateral or multilateral, regional or global – and constitutes the minimum threshold to start any type of cooperation. Usually, this level of regionalisation is coupled with a very loose spatial contiguity and a high level of generality in the provisions. This is the case, for instance, of the Group of Temperate Southern Hemisphere Countries on Environment (also known as Valdivia Group), whose geographical extension equals the looseness of the commitment. Cooperation is, in fact, limited to the identification of common interest and to grant communication among the scientific and environmental management communities in the member countries.

As far as consultation is concerned, the slight difference with respect to information exchange is the more open involvement of the political level through the convening of intergovernmental meetings and/or the institutionalisation

Table 2.2 The five stages of regional environmental integration

Degree of commitment	*Stages of regionalisation*	*Definition*	*Levol of generality*	*Degree of pervasiveness*	*Example*
Procedural	Information-sharing	Exchange of technical information and data	Very high	Very weak	Group of Temperate Southern Hemisphere Countries on Environment (Valdivia Group)
	Consultation	Involvement at a governmental level	High	Weak	Commission for Environmental Cooperation (CEC)
Substantial	Cooperation	Coordination of separate domestic activities	Medium	Medium	Association of the South East Asian Nations (ASEAN)
	Harmonisation	Shared actions carried out under the terms of formal agreement	Low	Strong	East African Community (EAC)
	Integration	Formal adoption of shared objectives through joint or linked policies	Very low	Very strong	European Union

Author's elaboration based on VanNijnatten, 2011

of some supranational council. It is also the case of the Commission for Environmental Cooperation (CEC), whose main task is to facilitate collaboration between Canada, the United States and Mexico in the context of the North American Free Trade Agreement (NAFTA). The main body of the organisation, the Council of the three environmental ministers, meets once a year and has restricted powers of inquiry and information-sharing. However, the close geographical ties between the member countries are lessened by their great territorial extension, which contributes to separating the priorities of each party and in preempting the agreement from its cooperative goals. The lack of a common position in relation to a pressing issue such as climate change is, in this sense, a reliable parameter to assess the low degree of integration reached by this potentially pivotal regional arrangement (Betsill, 2001).

If the first two steps can be defined as procedural, the three main steps represent the substantial core of the process of environmental regionalisation.

Cooperation is, in this sense, the first substantial step towards regional integration, as it goes beyond the mere intergovernmental level and provides a process of rule-making for the domestic enforcement of a legislation aimed at gaining mutual benefits and at promoting the effectiveness of the regional response. An example of cooperation on environmental matters comes from the Association of the South East Asian Nations (ASEAN). Even if the focus of this regional organisation was at first strategic and at present mainly economic, environmental cooperation has become a distinctive feature at the turn of the 21st century. This has happened through the so-called "ASEAN way", intended as a preference for soft institutionalism, non-binding agreements, non-interference and non-authoritative direction on the environmental practices of member states. All these typical characteristics, which at present are still guiding principles in the ASEAN action, have led to a reliance on national laws and policy-making as the basis of regional cooperation (Elliott, 2012).

Harmonisation represents, with respect to cooperation, a further step in the commitment to institutionalisation due to the existence of formal agreements aimed at setting common objectives to be achieved through shared – yet nationally implemented – courses of action. In this sense, a success story comes from the East African Community (EAC), an advanced laboratory of integration encompassing a customs union (since 2005) and a common market (since 2010). The localisation of these countries in the region of the African Great Lakes makes the environment an absolutely pivotal asset in building a sense of regional community and in fostering close cooperation among member states around specific issues and objectives. A paradigmatic example of such a vision comes from the Protocol on Environment and Natural Resources Management, which in Article 5 explicitly mentions the promotion of the development and harmonisation of policies, laws and strategies among member states.

The final step in regional environmental governance is the total integration of the legislation of member countries through common and linked policies. This elevated degree of interdependence can be reached, however, only by means of sovereignty cessions to a supranational organisation vested with quasi-legislative powers. The role model is, in this case, the European Union (EU), which will be the object of a thorough examination in the next chapter.

2.7 Final remarks: an *ex ante* justification for analysing the European Union

It is almost a commonplace to use the European Union as the most advanced laboratory of regional environmental governance, and the European continent as the territorial forefront of transnational ecological protection. Indeed, these assumptions possess a high degree of truth.

Europe has been the first abode of supranational environmental regulation in the 19th century, at first through bilateral treaties on fisheries, and progressively by expanding the range to multilateral agreements on the protection of watercourses, animals and plants. The European example stimulated in those pioneering years many attempts of imitation in other regional contexts, and particularly on the American continent. If other continents have followed the European example in the last part of the 19th century and in the first part of the 20th century, it is all the more true that Europe has maintained since then a sort of "comparative advantage" in the environmental field, which can be illustrated by recurring to the heterodox, physical idea of density. In fact, if the mass (that is the quantity) of environmentally related agreements and/or transnational institutions is compared to the tiny fraction of the globe occupied by Europe, the difference with respect to experiences on other continents is particularly perceivable.[10]

As far as the reasons of the advantage are concerned, it is possible to identify two sets of argumentation confirming that Europe is still the standard-bearer of regional environmental governance. The first is rather general and deals with historical reasons, while the second is the product of a teleologically oriented reading of an overarching principle of contemporary European Union law: the subsidiarity principle.

Historically, it is possible to identify an almost physiological lag separating the adoption of an agreement dealing with some type of ecological concerns in Europe and in the rest of the world. A particularly fitting case regards the regulation and management of transboundary watercourses. Looking at the database of the International Water Law Project, the first-ever multilateral agreement on this topic is the Mainz Convention on the Navigation of the Rhine River (1831), which established the principle of free navigation while institutionalising an ad hoc Central Commission. A first, partial attempt aimed at setting up a cooperative effort in the management of a transboundary river occurred more than 70 years later in North America. In the absence of multilateral treaties due to obvious geographical and political reasons, the first document regarding freshwater regulation – and not treating rivers as mere elements in boundary-marking – was the 1906 Convention between the United States and Mexico on issues of water distribution and allocation for the Rio Grande River. In the southern part of the continent, the development of a similar type of transnational regulation had its origin only in 1947 at the bilateral level through the Agreement Concerning the Utilization of the Rapids of the Uruguay River in the Salto Grande Area between Argentina and Uruguay, while the first multilateral agreement was reached in 1969, when the Treaty on the River Plate Basin was signed by Argentina, Bolivia, Brazil, Paraguay and Uruguay.

African and Asian efforts deserve a different discourse, as autonomous forms of cooperation were a consequence of the decolonisation process in those continents. Agreements on transboundary rivers were in fact already signed by the European colonising countries, but only after independence the negotiation of new arrangements gained a full political and regional dimension. In this sense, the first relevant document was the Act Regarding Navigation and Economic Co-operation between the States of the Niger Basin, signed in Niamey in 1963 by Benin, Burkina Faso, Cameroon, Chad, Guinea, Ivory Coast, Mali, Niger and Nigeria. In Asia, the tradition of non-interference in domestic politics led to an agreement only in 1995, when the Agreement on the Cooperation for the Sustainable Development of the Mekong River Basin was signed by Cambodia, Lao PDR, Thailand and Vietnam.

Rivers are, however, only the most evident example of the anticipatory nature of the European environmental multilateral tradition. Other relevant examples can be the regulation of transboundary mountains (i.e. the Alpine Convention) or lakes (i.e. the Convention Concerning Navigation on the Lake Constance).

A second array of reasons justifying a focus on the European continent, in general, and on the European Union, in particular, is linked to more strictly legal arguments. It is undeniable that Europe has witnessed an authentic turn in environmental regulation with the progressive institutionalisation of environmental issues and concerns at the regional level.

This has occurred especially since 1987, when the Single European Act (SEA) came into force and put economic and ecologic issues on a more equal footing through the express provision of environmental protection in the Treaty of the European Economic Community (EEC; McCormick, 2001), particularly by means of the new Article 130R, which imposed on the Community and on Member States the duty "to preserve, protect and improve the quality of the environment, to contribute towards protecting human health, and to ensure a prudent and rational utilization of natural resources", enunciating the precautionary principle, and specifying that the Community "shall take action relating to the environment to the extern to which the objectives referred to in paragraph I can be attained better at Community level than at the level of the individual Member States". This reference to the principle of subsidiarity has a different significance if referred to environmental concerns and does not forcefully limit the competence of the European institutions, considering the transboundary nature of many ecological concerns, which make of the supranational plan the most adequate regulatory level.

To verify the soundness of this last assumption, the next chapter will briefly examine all aspects of the environmental policy of the European Union, before performing a detailed analysis of the Union legislation in the field of biological invasions.

Notes

1 This approach is confirmed by the Malmoe Ministerial Declaration, adopted in 2000 in the framework of the Sixth Special Session of the Governing Council of the United Nations Environmental Programme (UNEP) and calling for greater coherence and coordination among international environmental instruments. After a first report, issued in 2001 by the open-ended group of ministries, the project was stationary until 2009, when the question was delivered to a group of regionally representative ministers with the task to elaborate a set of options for improving international governance. Similar initiatives were a report by the High-Level Panel on United Nations System-wide Coherence in the Areas of Development, Humanitarian Assistance and the Environment (*Delivering as One*, in Follow Up to the Outcome of the Millennium Summit, A/RES/61/583), and an options paper presented by the Informative Consultative Process on the Institutional Framework for the United Nations Environment Activities in June 2007 (www.un.org/ga/president/61/follow-up/environment/EG-OptionsPaper.PDF).

2 The first elements of the "polluter pays" principle are contained in the final decision of the Arbitral Tribunal in the *Trail Smelter* case (1938). In particular, lacking any international rule on the matter, the Tribunal used the principle set up by the United States Supreme Court in *Story Parchment Company v. Paterson Parchment Paper Company* (1931) that relief must be provided for the injured person and accountability to the wrongdoer in the form of monetary compensation.

3 In 1989, an oil tanker ran aground and over 300,000 barrels of crude oil poured into Alaskan waters. Exxon was in principle required to pay USD 125 million in fines to the US federal government and the state of Alaska, as well as USD 900 million for a fund to be doled out by government officials for environmental projects, among other things. In addition, Exxon was put under tremendous political pressure to restore the shoreline. It thus engaged in an extensive and costly clean-up operation, with controversial results.

4 The International Plant Protection Convention, signed in 1951 and revised in 1997, operates in the framework of the Food and Agriculture Organization (FAO) of the United Nations and currently has 181 signatories. As for animal health, a similar role is played by the Office International des Épizooties (OIE), an international organisation established in 1924 with the aims to prevent and control the spread of diseases with regard to trade in animals and animal products and to set out standards on import risk analysis and risk management measures for specific diseases, but does not cover related habitat and ecosystem issues. Like the IPPC (with its ISPM 6: *Guidelines for surveillance*, ISPM 9: *Guidelines for pest eradication programs*, and ISPM 17: *Pest reporting*), the OIE framework provides a legal basis for pest and disease surveillance, notification and control. OIE has a global network of over 150 Reference Laboratories working on the identification of new diseases and emerging hosts to develop harmonized detection and control methods.

5 An example of treaty congestion is given by the overlap of international instruments dealing with introductions to marine and coastal ecosystems, where the general jurisdiction of the United Nations Convention on the Law of the Seas (UNCLOS) registers meaningful interplays with regional systems, international

guidelines and codes of conduct dealing with particular matters (such as the reduction of the risk of escapes from mariculture operations, and the response to introductions and transfers of marine organisms caused by the release of ballast water or by land-based activities, including through sewage and runoffs).

6 A notable example comes from the international sanitary and phytosanitary treaty-system, which potentially covers all taxonomic groups and lower taxonomic categories, but only to the extent that these are injurious to animal or plant health (i.e. the IPPC's trigger for pest classification is "injurious to plants or plant products"). This covers alien organisms that could damage wild plants, but not explicitly those that may harm ecosystem function or plant genetic diversity.

7 Examples of those two extremes are, on the one hand, Article 17.1 of the Protocol on Nature Conservation and Landscape Protection to the Alpine Convention ("The Contracting Parties shall assure that no wild animal or plant species are introduced into a region that were not previously present naturally for a verifiable historic period. Exceptions can be made in cases in which such introducing is necessary for certain uses and will not lead to negative effects on nature and the landscape") and, on the other, Article 3.3(c) of the ASEAN Agreement on the Conservation of Nature and Natural Resources, which states that "Parties shall endeavor to regulate and, where necessary, prohibit the introduction of exotic species".

8 Principle 19 of the Rio Declaration, which is unanimously interpreted to be a customary set of rules for international environmental law, provides that "States shall provide prior and timely notification and relevant information to potentially affected States on activities that may have a significant transboundary environmental adverse effect and shall consult with those States at an early stage and in good faith". This principle is also formulated in several treaties including, as an example, the Convention on Environmental Impact Assessment (EIA) in a Transboundary Context (also known as the Espoo Convention, 1991).

9 In particular, Schmitt cites the Monroe Doctrine as an example of a regional tool of exercising hegemonic power, as a response to parallel hegemonic regional aggregations in other parts of the world.

10 It is, in fact, undeniable that still at present the European continent hosts a variety of environmental agreements dealing with the main natural elements present therein. The Alpine Convention, the Commission for the Navigation of the Rhine River, the Danube River Protection Convention, the Framework Convention on the Protection and Sustainable Development of the Carpathians, and the Landscape Convention all provide insightful examples of how territorial and environmental considerations have always been at the forefront of transnational cooperation on the continent.

Bibliography

Bälsiger, J. (2011), New environmental regionalism and sustainable development in *Procedia Social and Behavioural Science* 14: 44–48.

Bälsiger, J., Prys, M. and Steinhoff, N. (2012a), *The nature and role of regional agreements in international environmental politics: Mapping agreements, outlining future research* in GIGA Working Papers, No. 208.

Betsill, M.M. (2001), Mitigating Climate Change in U.S. cities: Opportunities and Obstacles in *Local Env* 6(4): 396–406.

Betsill, M.M. (2007), Regional governance of global climate change: The North American commission for environmental cooperation in *Global Environ Polit* 7(2): 11–27.

Biermann, F. and Dingwerth, K. (2004), Global environmental change and the Nation state in *Global Environ Polit* 4: 1.

Biggs, M. (1999), Putting the state on the map: Cartography, territory, and European state formation in *Comparative Studies in Society and History* 41: 374–399.

Birnie, P. and Boyle, A. (2002), *International law and the environment*, Oxford University Press, Oxford.

Boutros-Ghali, B. (1992), *An agenda for peace: Preventive diplomacy, peacemaking and peacekeeping*, report of the Secretary General of the United Nations, A/47/277, United Nations, New York, NY.

Boutros-Ghali, B. (2000), An agenda for democratization in B. Holden (ed.), *Global democracy, key debates*, Routledge, London.

Boyd, W. (2010), Climate change, fragmentation and the challenge of global environmental law: Elements of a post Copenhagen assemblage, in *U Pa J Int'l L* 32(2): 459–547.

Brown Weiss, E. (1993), International environmental law: Contemporary issues and the emergence of a new world order in *Geo L J*675: 697–702.

Brunckhorst, D. (2000), *Bioregional planning resource management beyond the new millennium*, Harwood Academic Publishers, Sydney, Australia.

Bull, H. (1977), *The anarchical society : A study of order in World Politics*, Palgrave Macmillan, London.

Cameron, J. and Abouchar, J. (1991), The precautionary principle: A fundamental principle of law and policy for the protection of the global environment in *Boston College Int Comp Law Rev* 14(1): 1–27.

Chasek, P. (1997), The convention to combat desertification: Lessons learned for sustainable development in *JED* 6(2): 147–167.

Chester, C. (2006), *Conservation across Borders: Biodiversity in an Interdependent World*, Island Press, Washington, DC.

Church, J.M. (2010), *The ideology of environmental regionalism under the test of the alpine convention, with comparative reflections from the Andes*, Regional Environmental Governance Workshop, Geneva, Switzerland.

Conca, K. (2012), The rise of the region in global environmental politics in *Global Environ Polit* 12(3): 127–133.

Connolly, W.E. (2000), Speed, concentric cultures, and cosmopolitanism in *Political Theory* 28(5): 596–618.

Convention on Wetlands of International Importance, especially as Waterfowl Habitat, also known as Ramsar Treaty (Ramsar, Iran, 1971).

Convention on International Trade in Endangered Species of Wild Fauna and Flora, also known as CITES (Washington, United States, 1973).

Convention on the Conservation of Migratory Species of Wild Animals also known as CMS (Bonn, Federal Republic of Germany, 1979).

Cooper, F. (2001), What is the concept of globalization good for? An African historian's perspective in *Afr Aff* 189: 189–190.

Crouch, C. and Streeck, W. (1997), The future of capitalist diversity in C. Crouch and W. Streeck (eds.), *Political economy of modern capitalism: Mapping convergence and diversity*, Sage, London.

Crumley, C. (1995), Heterarchy and the analysis of complex societies in *Archelogical Paper of the American Anthropological Association* 6(1): 1–5.

Debarbieux, B. (2012), How regional is regional environmental governance? in *Global Environ Polit* 12(3): 119–126.

Dodds, K. (1998), The geopolitics of regionalism: The valdivia group and Southern hemispheric environmental cooperation in *Third World Quarterly* 19(4): 725–743.

Elliott, L. (2012), Asean and environmental governance: Strategies of regionalism in Southeast Asia in *Global Environ Polit* 12(3): 38–57.

Evans, P. (2005), Between regionalism and regionalization: Policy networks and the Nascent East Asian institutional identity in T.J. Pempel (ed.), *Remapping East Asia: The construction of a region*, Cornell University Press, Ithaca, NY.

Fawcett, L. (2014), Exploring regional domains: A comparative history of regionalism in *Int Aff* 80(3): 429–446.
Fawcett, L. and Hurrell, A. (eds., 1995), *Regionalism in world politics: Regional organization and international order*, Oxford University Press, Oxford.
Gochhayat, A. (2014), Regionalism and sub-regionalism: A theoretical framework with special reference to India in *AJPSIR* 8(1): 10–26.
Grewe, W.G. (2000), *The epochs of international law*, DeGruyter, Berlin, Germany.
Grunwald, J., Wionczek, M.S. and Carnoy, M. (1972), *Latin American integration and US policy*, Brookings, Washington, DC.
Guruswamy, L. and Hendricks, B. (1997), *International environmental law*, West Publishing Company, St. Paul.
Halle, M. (2012), *Life after Rio: A commentary by Mark Halle*, IISD, Winnipeg.
Handl, G. (1991), The challenge to international law in W. Lang et al. (eds.), *Environmental protection and international law*, Dordrecht, London and Graham &Trotman, Boston.
Held, D. (1999), The transformation of political community: Rethinking democracy in the context of globalization in I. Shapiro and C. Hacker-Cordòn (eds.), *Democracy's edges*, Cambridge University Press, Cambridge.
Huber, V. (2006), The unification of the globe by disease? The international sanitary conferences on Cholera 1851–1894 in *Hist J* 49: 453–461.
Hurrell, A. (1995), Regionalism in theoretical perspective in L. Fawcett and A. Hurrell (eds.), *Regionalism in world politics: Regional organization and international order*, Oxford University Press, Oxford.
Hurrell, A. (2007), One world? Many worlds? The place of regions in the study of international society in *Int Aff* 83(1): 127–146.
Hutton, J.M. and Dickson, B. (eds., 2000), *Endangered species-threatened convention: The past, present and future of cites*, Earthscan Publications Ltd, London.
Jenkins, P. (1996), Free trade and exotic species introductions in O. Sandlund, P. Schei and A. Viken (eds.), *Proceedings of the Norway/UN conference on alien species*, Directorate for Nature Management Trondheim, Norway, Trondheim.
Koskenniemi, M. (2006), *Fragmentation of international law: Difficulties arising from the diversification and expansion of international law*, Report of the Study Group of the International Law Commission (A/CN.4/L.682).
Low, T. (1999), *Feral future*, Viking. Victoria, Australia.
McCormick, J. (2001), *Environmental policy in the European Union*, Palgrave Macmillan, Basingstoke.
McNeely, J.A. (2001), *The great reshuffling: Human dimensions on invasive alien species*, IUCN, Gland, Switzerland and Cambridge.
Omernik, J.M. (2004), Perspectives on the nature and definition of ecological regions in *Environ Manage* 1: 27–38.
Paasi, A. (2003), Region and place: Regional identity in question in *Progress in Human Geography* 27(4): 475–485.
Paradelll-Trius, L. (2000), Principles of international environmental law: An overview in *RECIEL* 9: 93–97.
Pigou, C.A. (1920), *The economics of welfare*, Palgrave MacMillian, London.
Rokkan, S. (1999), *State formation, nation building, and mass politics in Europe: The theory of Stein Rokkan*, P. Flora, S. Kuhnle and D. Urwin (eds.), Oxford University Press, Oxford.
Sands, P., Peel, J., Fabra, A. and MacKenzie, R. (2012), *Principles of international environmental law* (3rd ed), Cambridge University Press, New York, NY.
Sassen, S. (2007), *A sociology of globalization*, W.W. Norton and Company, New York, NY and London.

Secretariat of the Convention on Biological Diversity (SCBD, 2001), *Review of the efficiency and efficacy of existing legal instruments applicable to invasive alien species*, p. 42, Montreal, SCBD (CBD Technical Series no. 2).

Scelles, G. (1948), *Cours de droit international public*, Le Cours de Droit, Paris, France.

Schepin, O. and Yemarkov, W. (1991), *International quarantine*, International University Press Inc, Madison, CT.

Schmitt, C. (1950), *Der nomos der Erde: im Völkerrecht des Jus Publicum Europaeum*, Duncker & Humblot, Berlin, Germany.

Schmitter, P.C. (2000), *How to democratize the European Union . . . and why bother?* Rowmann & Littlefield, Lanham, MD.

Shine, C. (2005), *Overview of the management of invasive alien species from the environmental perspective* in *IPPC Secretariat, Identification of risks and management of invasive alien species using the IPPC framework*, Proceedings of the workshop on invasive alien species and the International Plant Protection Convention, Braunschweig, Germany, 22–26 September 2003. FAO, Rome, Italy.

Teló, M. (ed., 2007), *European Union and new regionalism: Regional actors and global governance in a post-hegemonic era*, Ashgate Publishing, Abington.

Trouwborst, A. (2009), Prevention, precaution, logic and law: The relationship between the precautionary principle and the preventative principle in international law and associated questions in *ELR* 2: 105–128.

Udvardy, M. (1975), *A classification of the biogeographical provinces of the world*, IUCN – The World Conservation Union, Gland, Switzerland.

Vandeever, S.D. (2003), Mapping institutional linkages in European air pollution politics in *Global Environ Polit* 3(3): 14–49.

Van Nijnatten, D. (2011), The North American case: Multi-level bottom-heavy and policy-led in L. Elliott and S. Breslin (eds.), *Comparative environmental regionalism*, Routledge/GARNET Series, Abingdon.

Veggeland, N. (2004), Post-national governance and transboundary regionalization: Spatial partnership formations as democratic exit, loyalty and voice options? In O. Kramsch and B. Hooper (eds.), *Cross-border governance in the European Union*, Routledge, Abingdon.

World Wide Fund for Nature. (WWF, 2000), *Global 200 ecoregions: A blueprint for a living planet*, Washington DC, United States.

Yang, T. and Percival, R. (2009), The emergence of global environmental law in *Ecol Law Q* 36: 616–667.

3 The European Union and its role in addressing the threat of biological invasions

Regional environmental governance at work

SUMMARY: 3.1. Introduction – 3.2. A brief overview on the development of a EU-wide environmental policy – 3.3. The institutional framework for the EU's environmental policy in the post-Lisbon scenario (a. Objectives and Principles; b. Allocation and exercise of competences; c. Actors and procedures) – 3.4. Binding force, cooperative implementation, judicial review: the European unicum *– 3.5. A continent under threat: the rationale for EU-wide action on biological invasions – 3.6. EU legislation on invasive alien species before the adoption of regulation 1143/2014 (a. The exogenous drivers of a EU-wide policy on biological invasions; b. The general picture:* Birds *and* Habitats *directives and the Natura 2000 network; c. Specific legislation on individual species. More is less?)*

3.1 Introduction

The process of European integration has been hailed as "one of the most remarkable political metamorphoses of modern times" (Weiler, 1991). Such a significant step-change in the way regional cooperation has been pursued is well exemplified by the progressive extension of the competences and regulatory powers of the European Union to the environmental sector. The rise of ecological concerns in the hierarchy of political and legal priorities at the regional level demonstrates, in fact, how the neo-functionalist paradigm – which is deeply embedded in Jean Monnet's idea of European integration – has created over the course of the decades room for a phenomenon known in international relations theory as "spill-over". According to this theoretical model, the establishment of supranational institutions designed to deal with functionally specific tasks sets in motion economic, social and political processes which generate pressures towards further integration (Tranholm-Mikkelsen, 1991). The use of the concept of "spill-over" for the explanation of the progressive interest that European institutions have developed towards environmental themes also facilitates any genuine effort to understand the dynamics of the gradual inclusion of environment inside the institutional and legal framework of the Union.

In fact, after the first phase of "functional spill-over" – during which the integration of basic industries, such as coal and steel, was the prelude to further integration in other energy and economic sectors – the process of region building has been characterised by a "political spill-over". Negative integration, based on the removal of discrimination between economic agents of different Member States, was initially combined with – and gradually exceeded by – positive models focused on the adoption of coordinated and common policies (Pinder, 1968) aimed at harmonising the pluralist nature of Western European social and legal systems. One consequence of the transition from "functional spill-over" to "political spill-over" was that European integration started to be perceived not only as a powerful driver towards the unity of an economical area, but also – and perhaps above all – as a more intense means to achieve new and more comprehensive sets of regulations. It is precisely in this transition that European integration has found its distinctive trait with respect to the traditional diplomatic negotiations: the provision of neutral institutions (such as the European Commission) called to mediate between conflicting state concerns towards a common interest have helped in moving beyond watered down compromises on the minimum common denominator. The most evident result of this process has been the converging process, according to which national political actors have shifted their loyalties and expectations, and ultimately transferred state sovereignty to an emerging political centre whose institutions demand jurisdiction over the pre-existing national states (Haas, 1961).

Even if this interpretative scheme has been challenged over the years by periods of stall which led a number of intergovernmentalist authors to emphasise how the overall political process has proved to be less deterministic and straightforward than assumed by neo-functionalists (Moravcsik, 1993), it is nonetheless true that the periods of expansion in European integration have showed how this explanatory paradigm retains at least part of its validity. The integration process did not stall even in the darkest hours of the "Eurosclerosis", as the competences of the European institutions continued to grow both in quantitative and qualitative terms even in the "absence of much visible institutional movement toward further integration" (Haas, 1975). In relation to environmental concerns, these remarks are all the more corroborated if confronted with the factual circumstances, which since the 1970s have followed the full realisation of the common market (Fligstein and Stone Sweet, 2002): the removal of direct restrictions on trade, in fact, shifted the attention to national regulatory standards on ecological and human health protection, which often worked as barriers to transnational exchange. The almost immediate consequence was an increasing pressure on European institutions to expand the reach of supranational competences to those new domains, thus deepening and broadening the process of integration.

Environmental policy and regulation have thus had a paramount role in the transformation of a resource-specific and economically focused organisation – the European Carbon and Steel Community (ECSC) – into a regional organisation capable of producing common policies and binding rules in a vast array of dimensions of the modern life of international relations.

In this sense, the chapter firstly presents the historical context in which a European environmental policy has developed throughout the decades, beginning with the establishment of the European Carbon and Steel Community up until the approval and entry into force of the Treaty of Lisbon (2007).

After this general overview, the chapter looks at the basic principles and objectives of the European environmental policy. Under these respects, some concepts which were already mentioned in chapter 2 – such as the precautionary principle, the principle of prevention, and the "polluter pays" principle – are analysed in context-specific detail which involves the relationship existing between these inspiring principles and other fundamental orientations of European integration, such as territorial cohesion. The logical prosecution of this general overview of the European Union's commitment to facing environmental concerns is the determination of the exact distribution of competences between Brussels' institutions and Member States on the matter on the one hand, and within the actors at the Union level on the other, in order to fully understand the "geography" of European environmental policy and law-making. Subsequently, the chapter presents the concrete unfolding of the environmental policy of the European Union in the field of biological invasions: first, a description of the current situation of biological invasions in the territories of the European Union gives a solid rationale for explaining the need for an EU-wide action against invasive species. This chapter is concluded by an overview of the European action in this sector. By way of introduction, the "exogenous" legal factors which have gradually led European institutions to progressively develop an embryonic normative framework in relation to biological invasions will be presented. After that, a thorough analysis of the most important by-products of such regulatory pressure – namely, the *Birds* and *Habitats* directives, the Natura 2000 network and the vast array of specific pieces of legislations dealing with peculiar aspects of the process of biological invasions – will reveal the existence of many regulatory gaps which have paved the way to the adoption of a comprehensive regulation on invasive alien species, the object of the next and final chapter.

3.2 A brief overview on the development of an EU-wide environmental policy

As stated above, the expansion of the European Union's environmental regulatory framework is one of the most telling demonstrations of the impact that the integration process has had, not only over governments, but also on industry and citizens in Member States. The perception of the better adequacy of the regional level in dealing with transboundary ecological concerns has, in fact, led to the current situation, in which a ponderous body of law – stretching from air and water quality to waste management, from the control of chemicals to energy efficiency and climate change (McCormick, 2001) – stands as the final outcome of a process which has mainly progressed through the often hidden action of supranational European institutions. This remark may well explain the stop-and-go pattern which has characterised

European integration in the environmental sector (Calfee, 1998), while at the same time emphasising a fundamental gap in the historical and political re-construction of such a fundamental process. Indeed, many authors have traced back the origins of European environmental policy to the Treaty of Rome establishing the European Economic Community (EEC). If this assumption is not contestable on the plan of the contents – since it is a matter of fact that the common market contained *in nuce* the germs of the future "ecological shift" of the Community – it is possible to advance some critical remarks under the functional and methodological standpoints. The bearing walls of the common European building had, in fact, already been laid down at the time of the establishment of the European Carbon and Steel Community (ECSC), which set up those supranational institutions that furthered European integration through cooperation and consultation.

In fact, the Treaty of Paris establishing the ECSC (1951) already designed the primary actors of the subsequent process of inclusion of the environmental concerns in the institutional, legal and regulatory framework of the European polity and, namely, the Court of Justice, the Assembly (which is now the European Parliament) and the High Authority (the forerunner of modern European Commission).

Furthermore, it is precisely in this historical timeframe that the basis for the adoption of the Treaties of Rome – and, primarily, of the EEC, the cornerstone of the future development of an integrated environmental policy – were laid out. Yet, when the Treaty of Rome establishing the EEC was signed in Rome in March 1957 the historical, political and economic context was such that the development of a common environmental policy and, *a fortiori*, the attribution of an environmental competence to the supranational institutions set up by the agreement were not a priority (Manservisi, 2012). Nor were the dangers and seriousness of ecological degradation sufficiently evident to justify a tendency towards shared responsibilities in the environmental field: a proof of validity of this assertion was contained, in the total absence of any reference to the environment, not only in the treaty establishing the EEC, but also in the "twin" agreement setting up the European Atomic Energy Community (EAEC or Euratom). As far as the field of atomic energy was concerned, the general objective of the treaty was to contribute to the formation and development of Europe's industries by ensuring energy supplies, with close regard to health and safety standards but without further consideration for the underlying ecological concerns. The only environmentally related provisions, in fact, were contained in Articles 35 and 37: the first entrusted each Member State with the task of monitoring the level of radioactivity in the air, water and soil; the latter put in place a plan for the disposal of radioactive forms so as to avoid contamination of the water, soil or airspace.

Despite this quite discouraging starting point, the environmental horizon of European integration progressively widened and deepened, at first outside the treaty framework, and subsequently through explicit provisions.

At first, ecological concerns appeared in the EEC agenda as a side effect of economic growth and increasing integration: agricultural and industrial activities in fact negatively affected the state of the environment because of the damages caused by intensive farming, uncontrolled use of chemical compounds, fertilisers and herbicides, and the augmented waste production and energy consumption. Furthermore, as a part of the international society, the EEC was also influenced by the environmentalist vogue which was at the time spreading at the global level.

It is precisely in this climate that the heads of state and government – convened in Paris in 1972 for one of those informal meetings developed outside the treaty framework to work as a counterbalance to the action of Community institutions – identified in environmental protection a determinant factor in the process of deepening and widening of European integration. In particular, the accent was posed on the achievement of the objective contained in Article 2 of the treaty regarding the substantial improvement of living conditions for all citizens of all Member States. The summit thus charged the European Commission with the task to "establish, before 31 July 1974, a programme of action accompanied by a precise timetable". Actually, the plan was ready well before, as in 1973 the European Commission drafted the Community's First Environmental Action Programme (EAP).

All those concerns had a transboundary nature which suggested Member States work cooperatively – and creatively – towards the individuation of ecologically sound and economically viable solutions.

Subsequently, a remarkable body of legislation on environmental matters was built on the basis of the provisions contained in the EAP. The overcoming of the economics-focused approach also produced a new way of enacting regulatory interventions. From this standpoint, the main innovation regarded the use, as a legal basis, of Article 235 the Treaty establishing the European Economic Community (TEEC) as a complement to Article 100 TEEC. In fact, if Article 100 was used as a legal basis in all those cases in which national environmental standards had a distortive effect on trade and on the realisation of the common market,[1] Article 235 displayed its effects when a direct economic link with the establishment or functioning of the common market was difficult to demonstrate and, therefore, the Community lacked direct competence to legislate (including the environmental sphere). Article 235 TEEC, in fact, authorised Community intervention not envisaged elsewhere to be enacted if "necessary to attain in the course of the operation of the common market one of the objectives of the Community". The treaty provision was further enhanced by the European Court of Justice, which in a preliminary ruling in 1985 (ADBHU case) recognised environmental protection as an essential objective of the Community (CJEC, 1985).[2]

By identifying environmental protection as a non-written objective of the EEC treaty, the decision of the Court made of Article 235 not only a supplementary legal basis to Article 100, but also – and above all – an autonomous juridical foundation for the achievement of a Community-level environmental policy. The Court, ruling "according to what it thought the law ought to be and not according to what the law was" (Hartley, 1988), took a decisive position in the ongoing debate on the modification of the treaty, and supported the proposals for the inclusion of a common environmental policy in the letter – and not only in the spirit – of the foundational agreement (Jordan and Adelle, 2005). Just as it did in other areas – such as human rights – the Court tried to unlock the political and legislative inertia through an evolutionist interpretation of the letter and spirit of the treaty, thus working as "praetorian developers" of European integration and opening the way to the formal inclusion of environment within the treaty.

As a consequence, in 1987 environmental protection was included within the objectives and legal competences of the European Economic Community through the Single European Act (SEA), which modified the Treaty of Rome. On the basis of the results of the European Council held in Luxembourg on December 1985, Member States "reached agreement in principle on a reform of the Community's institutions designed to improve its efficiency and extend its powers and responsibilities" in a vast array of sectors, including environmental protection and conservation. In particular, the environmental policy should have been integrated into any other action of the Community, as already emphasised by the European Council held in Brussels in March 1985, which identified the environment as "an essential component of the economic, industrial, agricultural, and social policies implemented by the Community and by its member states", since "isolated action is unlikely to prove effective and may even be harmful".

Entered into force on 1 July 1987, the Single European Act was mainly focused on the improvement of the economic and social situation of the EEC by extending common policies and pursuing new objectives. Focusing on environment, the Act added three new articles to the TEEC under a new, specific title (Title VII). The cornerstone of the new Community-wide environmental policy was, indeed, Article 130R. After having clarified that the overall objectives of the common action had to be "to preserve, protect and improve the quality of the environment; to contribute towards protecting human health; and to ensure a prudent and rational utilization of natural resources", it identified in the precautionary principle, preventive action and "polluter pays" principle the spearheads of the European environmental policy. Together with objectives and principles, Article 130R detailed the factors which should have been taken into account in preparing the Community's environmental policy (i.e. available scientific and technical data; environmental conditions in the various regions of the Community; the potential benefits and costs of action or lack of action; the economic and social development of the Community as a whole and the balanced development of its regions). At the same time, Article 130R inserted a fundamental caveat – inferred by the subsidiarity principle – that the Community should only intervene in environmental matters when this action could be better attained at the Community level than at the level of the individual Member States. With respect to this embryonic division of competences, Member States and European institutions were then invited to cooperate with third countries and international organisations. In turn, Article 130S established that the Council should use the unanimity rule when voting on Commission proposals for the

Community's environmental action, while Article 130T explicitly allowed for more stringent national protective measures with respect to the provisions contained in the TEEC, provided that they were compatible with other elements of the Treaty.

In addition to Title VII, Article 100A – whose primary aim was the harmonisation of measures for the establishment of the internal market – contained a "procedural" amendment concerning environmental policy: where legislation aimed at contrasting trade distortions concerned health, safety, environmental and consumer safeguards the Commission had the obligation to "take as base a high level of protection", and Member States were allowed to adopt more stringent and non-distortive national regulations.

In the years that followed the entry into force of the Single European Act, the environmental policy of the Community entered into a new dimension in which obligations upon Member States were finally clear and sanctioned through the enshrinement of objectives, principles and evaluation criteria in the language of the Treaty. Nevertheless, the SEA was just an intermediate passage towards the full re-construction of the European building in the 1990s and 2000s.

On 7 February 1992, in the Dutch city of Maastricht, Member States signed the Treaty on the European Union (TEU), which marked a new stage in the process of European integration through the achievement of an even closer union among the peoples of Europe.

While negotiating the treaty, Member States had in mind a set of historical goals: first and foremost, the establishment of an economic and monetary union; the strengthening of the democratic legitimacy of the institutions; the improvement of their effectiveness; the development of a Community-wide social action; and, last but not least, the pursuit of a common foreign and security policy. The treaty had a fairly complicated structure, and created a three-pillar European Union in which the supranational element – represented by the European Community (EC) – which bound together the EEC, the EAEC and the ECSC – was flanked by two intergovernmental policies: on the one hand, the Common Foreign and Security Policy (CFSP) and, on the other, the Police and Judicial Cooperation in Criminal Matters (PJCCM).

In relation to the environmental policy, however, the dualism between the supranational and intergovernmental arenas has no reason to exist, as the whole matter was regulated through the community method (Fois, 2005), to the extent that the pursuit of a common environmental policy became not simply an incidental task but an overall objective of European integration (Rizzo, 2012). The seventh clause of the Preamble to the Treaty on the European Union (TEU), as an example, described environmental protection as one of the main values in European integration, on an equal footing with the economic dimension.

As for operative clauses, the amended Article 2 numbered between the tasks of the Community the promotion of a "sustainable and non-inflationary growth respecting the environment". Furthermore, Title XVI of the treaty – completely devoted to the EU environmental policy – added significantly to the regulatory landscape set out by Title VII of the Single European Act. The first paragraph of Article 130R, enshrining the objectives of the common environmental policy, was complemented by a brand-new provision highlighting the role of the EU in "promoting measures at international level to deal with regional or world-wide environmental problems". Changes were far more substantial on the plan of principles, as a reference was made to two innovative elements whose importance has been paramount for the development of a Community-wide environmental policy. On the one hand, actions by European institutions should have been inspired to "a high level of protection taking into account the diversity of situations in the various regions of the Community";[3] on the other, the "precautionary principle" was added to the provisions already contained in Article 130R, par. 2. With regard to the inter-institutional dialogue on ecological matters, set forth in Article 130S, the Treaty of Maastricht provided for an almost complete passage from the principle of unanimity to the qualified majority voting system. Finally, as for the autonomous power of states to enact more stringent protective measures, Article 130T simply added the condition of a due notification to the Commission.

With the adoption of the Treaty of Amsterdam (1997), then, the European environmental policy underwent other major changes. First, the concept of sustainable development, which was already foreshadowed in the original version of Article 2, was finally introduced *apertis verbis* in the language of European institutions. In fact, if the Treaty of Maastricht inserted the goal of sustainability in a difficult cohabitation with economic growth (Haigh and Krämer, 1996), the Treaty of Amsterdam removed any ambiguity by separately mentioning the two goals. Even if the inclusion of sustainable development within the objectives of the Community did not imply any particular legal obligation for the institutions or the Member States, it generated both political and juridical consequences: on the one hand, the importance of environmental protection could not be denied without questioning the entire process of integration; on the other, the European Court of Justice could use sustainable development as an interpretative tool for any obligation deriving from the treaty, even in the intergovernmental pillars. To achieve the ambitious goal of sustainable development, and to translate it from paper into factual circumstances, the Treaty of Amsterdam stated in Article 6 that "environmental protection requirements must be integrated into the definition and implementation of the Community policies and activities referred to in Article 3, in particular with a view to promoting sustainable development".

Furthermore, the Treaty of Amsterdam amended the law-making procedure, thus removing a source of legal dispute originated by the Single European Act in the environmental sphere. The SEA, in fact, provided for co-decision for all those measures dealing with the approximation of internal legislations for the functioning of the common market (Article 100A) and for the cooperation procedure for all those acts related to environmental protection (Article 130S), thus causing uncertainty in all the borderline cases in which environmental considerations had to be taken into account when formulating rules related to the functioning of the internal market. The new formulation of Article 175, therefore, disposed that environmental policies should be adopted through co-decision, thus realizing a democratisation of the legal process in this field thanks to a greater and more substantial involvement of the European Parliament.

Further on, the Treaty of Nice – signed in 2001 and entered into force in 2003 – paved the way to the enlargement of the European Union towards the eastern part of the continent, but remained silent on environmental matters. Conversely, the Charter of Fundamental Rights of the European Union (CFREU) – prepared by the European Convention and solemnly proclaimed by the European Parliament, the Council and the Commission in 2001 – stated in its Article 37 that “a high level of environmental protection and the improvement of the quality of the environment must be integrated into the policies of the Union and assured in accordance with the principle of sustainable development”. The provision, evidently based on Articles 2, 6 and 174 of the Treaty establishing the European Union and on some national constitutions (i.e. Article 45 of the Spanish constitution, which entitles anyone to the right to enjoy an environment suitable for personal development), lays down the duties of public authorities in relation to environmental integration in policy-making and implementation without explicitly sanctioning an individual right to environment, or even including any specific procedural right such as access to environmental information, participation in the decision-making concerning the environment, and access to justice in environmental matters (Marin Duràn and Morgera, 2013). Certainly, the choice appears to be in line with the jurisprudence of the Court of Justice, which has traditionally been reluctant to attribute direct effects – meaning the possibility for individuals to immediately invoke a European provision before a national or European court – to the different pieces of legislation that the Community has adopted in the environmental sector.[4] Nonetheless, it is interesting to note how this lack of consideration for subjective situations risks overshadowing the participation of the European Union in the 1998 Aarhus Convention on Access to Information, Public Participation in Decision-making and Access to Justice in Environmental Matters.

3.3 The institutional framework for the EU’s environmental policy in the post-Lisbon scenario

The political shock caused by the popular rejection of the Treaty establishing a Constitution for the European Union in spring 2005 – as a consequence of referenda held in France and in the Netherlands – marked the beginning of a two-year period of reflection, during which the deepening and widening of European integration were put in a substantial stall. Under the German presidency, and pending the 50th anniversary of the signing of the Treaty of Rome in 2007, a Declaration (the so-called Berlin Declaration) was adopted by all Member States outlining the intention to agree on a new treaty before 2009 Parliamentary elections on the basis of the works of the Action Committee for European Democracy (the so-called "group of wise men" presided over by the Italian politician Giuliano Amato), which had already elaborated a new draft treaty devoid of any reference to a constitution (ACED, 2007).

The discussions required several months and led to the signing of the Treaty of Lisbon. In force since 1 December 2009, it abolishes the three-pillar structure of the Union and disposes the merger between the supranational Community and the two intergovernmental policies, while replacing the TEC with a Treaty on the Functioning of the European Union (TFEU), with the same legal value as the Treaty on European Union (TEU).

The Treaty of Lisbon marks a yardstick in European integration as it contains many relevant changes in the inter-institutional balance of powers and in the overall democracy of the Union. The qualified majority voting has been extended to new policy areas – with a double majority system based on the simultaneous presence of the majority of Member States and population – and co-decision has become the ordinary legislative procedure so that the Parliament could amplify its role of co-legislator in a *sui generis* bicameral system with the Council. From the institutional standpoint, the Treaty establishes the Presidency of the European Council, while the figure of the High Representative of the Union for Foreign Affairs and Security Policy – in turn Vice-President of the Commission – resulted from the combination of powers of the Commissioner for External Relations and of the High Representative of the Common Foreign and Security Policy, in an attempt at increasing the impact, coherence and visibility of the Union's external action.

Focusing on environmental issues, the Treaty of Lisbon is the most recent stage in the ongoing struggle for an ever-increasing inclusion of ecological concerns in the process of European integration. All the same, the changes brought together to the founding treaties in the Portuguese capital did not add anything to the *acquis communautaire* in the environmental field.

In fact, if the Treaty establishing a Constitution for the European Union had the ambitious objective to write *ex novo* the foundational charters of continental integration, the Treaty of Lisbon limits itself to re-affirm the old procedure of inserting new articles into the existing framework. For this reason, both the objectives and principles informing the European environmental policy underwent little more than a literal transcription of the provisions.

a Objectives and principles

The objectives of European environmental policy are dealt with through a three-layer approach, proceeding from general statements contained in the Treaty on European Union (TEU) to the framing of environmental concerns in the more comprehensive integration process, and finally, to the concrete exposition of environmental objectives *strictu sensu* in the Treaty on the Functioning of the European Union (TFEU). As far as the first, general layer is concerned, the reference to sustainable development made in the Preamble to the Treaty on European Union as amended in Lisbon seems rather watered down in comparison to what had been emphatically affirmed by the constitutional treaty. Whereas the fourth clause of the Preamble expressed in rather strong terms the awareness of a "responsibility towards future generations and the Earth", the ninth recital of the Preamble to the Treaty of Lisbon makes a plain reference to the need of promoting economic and social process "taking into account the principle of sustainable development and within the context of the accomplishment of the internal market and of reinforced cohesion and environmental protection". In Article 3, the commitment to sustainable development is reiterated and integrated with a reference to the high level of environmental protection that was introduced as a sectorial objective by the Single European Act, and elevated to a Union-wide policy by the amendments approved in Maastricht and Amsterdam. In the fifth paragraph of the same article, sustainable development is described as a specific goal of the Union's external action, whose aims are better specified in Article 21 TEU, which looks at an increasing presence of the EU in the global stage in order to "foster the sustainable economic, social and environmental development of developing countries . . . and help develop international measures to preserve and improve the quality of the environment and the sustainable management of global natural resources, in order to ensure sustainable development".

A more detailed overview of European environmental policy's objectives is provided in the Treaty on the Functioning of the European Union (TFEU). Its Title II on Provisions Having General Application presents two main objectives in relation to the environment: on the one hand, Article 11 – dealing with the integration of environmental policies into other areas of European action – almost literally transposes Article 6 TEC as lastly amended in Amsterdam. On the other, the respect for animal welfare provided for in Article 13 may be welcomed as a progressive recognition of the rights of all "sentient beings".

A third and far more specific layer of objectives is delineated in Article 191, which opens an ad hoc title (Title XX) on environment. Basically, it is a copy-pasted version of Article 174 as lastly amended in Amsterdam: the proper objectives of the Union's environmental policy are the preservation, protection and improvement of the quality of the environment; the safeguard of human health; the prudent and rational utilisation of natural resources; and the promotion, both at the regional and global levels, of measures aimed at dealing with "worldwide environmental problems, and in particular combating climate change". In the perspective of the goals set in Article 191, it is also possible to read the provisions contained in Article 194 (Title XXI) on the Union's energy policy: in fact, this addendum to the old versions of the TEC is the result of the combination of different norms related to competition, internal market and environmental protection. In this particular respect, EU energy policy shall aim to "promote energy efficiency and energy saving and the development of new and renewable forms of energy" and can be only pursued at the regional level "in the context of the establishment and functioning of the internal market and with regard for the need to preserve and improve the environment".

As for principles, Article 191, the second paragraph of the TFEU lists the principles guiding European environmental policy. Even if it is an almost unanimously agreed upon opinion among scholars that this cluster of norms has a binding legal status (Epinay, 1997; Winter, 2002; Hilson, 2008), it is nevertheless true that the paragraph in question does not go any further than a mere enunciation, probably in consideration of the highly contextual value inherent to the application of abstract norms to concrete situations of ecological concern. Yet, it is possible to enquire on the nature and content of such principles by putting secondary law – i.e. directives and regulations with an environmental focus – and relevant judgments by the Court of Justice of the European Union under scrutiny.

Indeed, the second paragraph of Article 191 opens with a reference to the need to ensure a high level of protection. This provision – also enshrined as a general aim in Article 3, paragraph 3 of the Treaty on European Union (TEU) and in Article 37 of the European Union Charter of Fundamental Rights – presents a rather hybrid nature: described as an "aim", it actually holds an intermediate role of cardinal principle under which all other principles are subtended. In this sense, the high level of protection can be qualified as a principle, yet of a different, coordinative nature. In fact, the attainment of a high level of environmental protection is a dynamic obligation, according to which European institutions and Member States are expected to take interventionist rather than conservative measures in order not only to protect but also to improve the overall quality of the environment (De Sadeleer, 2014).

If the content of the principle is clear, far more ambiguous is the way in which such a level of protection has to be attained and the degree of discretion that EU institutions and Member States enjoy in its regard. From the first point of view, a careful reading of the provisions contained in the second paragraph of Article 191 TFEU – corroborated by several judgments of the Court of Justice – reveal that the achievement of a progressively increasing level of environmental protection cannot be easily separated from the application of "secondary" principles such as precaution and prevention (Misonne, 2010).[5] As far as the degree of discretion enjoyed by European institutions and Member States is concerned, it is doubtless that a non-existent or objectively low level of protection would certainly violate the treaty obligation contained in Article 191, par. 2. However, this same norm explicitly allows for a minimum degree of flexibility in view of the differences between regional situations (Epinay, 2006). At the same time, the actual level of harm or impact could not be set once and for every situation, since the degree of intervention significantly varies according to the object of the act. As an example, in the chemical sector several regulations prohibit in peremptory terms the use of defined chemical substances, whereas under the European Parliament and Council regulation 1907/2006 for the Registration, Evaluation, Authorisation and Restriction of Chemicals (REACH), regarding carcinogenic risks, an adequate control is deemed to be sufficient.

For the aforementioned reasons, then, the most evident effect of the provision of a high level of environmental protection is to work as a connector of the "secondary" principles numbered in Article 191, par. 2. Some of them, such as the precautionary principle, the preventive principle and the "polluter pays" principle, have been drawn from multi-decennial experience at the universal level. Conversely, the proportionality principle and the integration of environmental policy into other areas of European intervention are exclusive features of the Union's legal framework.

Inserted in the spirit and letter of the treaties since Maastricht, the precautionary principle is the most direct expression of the link existing between international law and natural sciences: in recent decades, in fact, increasing calls for environmental protection have led law- and policy-makers to re-consider the relationship with the physical world, and subsequently to consult scientists in a vast array of situations of ecological concern. Nevertheless, some intrinsic aspects of law and science have led to a clash between the need for predictability – typical of regulatory endeavours – and the unpredictability of many natural phenomena. The precautionary principle, in this sense, became pivotal in responding to the limitations of science in assessing complex and uncertain ecological events (De Sadeleer, 2002), thus shifting the attention from how to prevent assessable, calculable and certain risks to how to anticipate risks permeated by a high level of uncertainty (De Sadeleer, 2010).

In the EU context, the role and extent of the precautionary principle have been clarified by a Communication from the Commission on February 2000: the primary role of the principle is to ensure a higher level of environmental protection through preventative decision-making in the case of a risk for nature and/or for the consumers whose dangerous effects have not been determined with sufficient scientific certainty. According to the Commission, the sphere in which the precautionary principle operates is that of potentiality, and it implies the recourse to risk analysis and risk management, but it cannot justify arbitrary decisions under any means. In fact, the precautionary principle may be invoked when three preliminary conditions are met: potentially adverse effects are identified; available scientific data are analysed; and a conclusive, univocal conclusion is impossible. Depending on the real extent of the scientific uncertainty, European institutions – or, more generally, the authorities vested with risk management – can decide to take action or to supersede. However, action is not an option but an obligation if the level of potential harm is high and a vast array of preventive measures – ranging from the adoption of proportionate legal acts to the financing of research programmes – can be deployed. In this case, five guiding elements are to be taken into consideration: the proportionality between the measures taken and the chosen level of protection; a non-discriminatory approach in applying the measures, so that comparable situations are not treated differently and different situations are not treated in the same way; the consistency of the measures with similar measures already taken in similar situations; the examination of the benefits and costs of action or lack of action; the review of the measures in the light of scientific development. Besides the comment by the Commission, the Court has confirmed, in the Waddenzee case (CJEU,

2004) regarding the issue of an authorisation for a plan likely to have effects on a Natura 2000 site, that both institutions and Member States are obliged to apply the precautionary principle when carrying out actions in the environmental field

> where doubt remains as to the absence of adverse effect on the integrity of the site linked to the pan or project being considered, the competent authority will have to refuse authorisation. The competent national authorities . . . are to authorise such activity only if they have made certain that it will not adversely affect the integrity of that site. That is the case where no reasonable scientific doubt remains as to the absence of such effects (CJEU, 2004).[6]

Immediately after – and in close connection to – the precautionary principle, the second paragraph of Article 191 TFEU refers to preventive action. At the Community level and later on at the Union level, this principle has been a constant presence since the embryonic phases of the European environmental policy. A reference to prevention was, in fact, already contained in the First Environmental Action Programme: in this document, focused on the need for a comprehensive assessment of the environmental impact of economic and social activities, the importance to "prevent, reduce and as far as possible eliminate pollution and nuisances" – as emerging from the outcomes of a meeting of the Ministers of the Environment held in Bonn in October 1972 – was underlined, and the idea was stressed that "the best environment policy consists in preventing the creation of pollution or nuisances at source, rather than subsequently trying to counteract their effects", with the help of technical and scientific progress. Paradoxically, the preventive approach found a first practical application in response to the industrial accident that happened in Seveso (Italy) in July 1976, which resulted in the highest known exposure to 2,3,7,8-tetrachlorodibenzo-p-dioxin (TCDD) in residential populations. The importance of the preventive principle in European environmental policy is witnessed, inter alia, by its early incorporation in the treaty framework through Article 130R of the Single European Act. Furthermore, reference to preventive measures is made in a number of secondary legislation norms, such as the Environmental Impact Assessment (EIA) Directive and the Industrial Emissions Directive (IED).

Continuing with the analysis of Article 191, par. 2, the so-called "source principle" implies that environmental damage should as a priority be rectified in loco rather than following "end-of-pipe" techniques. The rectification of environmental damage at source made its explicit appearance in the second EAP (1977), where it is stated that "effects on the environment should be taken into account at the earliest possible stage in all the technical planning and decision-making processes". Until its inclusion in the Single European Act, however, this principle remained "silent" and its content was clarified by the Court of Justice only in 1992, in a case regarding a Belgian national measure limiting the import of waste from other member countries – the *Walloon Waste* case (1992). The Belgian measure, which clearly failed to pass the test of non-discrimination, was nevertheless deemed justified as

> it is for each region, commune, or other local entity to take appropriate measures to receive, process, and dispose of its own waste. Consequently, waste should be disposed of as close as possible to the place where it is produced in order to keep the transport of waste to the minimum practicable (CJEC, 1992).[7]

The list of principles guiding the European environmental policy contained in the second paragraph of Article 191 TFEU is closed by a reference to the "polluter pays" principle (PPP), whose main function is to internalise the social costs borne by public authorities for all measures aimed at environmental prevention and control. The PPP, if conceived as a manifestation of the principle of equity aimed at obtaining an even-handed distribution of pollution damage costs between polluters and the general public – or as a specification of the principle of efficiency in terms of a better allocation of resources in economic production (Hilson, 2000; Bleeker, 2009) – is thus fundamental in delimitating the perimeter within which environmental protection and economic development may interact and in determining the extent to which economic operators have to take into account ecologic costs in designing industrial policies (Meli, 1996). Originally mentioned in 1972 by the OECD Council in the Guiding Principles concerning International Economic Aspects of Environmental Policies, the PPP made its appearance in the Community legal corpus a year later through the First Environmental Action Programme: its main role at the time was to reassure Member States that the introduction of a Community-wide environmental policy did not mean ipso facto an increase of their contribution to the common budget. In a context of market economy and for a good functioning of the internal market, it was up to the individual physical or juridical persons who damaged or polluted the environment – and not to Member States – to bear the costs of remedial measures. In 1975 the Council issued a recommendation regarding cost allocation and action by public authorities on environmental matters, whose main task was to establish a codified procedure for applying the "polluter pays" principle. The document described the PPP as

> a principle under which natural or legal persons who are responsible for pollution must pay the costs of such measures as are necessary to eliminate that pollution or to reduce it. Environmental policy should not in principle depend on policies which rely on grants of aid and place the burden of combating pollution on the tax-payer.

Once delineated in its main features, the PPP found application in several pieces of secondary legislation throughout the 1970s, with a particular impact on waste management.[8] After a period of decline, due to the diffuse practice by Member States to concede state aids in environmental matters during the 1980s, in the 1990s the Commission started to apply the PPP in full: in its 1994 Guidelines for State Aid for Environmental Purposes, in fact, the executive body of the Union clearly stated that the common environmental policy had to be understood not as a corrective policy but as a long-term objective aimed at reaching a more sustainable development (European Commission, 2001). As a consequence, state aids were peremptorily limited. In fact, they could be granted only in two cases: circumstances in which firms were not able to fully internalise the costs, or in cases in which state aid may also act as an incentive to firms to improve on standards or to undertake further investment designed to reduce pollution from their plants. Outside those few exceptions, the PPP can be defined as a general principle of the European environmental policy, and may be applied either *ex ante* as a "redistributive legal tool" in the form of taxation or *ex post* as a "curative instrument" through the transition from the public sphere to civil liability (De Sadeleer, 2012). As for the identification of the natural or legal person which has the duty to pay for pollution, the judgments delivered by the Court of Justice in the cases *Standley* (1999) and *Pontina Ambiente* (2010) greatly helped in shedding some light on the boundaries of application of the PPP by maintaining that a non-polluter or non-contributor to the risk of pollution cannot be held responsible, and therefore shall not be burdened by any charge (Lindhout and Van Broek, 2014).[9] Furthermore, in the *Erg and Others* case (2010), judges in Luxembourg allowed Member States to use presumptions in determining causation between certain activities and environmental pollution in order to identify the actual holder of the obligation to pay.[10] Finally, in the *Futura Immobiliare* case (2009) the Court reiterated a concept already expressed in *Standley*, clarifying that – in accordance with the principle of proportionality – polluters can be held responsible exclusively in relation to pollution to which they have actively contributed, so that they cannot be burdened by costs which are "manifestly disproportionate to the volumes or nature" of the environmental hazard they had caused.[11]

As a complementary strategy to the taxation of profits coming from polluting activities, in recent years the Commission has proposed the adoption of a directive on environmental liability (ELD), approved by the European Parliament and the Council in April 2004. Under this perspective, environmental liability has been identified as an *ex post* application of the PPP in those cases in which pollution could not be prevented and the polluter has to bear restoration costs for the environmental damage. Though limited in its strictness by the exclusion of a compensation scheme for private parties, the ELD has the explicit purpose to establish a legal and regulatory framework based on the "polluter pays" principle. In fact, it aims at ensuring that the financial consequences of certain types of harm caused to the environment (i.e. damage to protected species and natural habitats, water damage and land damage) are borne by the economic operator who caused that damage. In this respect, in the *Agusta* case (2010) the Court of Justice has underlined – in line with the precedent set out in the *Standley* case – how operators are exempted from bearing the costs of remedial actions if

> they can prove that environmental damage was caused by a third party and occurred despite the fact that appropriate safety measures were in place, since it is not a consequence of the 'polluter-pays' principle that operators must take on the burden of remedying the pollution to which they have not contributed (CJEU, 2010).[12]

In addition, judges dealt with the delicate interpretation of the ELD in cases of diffuse pollution in which multiple causes produce single effects and single causes produce multiple effects. In particular, in the *van de Walle* case (2004) relating to the responsibility for polluting activities deriving from the production and disposal of hydrocarbons, the Court drew a rather neat line between "practical recovery or disposal operations, which it makes the responsibility of any holder of waste, whether producer or possessor" and "the financial burden of those operations which, in accordance with the principle of "polluter pays", it imposes on the persons who cause the waste, whether they are holders or former holders of the waste or even producers of the product from which the waste came" (CJEU, 2004).[13] In concrete terms, if the responsibility for the recovery from waste production entirely falls on the material producer of waste, it is nevertheless possible that oil companies can be held liable under exceptional circumstances (such as oil leakage).

In conclusion, the Treaty of Lisbon has granted a "transition in continuity" to environmental principles from the three-pillar Union designed in Maastricht to the new regime, with a major insistence on their overarching role in guiding European policies in all relevant sectors. At the same time, however, the new treaty framework has provided for significant institutional changes in the subdivision of competences.

b Allocation and exercise of competences

The Treaty on the Functioning of the European Union has satisfied a need for clarification as far as the division of competences between the European Union and Member States is concerned. If such a remark does not imply any substantial or notable transfer of new competences from Member States to European institutions, it is nevertheless true that the TFEU introduces for the first time a precise classification in three main types of competences: exclusive, shared and supporting. This clarification has as a fundamental premise the abolition of the pillar structure and the conferral of legal personality to the Union, which eliminate at source a series of functional overlaps derived from the commingling of community and intergovernmental methods. At the same time, this new subdivision entitles European institutions to conclude treaties in the fields coming within their area of competence.

In substance, Title I (Articles 2–6) disciplines *in toto* the "categories and areas of Union competence". Article 2 is, in this sense, the cornerstone of a more general architecture regarding the conferral of competences, as it illustrates the implications of the *magna divisio* between the two main types of attribution. The first paragraph, in fact, clearly states that if the Union has exclusive competence in a specific area it has the absolute right to legislate and adopt legally binding acts, with the exception of measures which need implementation by member states or in case of specific "devolution" of powers by the Union. In the second paragraph the treaty deals with shared competences: in this case, "the Union and the Member States may legislate and adopt legally binding acts in that area". The provision translates in treaty terms the principle of preemption, which embeds a legislative *favour* for the Union since it allows Member States to exercise their competence "to the extent that the Union has not exercised its competence" or to take back their law-making power if the European institutions should decide to "cease exercising its competence".

According to the provisions laid out in Articles 3 and 4, which proceed to a more detailed enunciation of the areas of exclusive and shared competence, the environment undergoes a functional differentiation: if the conservation of marine biological resources under the common fishery policy is considered to be a field of exclusive competence, all other measures concerned with environmental issues are the object of shared competence between the Union and the Member States. This category is, indeed, residual, since paragraph 1 of Article 4 identifies as areas of shared competence all those sectors where the treaties do not confer to the Union an exclusive competence (under Article 3) or a supporting competence (under Article 6), that is, the competence "to carry out actions to support, coordinate, or supplement the actions of member states".

In exercising shared competences, European institutions are bound by three fundamental provisions contained in Article 5 of the Treaty on European Union: the principle of conferral limits the Union competences, while the principles of proportionality and subsidiarity deal with the way these competences are used. As far as the principle of conferral is concerned, the second paragraph of Article 5 states that "the Union shall act only within the limits of the competences conferred upon it by the member states in the treaties to attain the objectives set out there-in". As for the principles of subsidiarity and proportionality, the provisions contained in paragraphs 3 and 4 of Article 5 TEU are completed by an ad hoc document (Protocol n.2 on the application of the principles of proportionality and subsidiarity) which has been attached to the Treaty on European Union after Lisbon. The principle of proportionality regards actions taken by the Union at all levels and by virtue of any competence, and requests European institutions not to exceed in the form or in the content what is necessary to achieve the aims contained in the treaties. In turn, the principle of subsidiarity – contained in the third paragraph of Article 5 TEU – has to be applied in areas which do not fall within the Union's exclusive competence. In such sectors (i.e. the shared and supporting competences), the Union shall act only

> if and in so far as the objectives of the proposed action cannot be sufficiently achieved by the member states, either at central level or at

regional and local level, but can rather, by reason of the scale or effects of the proposed action, be better achieved at Union level.

The rigour of the subsidiarity principle is partly tempered by the insertion in Article 352 of the TFUE of the "flexibility clause", enabling the Union – under a strict procedure and in selected areas – to act beyond the powers of action conferred upon it by the treaties if the objective pursued so requires.

The post-Lisbon balance of competences between Member States and the European Union, when ingrained in the environmental sphere, can spark some insightful reflection on the modalities in which European institutions can address the common environmental policy: in this sense, particular attention must be devoted to the subsidiarity principle, interpreted as the key provision when translating the allocation of competences from theory to practice. Having as a fundamental aim the identification of the optimal level of action and of the most appropriate decision-maker, the subsidiarity principle has in environmental policy one of its main – and most controversial – fields of application. The matter of the discussion is polarised on the terms "sufficiently" and "better" as used in Article 5, paragraph 3 of the Treaty on European Union: if it is evident that some of the current threats to European ecosystems (i.e. climate change, loss of biodiversity, ozone depletion, air and water pollution) cannot be sufficiently dealt with at the state level, it is nevertheless true that it has to be demonstrated that action at the Union level can lead to "better" – that is, more effective – responses to such ecologically hazardous situations (Krämer, 2012). In this sense, a univocal response is not possible. Conversely, the assessment on the potential "added value" that a common action could bring in terms of the overall impact is deeply connected to the singularity of each situation and to the development of constructive relationships between Union and states, on the one hand, and within the European institutional framework, on the other.

c Actors and procedures

Guided by the principles set out in the second paragraph of Article 191 TFEU, with a view to the achievement of the objectives outlined in the first clause of the same provision, European institutions follow a complex path in the decision-making procedure leading to the adoption of legal acts in the field of environmental policy. Even considering the role of informal intra- and inter-institutional dialogue combined with pressures coming from forces which are external to the policy structure, it seems nevertheless useful for the ultimate aim and general structure of this work to dwell on the specific role of each institution in the regulatory chain leading to the formulation of the European environmental policy.

At first, and in accordance with what was disposed by Article 15 of the Treaty on European Union, the European Council has the duty to provide the necessary impetus to the integration process and to define the general political directions and priorities. For this reason, this institution does not enter into the detail of environmental policy, and it does not conventionally overpass the threshold of broad statements or solemn declarations. All the same, it would be erroneous to derive from such a general activity a total disinterest for ecological concerns on the part of the heads of state and government of the Union, since many political statements and declarations have had in the course of the decades fundamental importance in the development of a common environmental policy.[14]

On the basis of the policy priorities defined by the European Council, the European Commission exercises a central role as a forum for the exchange of policy ideas and as a mediator among Member States, as well as between national governments and supranational institutions in the long and often complex process of negotiation and elaboration of regulatory interventions (Mazey and Richardson, 1997). Once the decision to act in relation to some ecologically related question has been taken, the Commission prepares a draft document by virtue of its de facto monopoly on legislative initiative conferred by Article 17 of the Treaty on European Union. In particular, the Directorate General for Environment (EDG) and its group of experts prepare background position papers in which the scale of the problem, together with the costs and benefits of an action at the EU level, are assessed. This document triggers the discussion with other interested parties, including experts or government officials from Member States, representatives from other directorates general (DGs) and European institutions, industry, academia and pan-European NGOs (Krämer, 1996), on the way the proposal should be improved and/or its acceptability to the Member States maximised, to be then crafted in treaty-consistent language by the legal unit of the DG. After that, the draft is published in the *Official Journal of the European Union* and simultaneously sent out to the European Parliament and to the Council – together with national parliaments and, in some occasions, the Committee of the Regions and the Economic and Social Committee – for the debate on its adoption.

Since the entry into force of the Treaty of Amsterdam (1997), in fact, both the European Parliament (representing European citizens) and the Council (the seat for representatives from member countries) are vested with law-making power on the basis of the proposals received from the Commission. With the Treaty of Lisbon, the co-decision procedure became the ordinary legislative procedure, and its role has been confirmed as one of the cornerstones for the formulation of a Union-wide environmental policy, with room for some exceptions in sectors on which Member States are not keen to devolve additional quotes of sovereignty (such as provisions primarily of a fiscal nature; town and country planning; quantitative management of water resources; land use; measures affecting a Member State's choice between different energy sources). All the same, even in these sectors a unanimous agreement within the Council makes it possible to activate a *passerelle* clause, which allows the adoption of the ordinary legislative procedure in a way to greatly enhance the influence and authority of the European Parliament in the formulation of the European environmental policy.

Once the draft legislation is received, the President of the European Parliament refers it to the Committee on Environment, Public Health and Food

Safety (ENVI) or, in cases presenting cross-border issues, to associated or joint committees, which verify the legal basis and the financial implications of the proposal together with its compliance with the Charter of Fundamental Rights, nominate a *rapporteur*, and hold several meetings during which experts may be called in order to obtain more precise technical information, while the Commission may intervene to defend its position. On the basis of the report prepared by the *rapporteur* – and having heard the position of the Commission on the amendments adopted by the Committee – the plenary session of the Parliament discusses the legislative proposal. The usual outcomes of this discussion are the approval without modifications or the proposal of amendments to the initial draft legislation, while it is quite rare that Parliament requests the Commission to withdraw its proposal. Once approval by the Parliament is received – or as soon as the Commission deems "acceptable" the amendments proposed to the draft legislation through the adoption of a "modified proposal" – the text is forwarded to the Council. The representatives of states – usually within the framework of the COREPER – begin analysing the proposal simultaneously to the Parliament, but cannot formally conduct a reading before the assembly has issued its position. The Council can, at this point, accept or reject the position emerged in the Parliament during the first reading or propose its own amendments. In case of acceptance, the act is considered to be adopted and is sent for signature to the Presidents and Secretaries-General of the European Parliament and of the Council, and later published in the *Official Journal of the European Union*. If, in turn, the Council decides to adopt only a part of the amendments proposed by the Parliament, or if it adds its own modifications to the draft legislation, a position in first reading is adopted and sent to the Parliament together with a statement of reasons. At this stage, Article 294 TFEU sets a precise timeframe for the progress of the procedure. Within three months the Parliament examines the Council's position, while informal contacts with the Council and the Commission take place in order to facilitate the adoption of an early second reading agreement. At the end of this period the Parliament can approve the Council's position – or fail to take a decision within the time limit – leading to the adoption of the act; it can reject the Council's provision, so putting an end to the legislative procedure; finally, it can propose limited amendments and forward them to the Council for a second reading. At this point the Council has a further three months to examine the Parliament's second reading position and to be informed about the Commission's stance with regard to the amendments proposed by the assembly. If the Council approves all of the Parliament's amendments, the act is clearly adopted and published in the *Official Journal* after signature by the Presidents and Secretaries General of the Parliament and Council. If the Council does not approve all the amendments proposed by the Parliament, a third, decisive phase is opened by the convening of a Conciliation Committee – composed by an equal number of representatives from the European Parliament and the Council, under the supervision of the Commission (usually represented by the Director-General for Environment) – within six weeks of the failed approval of the draft legislation. This Committee has six weeks to agree upon a joint text based on a compromise between the different versions of the proposed legislation emerging from the second reading positions of the two co-legislators. If the delegations fail to reach an agreement the whole proposal sinks, and the only possible option to legislate in the matter is a new procedure based on a new Commission proposal. Conversely, if an agreement is reached and a "joint text" approved, the Parliament and the Council have six weeks to vote on the compromised text without any possibility of further amendments; if one or both institutions reject the compromise or do not respond in time the legislation falls and the procedure is ended. In turn, if each legislator separately approves the joint text in a third reading, the draft legislation becomes a fully legal act after the signature by the Presidents and Secretaries-General of the Parliament and of the Council and the publication in the *Official Journal of the European Union*.

This description of the law-making procedure emphasises one of the main differences between the European Union and other regional or universal regulatory actors: it is only in the EU framework that a "democratic actor" such as the Parliament, which represents European citizens, participates in environmental regulation. And yet, the main peculiarities and the main reasons for the diversity of the European action in the field of ecological regulation lie in the binding nature of the acts and on the role played by supranational institutions, such as the Commission and the Court of Justice, in their implementation and enforcement.

3.4 Binding force, cooperative implementation, judicial review: the European *unicum*

According to Article 289 TFEU, the ultimate outcome of the ordinary legislative procedure "shall consist in the joint adoption by the European Parliament and the Council of a regulation, directive or decision". These instruments of secondary legislation are, in turn, detailed in Article 288 TFEU as the means by which the European Union "shall exercise its competences". As expressions of the sole normative will of European institutions and by virtue of their explicit mention in the treaties, these three acts are usually called "unilateral" and "typical". More importantly, all of these acts have binding force upon states.

With particular regard to environmental legislation, directives and regulations have been by far the primary regulatory tools used by European institutions, and have thus originated over the decades a substantial corpus of laws detailing the objectives and principles set in the treaties in a fairly sectorial and precise secondary legislation. United by their scope, however, regulations and directives are characterised by peculiarities – sketched out in Article 288 TFEU – which greatly contribute to differentiating one from the other. Regulations are, in fact, the most powerful regulatory tool in the hands of European institution as they are binding in all their aspects upon each and every Member State, with a self-executing nature which deprives national authorities of any potential interference from the application of the norm within the domestic legal system. Because of these characterising elements – and of the technical nature of many environmental problems – regulations are the most useful tool in developing a uniform body of law through the formulation of common rules of procedure or the establishment of technical standards. Directives, in turn, are binding on Member States to which they are addressed as they contain obligations of result, but national authorities are free to choose the most adequate forms and methods through which to attain the objectives laid down by the norm. By virtue of their non-self-executing nature directives are not directly applicable in the domestic legal order, as they need an intervention in the part of the state to be implemented. Nonetheless, the well-established case law of the European Court of Justice has found that directives imposing clear, unconditional and unambiguous obligations on Member States – which have not been transposed within the relevant deadline – can be invoked by individuals before national courts, thus recognising a direct effect to these acts. In relation to the environment, directives can be useful tools of harmonisation and approximation of national legislations in certain areas: examples include the directives on waste (75/442), dangerous substances (76/464), pollution from industrial plants (84/360), surface water quality (75/440), bathing water (76/160), drinking water quality (80/778), pollution from large combustion plants (88/609), and urban waste water treatment (91/271).

Both regulations and directives have been abundantly used by European institutions in the last four decades, to the point that there is a substantial uncertainty in relation to the actual dimensions of the environmental *acquis*, with numbers greatly varying from 250 to 500 pieces of legislation (Vogel and Kessler, 1998) on issues ranging from climate change to air quality, from waste management to the protection of water resources and biodiversity, and from the controls on chemicals to the conduction of environmental impact assessment.

As the abundance of the environmental "normative output" demonstrates, however, a great effort has to be made by European institutions and Member States to ensure an effective and uniform implementation of existing legislation. In this sense, a real change of attitude from the quantitative aspect of law-making to the qualitative research of effectiveness can be traced back to the Fourth Environmental Action Programme (1987) and to a declaration of the Dublin European Council (1990) on the need for Member States to give full implementation to the community environmental legislation. A first great development in this sense was the launch, in 1992, of the European Union network for the Implementation and Enforcement of Environmental Law (IMPEL). Set up as an informal network of regulators and authorities concerned with the implementation and enforcement of the already conspicuous body of European environmental norms, IMPEL brought national enforcement agencies to meet biannually with the DG Environment in order to exchange information and experiences on the way to "connect" the Community and national levels.

Besides the important role played by this "external" agency, there are two institutions which – more than others – are vested with the task of the implementation and enforcement of existing environmental legislation: the Commission and the Court of Justice of the European Union. Article 17 TEU, in fact, gives to the European Commission – in cooperation with national authorities and agencies – the responsibility for overseeing the correct application of the treaties and of the measures adopted pursuant to them "under the control of the Court of Justice". The Commission, the Court of Justice and national authorities are thus the three sides of the "triangular relationship" forging the uniqueness of the European regional approach to the implementation and enforcement of regional environmental regulation (European Commission, 2008b).

The multiplicity of objectives and tools, combined with the presence of significant public and private interests on the conditions of the environment, makes implementation a real challenge for the Union. In this respect, the Commission – and particularly the DG Environment – has developed a "road map" towards effective implementation and enforcement of the environmental *acquis* through a combination of preventive and corrective measures. As prevention is a guiding principle in designing environmental policy, the most effective way to tackle ineffectiveness and grant coherence to European legislation in this field is the prevention of breaches by virtue of a life-cycle approach by the Commission, from the design and drafting of new norms to the systematic revision of existing policies. If preventive measures display their effects in a relationship of cooperation with national and local authorities and environmental agencies within Member States, there are cases in which these functional linkages enter a "pathological phase" as a consequence of a panoply of challenges to the effective implementation of the relevant legislation put forward by European institutions. The Commission has emphasised, at a general level, the insufficient attention being paid to deadlines and completeness during the adoption of national and regional pieces of legislation transposing Union norms; shortcomings in knowledge and awareness – as well as in administrative capacities – by national and regional authorities; and weak enforcement policies and practices both at the state and local levels. In these cases, the preventive approach gives way to corrective measures, and the role of the judiciary emerges powerfully as a differentiating factor between the way European environmental governance is carried out with respect to the failures in implementation and enforcement at the universal level.

In this sense, two great "enforcing hallways" open up in order to guarantee an effective implementation of the environmental *acquis*. On the one hand, the Commission has the possibility to start an alternative path of law-enforcement based on the infringement procedure described in Articles 258–260 TFEU for those cases in which national authorities have not correctly transposed a directive or strictly complied with a regulation. On the other, the provision contained in Article 267 TFEU allowing national judges to refer a case already underway to the Court of Justice can realise the principle of loyal and active cooperation between courts enounced in

Article 4 TEU and ensure the correct interpretation or verify the validity of a European norm.

The infringement procedure is the bridge between the cooperative implementation and the legal enforcement, as it involves at the same time the Commission, the Member State to whom a breach is contested, and the Court of Justice in its role of "guarantor" of the interpretation and application of EU law according to Article 19 TFEU. Under Article 258 TFEU, in fact, the European Commission can launch this formal procedure in cases it considers "that a member state has failed to fulfil an obligation under the treaties", while Article 259 TFEU gives to each Member State the possibility to bring failures by other states to fulfil an obligation under the treaties to the attention of the Commission before bringing the matter to the Court of Justice. In its first phase, the infringement procedure has an "administrative" nature, given its pre-litigation character: at first, in fact, the Commission issues a letter of formal notice against a Member State's alleged infringement of European law in order to give to national authorities the occasion to present observations in discharge. If the Commission does not deem the justifications to be sufficient and the infringement is not repaired, it can issue a reasoned opinion against the Member State, containing a deadline by which it shall comply with the allegedly breached legislation. In case of inaction, or insufficient action, by Member States, the Commission can pass from the pre-litigation to the litigation phase, referring the case to the Court of Justice. The Court shall deliver a declaratory judgment on the actual subsistence of a case of non-compliance by the Member State, which has in turn the duty to take all the necessary measures in order to bring its national law in line with the requirements of the breached Union law (Krämer, 2008). Subsequently, if a state fails to comply with the obligations stemming from the declaratory judgment of the Court, it is possible for the Commission to start a second infringement procedure for violation of its obligations under Article 260 TFEU, which explicitly mentions the possibility to bring the case before the Court of Justice requesting the imposition of a lump sum or a penalty payment on the Member State.

A general trend emerging from the Annual Reports of the Court of Justice shows how the environment has been one of the most infringement-prone areas: in 2015 – the date of the most recent data – the Commission detected 84 possible infringements in the environmental sector, with 363 complaints presented by members of the public, businesses, NGOs and other organisations reporting potential breaches of relevant EU law provisions (38 of them leading to formal infringement procedures). The infringement procedures that have been opened in the environmental sector have led the Commission to send 40 reasoned opinions to Member States. In total, pending procedures regarding the non-transposition, incorrect transposition or incorrect application of secondary legislation in the environmental sector total 276 cases (European Commission, 2016).

Complementarily to the infringement procedures, another way to legally enforce the application of European environmental legislation rests upon the loyal cooperation between the European Court of Justice and national judges pursuant to Article 4 TEU. In this sense, Article 267 TFEU disposes that national judges can – or, in cases where there is no judicial remedy under national law, shall – refer an ongoing case to the Court of Justice of the European Union to obtain preliminary rulings concerning the interpretation of the treaties and/or the validity and interpretation of the acts of the institutions. As is evident, the Court of Justice cannot settle the dispute, but it can give unparalleled assistance in clarifying the interpretation of a piece of environmental legislation and ensure its correct and uniform application, thus contributing to solving a problem connected to the implementation of the common legal framework set up to protect the environment. However, preliminary rulings still play a secondary role in the overall architecture presiding over the implementation of the environmental *acquis*, considering that less than 200 relevant cases have been referred as of 2014 – even though there has been a significant acceleration since the 1990s – and their impact is further limited by the impossibility for environmental NGOs to bring suits before national courts (Somsen, 2000). Besides this significant limitation, however, the possibility for one of the parties in a dispute to ask for the referral is a *unicum* which gives further credibility to the role of the European Union as a valid actor in environmental governance.

3.5 A continent under threat: the rationale for EU-wide action on biological invasions

As authoritatively stated by the European Environmental Agency, biological invasions are a large-scale phenomenon constituting the second major current threat to European biodiversity (EEA, 2003). In fact, the introduction and transfer of invasive alien species among distant regions as a consequence of the increased flows in trade and tourism have created significant disturbances to the recipient aquatic and terrestrial ecosystems (McNeely, 2001). The pressure of evidence suggesting a significant change of magnitude in the scale of introductions since the times of the Industrial Revolution is, in this sense, fuelling a revisionist lecture of the conventional ideas of Europe as a "more resistant ecosystem" and as a "net exporter" of invasive species to other continents (Hulme, 2007). Increasingly since the end of the 19th century, in fact, the European territory has been invaded by a vast array of different biomes: exotic plants and animals have been imported for economic return – such as in the cases of the American mink (*Neovison vison*), initially imported for commercial purposes in fur farms – or recreation, as happened with the pheasant (*Phasianus colchicus*), introduced as a game animal, or with the purple-flowered rhododendron (*Rhododendron ponticum*), which arrived in Europe as an ornamental plant. In cases of animals and plants introduced in managed environments (i.e. zoological or botanical gardens), it is not rare that individuals may accidentally (but not unpredictably) escape into the wild, as was the case for the ruddy duck (*Oxyura jamaicensis*) in the animal realm, or the Japanese plant *Fallopia japonica* (most commonly known as knotweed).

The situation has been further deteriorated by the unintentional diffusion of flora and fauna which lands in Europe as "contaminants" of particular commodities – as in the case of the Colorado beetle (*Leptinotarsa decemlineata*), usually imported with potatoes – or as "hitchhikers" in cargo ships, by far the most used vectors in transcontinental trade. Indeed, together with goods, vessels carry an amount of ballast water which, together with ships' hulls, is the ideal means of transportation for alien species of small dimensions, such as microbes, larvae, eggs, plankton, crustaceans and bivalves.

Once introduced, alien species usually find particularly suitable environments in Europe for thriving and establishing colonies, for a combination of geographical and anthropogenic reasons. On the one hand, Europe is one of the richest regions in the world when it comes to vulnerable ecosystems such as islands, lakes, rivers and in-shore marine areas (Heywood, 1995), while at the same time it presents contiguous and transboundary coastlines, mountain ranges and watercourses. On the other hand, human activity has been particularly intense on the continent for millennia, thus determining a progressive weakening in the ecological resilience of native species through a constant subtraction of space from the surrounding environment and modifications of the existing habitats (Hulme, 2003).

Given these assumptions, it is particularly difficult to outline a reliable and unitary picture of the "state of the Union" in relation to biological invasions.

Despite these difficulties, a common agreement exists on the severity of the damages produced by invasive species: data recently collected by experts from the DAISIE (Delivering Alien Invasive Species Inventory for Europe) have shown that at least 11% of alien species have produced adverse ecological effects in the EU territory, while this percentage rises to 13% if economic damages are taken into account. Alien species can, in fact, alter ecosystems processes, reduce biodiversity, change landscapes, and reduce the value of land and water for human activities.

Following a classification used by the European Environmental Agency in its report on the impacts of invasive alien species in Europe (EEA, 2012), it is possible to identify four major groups of hazardous effects: impacts on biodiversity; impacts on ecosystem services; impacts on human health; and impacts on human activities.

From the first point of view, invasive alien species can affect biological diversity at the gene, species and ecosystem levels by means of hybridisation, pathogen diffusion, predation and/or competition for resources. As far as hybridisation is concerned, high rates of reproduction between alien and native species may result in the conception of infertile or genetically faulty hybrids, thus causing the decline of autochthon populations. Trade-related movements across Europe caused, as an example, the hybridisation of the Mediterranean subspecies of the honeybee (*Apis mellifera*) and bumblebee (*Bombus terrestris*) with northwestern European local subspecies. At the species level, the most pressing issues are the transmission of diseases, predation and competition for resources. As far as the transmission of diseases is concerned, non-native species can be unconscious vectors for parasites and pathogens which adversely impact on native wildlife, as in the case of amphibians infected by *Batrachochytrium dendrobatidis*, a chytrid fungus originated in Africa and subsequently spread in Europe by trade of African clawed frogs (*Xenopus laevis*). Furthermore, predation can cause severe population declines and, in the long term, threats of extinction. As an example, the harlequin ladybird (*Harmonia axyridis*), a coccinellid beetle native to Central and East Asia used in European greenhouses as a bio-control agent, has voraciously preyed on aphids and scales, but also on local ladybird species, thus causing a sudden decline in native populations. Finally, it is far from infrequent that alien species outcompete and eventually displace native wildlife as a consequence of their higher adaptability or more aggressive behaviour. In Northern Europe the Canadian beaver (*Castor canadensis*) is reported to have almost totally displaced the smaller and less aggressive European beaver (*Castor fiber*) in the maritime ecosystem, and in the Mediterranean two types of alien algae (i.e. the tropical *Caulerpa taxifolia* and the *Caulerpa racemosa* native to the Red Sea) that have arrived on ships' hulls or in ballast water have overgrown and substantially replaced native seagrass. More rarely, it can also happen that the impact of an exotic biome on the wider ecosystem results in significant and, sometimes, irreversible modifications in terms of biochemical, geo-morphological and hydrological processes. In this sense, an interesting case regards the introduction of four different species of Australian acacias (*Acacia longifolia*, *Acacia saligna*, *Acacia melanoxylon*, *Acacia cyclops*) to Portugal with the aim to stabilise dune ecosystems. Actually, these species entered into a relationship of biological facilitation with nitrogen-fixing bacteria, causing an increase in availability of soil nitrogen and carbon. This symbiosis significantly impacted on native species and favoured further invasions by acacia itself, thus causing structural change to the entire ecosystems, which became a mono-specific habitat. The impact of invasive alien species on ecosystem services – intended as the complex of direct and indirect contributions of ecosystems to human wellbeing (i.e. production of food, water, wood; regulation of climate, flood control, waste management; habitat support; cultural and recreational activities) – provides a link between ecological and economic impacts, as changes in the ecosystem have an impact on the overall human wellbeing. Although this impact can regard specific ecosystem services, it is likely that adverse effects are not restricted to a single aspect and may profoundly change the ecosystem functioning by altering at the same time supporting, regulating and provisioning regimes. An example comes from the aquatic ecosystem, where the zebra mussel (*Dreissena polymorpha*) – a small freshwater mussel originally native to the lakes of southern Russia and now widely spread in Great Britain, Ireland, Italy, Spain and Sweden – can alter water quality and bioaccumulation, thus undermining the production of native fish or the filtration of polluting substances.

With regard to direct impacts on human health, invasive species can be vectors of specific diseases, such as in the case of the outbreaks of *chikungunya* fever in northeastern Italy (2007, and again in September 2017) or *dengue* fever in Corsica (2010) as a consequence of the spread of the Asian tiger mosquito (*Aedes albopictus*), or cause direct threats, as in the case of the giant hogweed (*Heracleum mantegazzianum*), a species native to the Caucasus region whose sap causes a severe skin inflammation known as *phytophotodermatitis*. Finally, biological invasions also have dramatic economic consequences both in terms of direct expenses for prevention, eradication or mitigation and with regard to indirect costs related to damages to infrastructure, landscapes and agriculture. From the first point of view, a good yardstick is represented by the already mentioned *Rhododendron ponticum*: this plant, native to the Iberian Peninsula, Turkey, Bulgaria and the Balkans, is a highly invasive species in forests and semi-natural woodlands of the British Isles, where expenses for its control in a restricted area (the Snowdonia National Park in Wales) have reached the impressive amount of £45 million since 1992 (Jackson, 2008). As far as indirect costs are concerned, a paradigmatic case regards the damages caused to British and Irish agricultural and forestry industries by the red (*Cervus elaphus*), fallow (*Dama dama*) and roe (*Capreolus capreolus*) deer (Putnam and Moore, 1998).

In conclusion, the combination of ecological damages, loss of ecosystem services, threats to human health, and increasing economic costs for biological invasions in Europe has stressed the need for a coordinated regulatory approach at the regional scale. Before focusing on the recently enacted and all-encompassing regulation on the prevention and management of the introduction and spread of invasive alien species (Regulation 1143/2014/EU), which will be analysed in the next chapter, it is interesting to note that the first steps in the EU-wide action in the field of biological invasions clearly pre-date 2014. Pressures for a regulatory action started well before and outside the Community institutional framework and then made their entrance to EU law with different degrees of pervasiveness.

3.6 EU legislation on invasive alien species before the adoption of regulation 1143/2014

The normative horizon within which the European Union has pursued its strategy of conservation of native wildlife and – more recently – of complementary prevention or mitigation of damages caused by invasive alien species only partially coincides with the "space of governance" created through, and progressively evolved from, the Treaty of Rome in 1957. Looking at the gradual shaping of a supranational *corpus* of norms dealing with biological invasions, there are in fact two interconnected dynamics: on the one hand, agreements negotiated and adopted by Member States outside the Community framework that originated an authentic "ecological spill-over" between national authorities and European institutions; on the other, a slow but non-regressive transfer of regulatory and enforcement powers from the national to the Community level.

a *The exogenous drivers of an EU-wide policy on biological invasions*

A question of primary interest is to observe how important milestones at both the universal and continental levels have impacted on the design of a Community, first, and Union-wide, later, regulatory response to biological invasions. Following a strictly chronological order, the most important treaties which produced a direct impact on European legislative output have thus been the Convention on International Trade of Endangered Species of Wild Fauna and Flora (CITES) (opened for signature in 1973 and entered into force in 1975), the Bonn Convention on the Conservation of Migratory Species of Wild Animals (opened for signature in 1979 and entered into force in 1983), the Bern Convention on the Conservation of European Wildlife and Natural Habitats (opened for signature in 1979 and entered into force in 1982), and the Convention on Biological Diversity (opened for signature in 1992 and entered into force in 1993).

European institutions, indeed, became progressively more involved in the implementation of these international agreements: at first, in fact, the Community developed a non-protagonist yet fundamental role in the implementation of the CITES by enacting relevant pieces of internal legislation aimed at facilitating states' compliance, to become at a later moment an active player even in the exercise of its external competences.

With regard to the CITES, the European Economic Community was not directly involved, as the Gaborone amendment authorising regional economic integration organisations (REIOs) to become contracting parties only came into force in 2013. Nevertheless, the implementation of the convention by member countries became a matter of regional interest as the absence of border controls within the Community made a harmonising intervention by European institutions of paramount importance. In 1983, Council regulation 3626/82/EEC provided for even stricter controls on trade of wildlife specimens than those laid out in the text of the CITES. In fact, import permits had to be presented not only for species threatened with an immediate risk of extinction catalogued in Appendix I of the convention, but also for less imperilled species included in Appendixes II and III (Valaoras, 1998). In relation to biological invasions, the revised version of this regulation (i.e. Council regulation 338/97/EC on the protection of species of wild fauna and flora by regulating trade therein) contains a significant evolution. Article 4, sixth paragraph, confers to the European Commission the power to establish general restrictions on the import of specimens whose introduction into the natural environment of the Community should present an ecological threat to "indigenous" wild species of fauna and flora.

It was, however, in 1979 that European institutions reached a turning point in the way they pursued the objective of nature conservation, as the European Economic Community directly took part in the negotiation processes for the adoption of relevant agreements at both the universal and regional levels: the CMS, negotiated under the aegis of the United Nations

Environmental Programme (UNEP) in Bonn; and the Bern Convention, stipulated in the framework of the Council of Europe.

The first multilateral instrument in which the European Economic Community directly took part was the Bern Convention on the conservation of European wildlife and natural habitats. Adopted in the framework of the Council of Europe in 1979 with the aim to ensure conservation of wild flora and fauna species and their habitats in the European continent, the Convention contained a dedicated provision for invasive alien species, as the second paragraph of Article 11 required that contracting parties must "strictly control the introduction of non-native species". Council Decision 82/72/EEC approved the text of the Convention and declared its implementation "necessary in order to attain one of the objectives of the Community" under Article 235 TEEC. Since its adoption, the Bern Convention has produced recommendations and technical reports, both on general and specific problems. With reference to non-native species, in 1984 the Committee of Ministers adopted Recommendation n. 14 calling parties to prohibit the voluntary introduction and to prevent the accidental spread of non-native species into the natural environment in a framework of international cooperation (Council of Europe, 1984). In the 1990s, the important gaps and differences found in the implementation by Member States of Article 11.2 led the Standing Committee to create a specialised group of experts (Trinquelle, 1992),[15] whose work, firstly condensed in Recommendation n. 57 on the introduction of organisms belonging to non-native species into the environment (1997), had as a salient result the preparation and negotiation of a pan-European strategy on invasive alien species largely built on the Guiding Principles developed by the CBD (SCBD, 2002). Yet, if the guidelines elaborated at the universal level mainly focus their attention on the three-tier approach (prevention, eradication, management), the strategy elaborated by the group of experts of the Bern Convention promotes the development and implementation of coordinated measures and cooperative efforts throughout Europe to prevent and minimise the impacts of invasive alien species on local biodiversity, human health and wealth (Genovesi and Shine, 2003). Besides its problematic implementation, the role of the Bern Convention as an "accelerator" for a Community-wide conservation policy is evident, particularly in the light of the immediate evolutions. Already in November 1979 the Council approved a directive on the conservation of wild birds (Council Directive 79/409/EEC, or *Birds* directive), which was intimately connected to the objectives of the pan-European agreement even if with a narrowed focus *ratione materiae*. With particular regard to invasive species, Article 11 of the directive affirmed that Member States should ensure that any introduction of species of birds from outside the European territory of the Member States did not prejudice the local flora and fauna. Furthermore, in 1992 the European Community passed a new directive, the Council Directive 92/43/EC on the conservation of natural habitats and of wild fauna and flora (or *Habitats* directive), which improved the implementation of the Bern Convention within the Community, and took from this agreement much of its language and structure (Epstein, 2014). In particular, in relation to invasive species, Article 22(b) of the directive established that Member States should ensure that the deliberate introduction into the wild of any alien species would happen so as not to prejudice natural habitats or the wild fauna and flora. In extreme cases, national authorities were also authorised to prohibit threatening introductions.

Both the *Birds* and *Habitats* directives have been tools of implementation not only for the Bern Convention, but also for another intergovernmental agreement negotiated in the same year. In fact, the 1979 Convention on Migratory Species of Wild Animals (CMS) – better known as the Bonn Convention – had as its fundamental aim the conservation of migratory species, seen as a category worthy of reinforced protection because of environmental, ecological, genetic, scientific, recreational, cultural, educational, social and economic reasons. Moreover, migratory species particularly seemed to fit a supranational regime of conservation because of their cyclical movements across national jurisdiction boundaries. In addition, the Bonn convention has the unique characteristic – among the main multilateral conservation treaties signed at the universal level in the 1970s – of explicitly mentioning invasive species in its operative clauses. Article III.4(c) states, in fact, that

> parties that are range states of a migratory species listed in Appendix I shall endeavour . . . to the extent feasible and appropriate, to prevent, reduce or control factors that are endangering or are likely to further endanger the species, including strictly controlling the introduction of, or controlling or eliminating, already introduced exotic species.

Furthermore, Article V.5 states that agreements adding to Appendix II should provide for the

> conservation and, where required and feasible, restoration of the habitats of importance in maintaining a favourable conservation status, and protection of such habitats from disturbances, including strict control of the introduction of, or control of already introduced, exotic species detrimental to the migratory species.

An example of an agreement concluded in accordance with Article V.5 of the CMS and directly involving the European Union, through Council decision 2006/871/EC, is the Agreement on the Conservation of African-Eurasian Migratory Waterbirds (AEWA). This agreement establishes an ad hoc multilateral conservation regime for 255 species of migratory waterbirds dependent on wetlands for at least part of their annual cycle through coordinated measures aimed at achieving and maintaining a "favourable conservation status" in an area of 60 million square kilometres encompassing 118 states. Under the AEWA framework, parties are bound to prohibit the "deliberate introduction of non-native waterbird species into the environment" while at the same time taking "all appropriate measures to prevent the unintentional release of such species if this introduction or release would prejudice the conservation status of wild flora and fauna" or – once non-native waterbird species have already been introduced – "to prevent these species from becoming a potential threat to indigenous species".

Doubtlessly, the increasing attention devoted by European institutions to the question of invasive species has been a consequence of the negotiation and entry into force of the Convention on Biological Diversity (1993), an international binding agreement negotiated under the direct aegis of the United Nations and aimed at three fundamental objectives: the conservation of biological diversity, its sustainable use, and the fair and equitable sharing of the revenues coming from the use of natural resources. Indeed, a substantial role in the general aim of conserving and sustainably using biological diversity is played by the obligation contained in Article 8(h) CBD, which calls all parties to "prevent the introduction of, control or eradicate those alien species which threaten ecosystems, habitats or species". Such a general provision has been further reinforced – at least with regard to its interpretation and implementation – by the adoption, during the Sixth Conference of the Parties to the CBD held in The Hague in 2002, of a set of non-binding Guiding Principles for the action of contracting parties towards invasive alien species. These guidelines are based on a three-tier approach according to which prevention is the most effective, environmentally desirable, and at the same time least costly response, followed by early detection and eradication, while management and control are seen as palliative and expensive methods of last resort. The European Union has been a party to the CBD since 1992 and has been an active implementer of the agreement. In 1998, a communication from the Commission to the European Parliament and the Council on the development of a Community-wide biodiversity strategy was issued in compliance with Article 6 of the CBD, which requires each contracting party to set out a strategy for the conservation and sustainable use of biological diversity. According to this document, the final aim of the Community-wide strategy was to prevent and attack the cause of significant reduction or loss of biodiversity at the source, with a particular emphasis on the question of biological invasions. The document stressed how

> the presence or introduction of alien species or sub-species can potentially cause imbalances and changes to ecosystems. It can have potentially irreversible impacts, by hybridisation or competition, on native components of biodiversity. Applying the precautionary principle, the Community should take measures pursuing to prevent that alien species cause detrimental effects on ecosystems, priority species or the habitats they depend on and establish measures to control, manage and, wherever possible remove the risks that they pose.
>
> (European Commission, 1998)

The 1998 communication signs an important historic caesura, as European institutions underlined with unprecedented emphasis the role of biological invasions in the regulatory approach to nature conservation, thus laying down the political foundations for subsequent action against invasive alien species.

b The general picture: **Birds** *and* **Habitats** *directives and the Natura 2000 network*

As already stated, the first dedicated piece of legislation enacted by the Community in the field of biological invasions dates back to 1979, an epoch in which limited powers in the environmental field had to be combined with public disquiet over the decline of a large number of bird species (DG Environment, 2004). Following a petition presented by national and international organisations to the Parliamentary Assembly, Commission and Council "on the need to save migratory birds", in 1974 the assembly adopted a resolution urging the Commission and the Council to "propose and adopt in the near future practical measures for the protection of migratory birds". The activity of the Parliament as an "advocate" of nature conservation eventually incepted the legislative mechanism which brought about the adoption of Council directive 74/409 on the conservation of wild birds. According to the directive, Member States had to adapt national and/or regional legislation before May 1981 in a way to maintain populations of wild bird species by ensuring the appropriate classification and management of protected sites (named Special Protection Areas, SPAs). The role of SPAs was specifically to preserve, maintain or re-establish sufficient diversity for birds by applying measures aimed at properly protecting animals from hunting and other hazardous practices (such as deliberate killing or capture, the destruction of nests or the taking of eggs, and disturbances of any kind, particularly in the time of breeding and rearing). The *Birds* directive is also the first official document by the European Communities explicitly mentioning biological invasions. Article 11 of the directive, in fact, constitutes the seminal – though limited to birds' conservation – piece of Community law regarding a response to the damages caused by invasive alien species, as it posits that

> member states shall see that any introduction of species of bird which do not occur naturally in the wild state in the European territory of the member states does not prejudice the local flora and fauna. In this connection they shall consult the Commission.

This rather vague formulation did not provide the executive European body with substantial powers, while on the other hand it seemed to be quite reticent on the corresponding obligation by Member States to report on its implementation. It has not been a case, then, of "reporting on introduced species has not been consistent over the years" or of most of the information available having failed to distinguish between deliberate and accidental introductions (European Commission, 2007). Furthermore, national reports have often neglected to specify whether and to what avail control measures had been taken, thus contributing to an incomplete control by the Commission and to a generally scarce implementation of the specific provision, with only limited action taken in most Member States to ensure that introduced species do not prejudice the local fauna and flora (European Commission).

Modelled after – and based on – the *Birds* directive, Council directive 92/43/EC on the conservation of natural habitats and of wild fauna and flora (the *Habitats* directive) updated and enhanced natural protection in the wake of the extension of Community competences in environmental matters (Machado, 1997). Composed of a preamble, 24 articles and six annexes, the *Habitats* directive had as its general aims – listed in Article 2 – to "contribute toward ensuring biodiversity through the conservation of natural habitats and of wild fauna and flora in the European territory of member states" and to "maintain or restore, at favourable conservation status, natural habitats and species" listed in the annexes. The most important means of conservation was, according to the directive, the establishment pursuant to Article 3 of a coherent European ecological network of "special areas of conservation" (SACs) for listed types of habitats and species. This network, set up under the title of Natura 2000, incorporated those ecological hotspots classified as Special Protection Areas (SPAs) by Member States pursuant to the *Birds* directive while introducing the possibility for national authorities to identify the areas of conservation not on the basis of state boundaries but according to bio-geographical regions (Alpine, Atlantic, Boreal, Continental, Macaronesian, Mediterranean and Pannonian). With particular regard to the protection of habitats and native species from unwanted and potentially threatening introductions, Article 22 of the *Habitats* directive establishes that, for Member States, "the deliberate introduction into the wild of any species which is not native to their territory is regulated so as not to prejudice natural habitats within their natural range or the wild native fauna and flora and, if they consider it necessary, prohibit such introduction". This provision can be read in conjunction with the third paragraph of Article 6, particularly if the release, translocation or introduction of exotic biomes is intended as a "plan or project not directly connected with or necessary to the management of the site but likely to have a significant effect thereon, either individually or in combination with other plans or projects". In practical terms, if the *Birds* and *Habitats* directives have set the normative scene for a general policy of conservation and prevention of biological invasions, the technical instrument which has made its implementation possible has been Council regulation 1973/92/EC, which established the Financial Instrument for the Environment (*L'Instrument Financier pour l'Environnement*, LIFE). Since the first instrument was adopted, as many as 14% of the total funded projects have included actions dealing with the management of exotic species in its various phases (prevention of the introduction, early detection and eradication, mitigation of the adverse effects, restoration of habitats and recovery of affected species). In fact, through the LIFE and LIFE+ financing schemes the European Community has contributed to funding almost 300 projects addressing invasive alien species issues for a total budget exceeding €132 million.

Though significant, these interventions are a drop in the ocean of the threats posed by biological invasions to European habitats and species. If put to the test of time – and results – the provisions contained in Article 11 of the *Birds* directive and in Article 22 of the *Habitats* directive have shown poor implementation, in complete antithesis to the strong legal basis which both of them provided for Member States in order to develop more robust preventive measures based on a white list approach.[16] In practice, they have not been consistently and uniformly applied, thus showing them to be ineffective in preventing the continued introduction and spread of invasive alien species on European territory (Shine et al., 2010). Besides the various degrees of commitment by individual Member States – a danger which is deeply connate to the nature of a highly decentralised mechanism such as the directive – one of the main reasons for such a poor performance relies in the inapplicability of the legal framework to species that are not directly hazardous to native wildlife but to vector pathogens or parasites threatening to European biodiversity. At the same time, both directives ignore the phenomenon of exotic species kept in captivity or in managed environments while arbitrarily ignoring the EU's outermost regions, which, in turn, are particularly exposed to the threat of biological invasions given their isolated nature. Given these gaps and inconsistencies, ad hoc normative approaches have been put in place with regard to specific dangers and/or particularly threatened species and ecosystems.

c Specific legislation on individual threats and species. More is less?

Throughout the decades – partially as a reaction to the inapplicability of the two main pieces of European legislation on nature conservation to specific situations, and partially as a consequence of factual circumstances – a vast array of ad hoc norms have been developed to deal with very specific issues. It is thus interesting to assess the contribution of such normative evolutions to the overall functioning of the European Union's response to biological invasions. For this reason, this subsection will illustrate the most relevant examples of the intervention of European institutions in specific ambits such as animal and plant health and trade and marine and freshwater ecosystems.

As far as animal health and welfare is concerned, in 2007 the European Union developed an Animal Health Strategy and Action Plan focused on an integrated approach through the modernisation and harmonisation of a dispersed and sometimes chaotic body of norms, including both general legislation and species-specific instruments, with the final aim to support risk-based prioritisation of EU interventions together with enhancing border control and on-farm biosecurity (European Commission, 2008a). With relation to invasive species, this strategy has the merit of regulating import and intra-Union movement of animals that can work as vectors of diseases to other animals or humans, as in the case of the EU-wide prohibition on import of wild birds as a preventive measure against the transmission of avian flu. At the same time, however, this general strategy did not consider environmental risks associated with the import, release and/or escape of alien animals for non-commercial purposes while completely setting aside the question of early warning and rapid response. In this respect the Animal Disease Notification System, which provides for reporting and diagnosis of detected diseases, plays an important role, with an auxiliary role entrusted to the EU Veterinary Emergency Team, established in 2007.

In relation to plants, the framework regime is provided by the Plant Health directive (Council directive 2000/29/EC, as amended), with ad hoc complementary regulations for particular types of pests. This directive establishes a normative protection against the introduction into the European Union – or the circulation within its territory – of organisms harmful to plants or plant products, defined as "pests of plants or of plant products, which belong to the animal or plant kingdoms, or which are viruses, mycoplasmas or other pathogens". A limit of the directive is its focus on agriculture and forestry pests, leaving little room for those species constituting a biological hazard for the diversity of the ecosystems or for human health. This lack of consistency in the approach has been referred to as one of the main reasons for those situations in which a preventive approach has failed – such as in the case of the red palm weevil. The situation is further endangered by the choice to allow "free movement" of plants, both those that have been imported from outside the Union borders and those traded within its boundaries. Derogation is only possible in case of request by a Member State to activate a "protected zone" in order to prevent hazardous organisms from spreading from areas where they had already thrived into non-invaded areas with favourable conditions for their establishment. In cases where pests succeed in spreading within a native ecosystem, early warning and rapid response are managed by Europhyt, an electronic system shared by the Commission and Member States. The provision for an emergency procedure (the so-called "fast track Pest Risk Assessment") for non-listed hazardous organisms is not combined with an EU-level emergency team as it is in the case of animal health.

Furthermore, trade of animals and plants is one of its most recognised and effective drivers of the introduction of invasive alien species. In this sense, the wild trade regulation (Council regulation 338/97/EC) – primarily aimed at implementing the CITES – is at the forefront of the Union's regulatory approach for border, import and transit controls in relation to trade in protected species of wild fauna and flora. In its Article 4, the regulation sets up the legal basis to suspend the import into the EU of "live specimens of species for which it has been established that their introduction into the natural environment of the Community presents an ecological threat to wild species of fauna and flora indigenous to the Community",[17] while stand-alone provisions to address intra-EU movements of species native in some parts of the EU and alien and potentially invasive in others are not contemplated. The mechanism of functioning of such normative provisions is delegated to Member States' customs authorities, which perform border and internal trade controls, with the technical support by the EU Trade in Wildlife Information Exchange Initiative (EU-TWIX), an online database set up in 2005 to help enforcement personnel undertake risk analysis and coordinate joint investigations. Given its focus on prevention, the Wildlife trade regulation does not have any provision regarding rapid response or control, thus limiting the impact of this piece of legislation on the safeguarding of European biodiversity.

Shifting the focus of attention to seas and freshwaters, some important legislative acts regard aquaculture and the safeguard of the marine ecosystems. As far as aquaculture is concerned, Council regulation 708/2007/EC concerning use of alien and locally absent species in aquaculture sets up a legal framework under which Member States are obliged to take appropriate measures to prevent, assess and minimise the potential hazardous impacts of alien and locally absent species used in aquaculture on the aquatic environment, thus contributing to the sector's sustainable development (Shine et al., 2010). National authorities are the primary actors in the implementation of the regulation as they have the duty to conduct risk assessments, issue permits and perform follow-ups on the introduction or translocation of exotic species, ensuring that only those species that meet the requirements of an environmental risk assessment may be allowed. The introduction of such detailed assessment procedures, combined with the restrictive approach of the white list – under which species are considered "guilty until proven innocent" – has not completely eliminated the influence of external (and sometimes unpredictable) factors in the determination of a ban to the introduction. It may be the case, in fact, that the risk level can be different for some species depending on the particular ecosystem of Member States or as a consequence of their higher degree of adaptability to a new environment. A framework directive enacted in 2000 (Council directive 2000/60/EC, also known as Water Framework Directive or WFD) in turn, aims at harmonising national measures for the achievement and/or the maintenance of a good ecological status for European inland, transitional and coastal waters. The WFD does not directly mention invasive species, whose coverage is granted by the provision regarding "potential anthropogenic impact" contained in Annex V. In 2009, a consultative process (ECOSTAT, 2009) revealed how the incorporation of considerations on invasive species on the implementation of the Water Framework Directive was still poor as a consequence of the lack of adequate information tools – inter alia, the analysis emphasised the lack of a coordinated monitoring activity at the national level and the almost non-existent long-term approach taken by the few existing reports, often focused on particular regional situations or driven by human health, livestock or economic needs rather than environmental needs – and of the vast range of potentially covered *taxa*, as plants, invertebrates and fish are equally covered.

Finally, with regard to the marine environment, the Marine Strategy Framework Directive (2008/56/EC) requires Member States to develop – on the basis of the ecosystem approach – a marine strategy aimed at creating and maintaining a "good environmental status" by the year 2021 through the combined use of three of the main principles of the European environmental policy (i.e. the principles of preventive action, rectification of environmental damage at source, and the "polluter pays" principle). As far as invasive species are concerned, reports by Member States on the implementation of the directive should include an inventory of the disturbances caused by the spread of exotic biomes.

This brief yet thorough review of the existing European legal response to biological invasions has emphasised the existence of some very well regulated categories of invasive alien species and pathways, such as in the case of aquaculture or animal and plant diseases, and conversely, the absence of similar coverage for other categories (such as mammals and fishes) or situations (such as the establishment of a centralised system of border controls or the regulation of ballast waters). More importantly, the regulatory response set up by the European Union has been conventionally marked by the lack of an overall framework for their control and management, and by the absolute decentralisation to Member States in terms of implementation. These reasons have led to a substantial re-thinking of the way the issue of biological invasions had to be approached by European institutions, perhaps fuelled by the evident need of a more streamlined and comprehensive action capable of taking into account, inter alia, the intrinsic transboundary nature of biological invasions, the increasing number and magnitude of threats posed by invasive alien species to European biodiversity, and the close connection between the spread of exotic biomes and the growth of international trade, an exclusive competence of the Union. Those considerations have thus led European institutions, in general, and the European Commission, in particular, to start a process of slow convergence towards a more general strategy on invasive alien species, which culminated in September 2014 in the adoption of an all-encompassing regulation on invasive alien species.

Notes

1 A good example on the matter is the so-called *Danish bottle* case (*Commission v. Denmark*, C-302/86): in this infringement procedure, in which the Danish government was accused of distorting trade of containers for beers and soft drinks through an internal provision establishing the obligatory disposal of empty cans and bottles, the Court ruled that environment was a fundamental objective for the Community, and national legislation which in principle would obstruct trade is nevertheless compatible with Article 30 of the TEEC (prohibiting quantitative restrictions on imports and measures having an equivalent effect between Member States) as long as the Community has not already regulated the same activity and the national legislation is purely environmental in purpose and is applied evenly to imported and domestic products.

2 Court of Justice of the European Communities, case *Procureur de la République v. Association de défense des brûleurs d'huiles usagées* (C-240/83). This particular case regarded a reference for a preliminary ruling (Article 177, TEEC) from the Tribunal de Grande Instance in Créteil, in a dispute over the interpretation and validity of Council Directive 75/439/EEC on the disposal of waste oils in exclusive zones and following a licensing and authorisation process. The disposition was challenged on the ground of free movement of goods and freedom of competition. The Court underlined how French national legislation was coherent with the scope of the Directive, since "disposal of waste oils is carried out in a way which avoids harm to the environment". The principle of freedom of trade, in fact, is "not to be viewed in absolute terms but is subject to certain limits justified

by the objectives of general interest pursued by the Community provided that the rights in question are not substantively impaired".

3 In relation to the precautionary principle, it is evident the influence exercised – pending the negotiation of the TEU – by the United Nations Conference on Environment and Development (UNCED), where the precautionary principle was included in Principle 15 of the Rio Declaration and defined as follows: "where there are threats of serious or irreversible damage, lack of full scientific certainty shall not be used as a reason for postponing cost-effective measures to prevent environmental degradation".

4 See, as an example, case *Aannemersbedriff P.K. Kraaijeveld BV e. a.* c. *Gedeputeerde Staten van Zuid-Holland* on the application of Directive 85/337/EEC on the environmental impact assessment (EIA) for public and private projects. In particular, the claimants relied on the direct effect of the directive in order to ask an EIA for the construction of a dyke which would allegedly prevent them from access to water. The Court replies that – also in case of a State measure declared inapplicable – it is not always possible to secure for the private individual the exact legal position which he would have enjoyed if the State had taken the correct implementing measure.

5 Under this respect, two cases hold a paramount importance: in a reference for preliminary ruling (*ARCO Chemie Nederland*, joined cases C-418 and C-419/97), the Court has emphasised the mutually supportive relationship between the high level of environmental protection and the precautionary and preventive principles; similarly, in the *Thames Water Utilities* case (C-252/05), the provision of a high level of environmental protection has been considered by judges in Luxembourg as a cornerstone in applying the precautionary and preventive principles and as an interpretative tool for clarifying the content of an obligation stemming from a piece of environmental legislation of the Union.

6 Court of Justice of the European Union (2004), *Landelike Vereniging tot Behoud van de Waddenzee and Nederlandse Verniging tot Bescherming van Vogels v. Staatssecretariats van Landbouw, Naturbeheer en Visserij* (C-172/02).

7 Court of Justice of the European Communities (1992), *Commission v. Kingdom of Belgium* (*Walloon Waste* case, C-2/90), 9 July 1992.

8 From this point of view, an interesting case regards the disposal of waste oils: Council Directive 75/439/EEC, in its Article 14, made explicit reference to the "polluter pays" principle as the inspirational basis for financing indemnities to be accorded to those undertakings charged with the collection and/or disposal of waste oils. In 1983, then, the Court of Justice, in the case *Syndicat national des fabricants raffineurs d'huile de graissage and others v. Groupement d'intérêt économique "Inter-Huiles" and others* (case c-172/82), gave an interpretation of the "polluter pays" principle by condemning a prohibition on the export of waste oils outside of France on the grounds of an incompatibility with the free movement of goods within the Community: in particular, the Court refused the economic argument defended by the French authorities that "only the collection of all waste oils" would be "sufficient to ensure the profitability of undertakings approved for the disposal" in the light of Articles 13 and 14 of the Waste Oils directive providing that "by way of compensation for the obligations imposed on the undertakings for the implementation of Article 5, member states may, without placing restrictions on exports, grant to such undertakings indemnities financed in accordance with the principle of the polluter pays".

9 In the *Standley* case (1999, C-293/97), regarding the reduction of water pollution from nitrates discharged into water from agricultural sources, the Court affirms that the obligation posed by the Nitrate directive does not mean that "farmers must take on burdens for the elimination of pollution to which they have not contributed". In the subsequent *Pontina Ambiente* case (2010, C-172/08), dealing with the possibility for Member States to introduce a levy on the operator

of a landfill in order to cover all the operating costs provided that the actual producer of waste would reimburse the operator, the Court found the levy allowable "on the condition that the fiscal provision in question is accompanied by measures to ensure that the levy is actually reimbursed within a short time so as not to impose excessive operating costs on the operator on account of late payment", considering that "causing the operator to bear such charges would amount to charging to him the costs arising from the disposal of waste which he did not generate but of which he merely disposes in the framework of his activities as a provider of services".

10 Court of Justice of the European Union (2010), *Raffinerie Mediterranee (ERG) SpA, Polimeri Europei SpA and Syndall SpA v. Ministero dello Sviluppo Economico and Others* (C-378/08). In determining the link between a certain activity and an environmental hazard, competent authorities "must have plausible evidence capable of justifying its presumption, such as the fact that operator's installation is located close to the pollution found and that there is a correlation between the pollutants identified and the substances used by the operator in connection with his activities".

11 Court of Justice of the European Union (2009), Futura Immobiliare case (C-254/08), par. 56.

12 Court of Justice of the European Union (2010), Agusta case, C-373/08.

13 Court of Justice of the European Union (2004), van de Walle case, C-1/03.

14 Paradigmatic are, in this sense, the 1972 Paris Summit, with its embryonic formulation of a common environmental policy; the 1983 Stuttgart European Council, which addressed the European response to acidification; the 1985 Brussels meeting, which anticipated the principle of integration of environmental protection in the economic, industrial, agricultural and social policies; and the 1990 Dublin summit, which issued a declaration on the "environmental imperative" and on the necessity to coordinate environmental action on the basis of sustainable development and precautionary principle.

15 The Group of Experts on Invasive Alien Species decided, during its first meeting in March 1993, to collect and analyse national laws dealing with biological invasions with a view to harmonisation in the fields of definitions, territorial scope of regulation, listing of species whose introduction was undesirable, and identification of the authorities responsible for the issue of permits (together with its conditions). In 1995, it decided to broaden its scope to the centralisation of existing information on a European Clearing House Mechanism on Introductions, the analysis of legal and administrative measures taken by states, the design of an overall risk management policy, the elaboration of guidelines and codes of conduct, and the identification of sensitive areas and emergency situations.

16 According to this particular method, exotic species undergo a general presumption of "no release" into the wild in absence of a permit by national authorities. A valid example is, within the European legal framework, the approach followed by Council regulation 338/97/EC on the protection of species of wild fauna and flora by regulating trade therein, which contemplates the obligation to present an import permit for all imported specimens of endangered species, particularly if alleged to be a threat to native flora and fauna.

17 Council regulation 338/97/EC, Article 4, paragraph 6(d). Since 1997, the ban on the import has been necessary for four species: the red-eared slider (*Trachemys scripta elegans*), the American bullfrog (*Lithobates catesbeianus*), the painted turtle (*Chrysemys picta*), and the American ruddy duck (*Oxyura jamaicensis*).

Bibliography

Action Committee for European Democracy. (2007), *A new treaty and supplementary protocols.* Contribution to the debate on Europe's political prospects in the

Perspective of the European Council of 21–22 June 2007 – Explanatory Memorandum, Brussels, Belgium, 4 June.

Bleeker, A. (2009), Does the polluter pay? The polluter pays principle in the case law of the European Court of Justice in *EEEL Review*, December: 289–306.

Calfee, C.H. (1998), Europe's "Jolly Green Giant": Environmental policy in the European Union in *Environs Envtl L & Pol'y J* 22(1): 45–58.

Council of Europe. (1984), *Recommendation No. R(84) 14 of the Committee of Ministers to member states concerning the introduction of non-native species*, adopted on 21 June.

Court of Justice of the European Communities (1985), case Procureur de la République v. Association de défense des brûleurs d'huiles usagées (C-240/83).

Court of Justice of the European Communities (1992), case Commission v. Kingdom of Belgium (Walloon Waste case, C-2/90), 9 July 1992.

Court of Justice of the European Union (2004), case Landelike Vereniging tot Behoud van de Waddenzee and Nederlandse Verniging tot Bescherming van Vogels v. Staatssecretariats van Landbouw, Naturbeheer en Visserij (C-172/02).

Court of Justice of the European Union (2004), Judgment of the Court (Second Chamber) of 7 September 2004. Criminal proceedings against Paul Van de Walle, Daniel Laurent, Thierry Mersch and Texaco Belgium SA (C-1/03).

Court of Justice of the European Union (2010), Judgment of the Court (Grand Chamber) of 9 March 2010, Raffinerie Mediterranee (ERG) SpA, Polimeri Europa SpA and Syndial SpA v Ministero dello Sviluppo economico and Others (case C-378/08).

De Sadeleer, N.M. (2002), *Environmental principles: From political slogans to legal rules*, Oxford University Press, Oxford.

De Sadeleer, N.M. (2010), The principle of prevention and precaution in international law: Two heads of the same coin? in M. Fitzmaurice, D.M. Ong and P. Merkouris (eds.), *Research handbook on international environmental law*, Edward Elgar, Cheltenham and Northampton, MA.

De Sadeleer, N.M. (2012), The polluter-pays principle in EU law – bold case law and poor harmonisation in *Pro Natura: Festskrift Til H. C. Bugge*, Universitetsforlaget, Oslo, 405–419.

De Sadeleer, N.M. (2013), The principle of a high level of environmental protection in EU Law: Policy principle or general principle of law? In Gipperth, L. and Zetterberg, C. (eds.), *Mijörättsliga Perspektiv Och Tankevändor, Vänbok Till Jan Darpö & Gabriel Michanek*, Iustus Förlag, Uppsala, Finland.

De Sadeleer, N.M. (2014), *EU environmental law and the internal market*, Oxford University Press, London.

DG Environment. (2004), *25 years of the Birds Directive, challenges for 25 countries – Implementation report*, Report by the European Commission, Brussels, Belgium.

ECOSTAT (2009), Workshop on Alien Species and the EC Water Framework Directive, Final Report of a workshop prepared by Alison Lee, UK Joint Nature Conservation Committee (Ispra, Italy, 17–18 June 2009).

Epiney, A. (1997), *Umweltrecht in der Europäischen Union*, Heymanns, Cologne, Germany.

Epiney, A. (2006), *Environmental principles in principles of European environmental law*, Europa Law Publishing, Groeningen, The Netherlands.

Epstein, Y. (2014), The habitats directive and Bern convention: Synergy and dysfunction in public international and EU law in *Geo Int'l Envtl L Rev* 26(2): 139–173.

European Commission. (1998), *Communication from the Commission to the European Parliament and the Council on a EC strategy on biological diversity*, COM(1998)42, 4 February 1998, Brussels, Belgium.

European Commission. (2001), Guidelines for state aid for environmental purposes in *Official Journal of the European Union* 37: 3.

European Commission. (2007), *Report from the Commission on the implementation of Directive 79/409/EEC on the conservation of wild birds* (period covered 2005–2007).

European Commission. (2008a), *Communication to the European Parliament, the Council, the European Economic and Social Committee and the Committee of the Regions on implementing European Community Environmental Law*, COM(2008) 773, Brussels, Belgium.

European Commission. (2008b), *Communication laying down the Action Plan for the implementation of the EU Animal Health Strategy for 2007–2013*, COM(2008)545, 10 September 2008, Brussels, Belgium.

European Commission. (2016), *33th annual report on monitoring the application of EU Law*, July.

European Environmental Agency. (2012), *The impact of invasive alien species in Europe*, EEA Technical Report 16/2012, Copenhagen, Denmark.

European Environmental Agency. (EEA, 2003), *Europe's environment: The 3rd assessment*, Environmental assessment report n.10, Office for Official Publications of the European Communities, Luxembourg.

Fligstein, N. and Stone Sweet, A. (2002), Constructing markets and polities: An institutionalist account of European integration in *Am J Sociol* 107: 1206–1243.

Fois, P. (2005), Il diritto ambientale nell'ordinamento dell'Unione Europea in G. Cordini, P. Fois and S. Marchisio (eds.), *Diritto ambientale: profili internazionali, europei e comparati*, G. Giappichelli Editore, Turin, Italy.

Genovesi, P. and Shine, C. (2003), *European strategy on invasive alien species*, Nature and Environment Series n. 137, Council of Europe Publishing, Strasbourg, France.

Haas, E.B. (1961), International integration: The European and the universal process in *International Organization* 15(5): 366–392.

Haas, E.B. (1975), *The obsolescence of regional integration theory*, Berkeley Institute of International Studies, University of California, Berkeley, CA.

Hartley, T.C. (1988), *The foundations of European community law* (2nd ed.), Clarendon Press, Oxford.

Heywood, V. (1995), *Global biodiversity assessment*, Cambridge University Press, Cambridge.

Hilson, C. (2000), *Regulating pollution: A UK and EC perspective*, Hart Publishing, Oxford.

Hilson, C. (2008), Rights and principles in EU law: A distinction without foundation in *Maastricht Journal of European and Comparative Law* 15(2): 193–215.

Hulme, P.E. (2003), Biological invasions: Winning the science battles but losing the conservation war? in *Oryx* 37: 178–193.

Hulme, P.E. (2007), Biological invasions in Europe: Drivers, pressures, states, impacts and responses in R.E. Hester and R.M. Harrison (eds.), *Biodiversity under threat*, The Royal Society of Chemistry, Cambridge.

Jackson, P. (2008), *Rhododendron in Snowdonia and a strategy for its control*, Awdurdod Parc Cenedlaethol Eryri/Snowdonia National Park Authority, Penrhyndeudraeth, Wales.

Jordan, A. and Adelle, C. (2005), *Environmental policy in the European Union: Actors, institutions, and processes* (2nd ed.), Earthscan, London.

Krämer, L. (1996), The elaboration of EC environmental legislation in G. Winter (ed.), *European environmental law: A comparative perspective*, Dartmouth Publishing Co., Aldershot.

Krämer, L. (2008), *Environmental judgments by the court of justice of the European Union and their duration*, Research Papers in Law, Cahiers Juridiques, 4/2008.

Krämer, L. (2012), *European union environmental law* (7th ed.), Sweet and Maxwell, London.

Lindhout, P.E. and Van Broek, B. (2014), The polluter pays principle: Guidelines for cost recovery and burden sharing in the case law of the European court of justice in *Utrecht L Rev* 10(2): 46–59.

Machado, A. (1997), *Guidelines for actions plans for animal species: Planning recovery*, Council of Europe Publishing, Strasbourg, France.

Manservisi, S. (2012), Le norme ambientali del diritto primario dell'Unione Europea in L. Costato and S. Manservisi (eds.), *Profili di diritto ambientale nell'Unione Europea*, Quaderni del Centro di Documentazione e Studi sulle Comunità Europee – Università degli Studi di Ferrara, CEDAM, Padova, Italy.

Marin Duràn, G. and Morgera, E. (2013), Commentary on article 37 of the EU charter of fundamental rights – environmental protection in S. Peers, T. Hervey, J. Kenner and A. Ward (eds.), *Commentary on the EU charter of fundamental rights*, Hart Publishing, Oxford.

Mazey, S. and Richardson, J. (1997), The commission and the lobby in G. Edwards and D. Spence (eds.), *The European commission* (2nd ed.), Catermill, London.

McCormick, J. (2001), *Environmental policy in the European Union*, Palgrave Macmillan, Basingstoke.

McNeely, A. (2001), *The great reshuffling: Human dimensions on invasive alien species*, IUCN, Gland, Switzerland and Cambridge.

Meli, F. (1996), *Il principio comunitario "chi inquina paga"*, Giuffrè, Milan, Italy.

Misonne, D. (2010), *Droit européen de l'environnement et de la santé: l'ambition d'un niveau élevé de protection*, Anthémis, Luvain, Belgium.

Moravcsik, A. (1993), Preferences and power in the European community: A liberal intergovernmentalist approach in *J Common Mark Stud* 31(4): 473–524.

Haigh, N. and Kraemer, R.A. (1996), Sustainable development in den Verträgen der Europäischen Union in *ZUR* 5: 239–242, Berlin, Germany.

Organization for the Economic Cooperation and Development (OECD, 1972), *Guiding principles concerning international economic aspects of environmental policies*, Recommendation C(72)128, Paris, France.

Pinder, J. (1968), Positive integration and negative integration: Some problems on economic union in the EEC in *World Today* 24(3): 88–110.

Putnam, R.J. and Moore, N.P. (1998), Impact of deer in lowland Britain on agriculture, forestry and conservation habitats in *Mamm Rev* 28(4): 141–164.

Rizzo, A. (2012), L'affermazione di una politica ambientale dell'Unione Europea in R. Giuffrida (ed.), *Diritto europeo dell'ambiente*, G. Giappichelli Editore, Turin, Italy.

Secretariat of the Convention on Biological Diversity (SCBD, 2002), Guiding Principles for the Prevention, Introduction and Mitigation of Impact of Alien Species that Threatens Ecosystems, Habitats or Species – Decision VI/23 of the 6th Conference of Parties to the Convention on Biological Diversity.

Shine, C., Kettunen, M., Genovesi, P., Essl, F., Gollasch, S., Rabitsch, W., Scalera, R., Starfinger, U. and Ten Brink, P. (2010), *Assessment to support continued development of the EU Strategy to combat invasive alien species.* Final Report for the European Commission, Institute for European Environmental Policy (IEEP), Brussels, Belgium.

Somsen, H. (2000), The private enforcement of member states compliance with environmental EC law: An unfulfilled promise? in H. Somsen (ed.), *Yearbook of European environmental law*, Oxford University Press, Oxford.

Tranholm-Mikkelsen, J. (1991), Neo-functionalism: Obstinate or obsolete? A reappraisal in the light of the new dynamism of the EC in *Millennium J Int Stud* 20(1): 4–6.

Trinquelle, I. (1992), Legal aspects of the introduction and re-introduction of wildlife species in Europe, *TPVS* 92: 7.

Valaoras, G. (1998), *Monitoring of wildlife trade in the European Union: Assessing the effectiveness of EU CITES import policies*, TRAFFIC Europe, Brussels, Belgium.

Vogel, D. and Kessler, T. (1998), How compliance happens and doesn't happen domestically in E. Brown Weiss and H.K. Jacobsen (eds.), *Engaging countries, strengthening compliance with international environmental accords*, The MIT Press, Cambridge, MA.

Weiler, J.H.H. (1991), The transformation of Europe in *Yale Law J* 100: 2403–2483.

Winter, G. (2002), Constitutionalizing environmental protection in the EU in Somsen, H. (ed.), *YEEL* 2: 67–88.

4 EU regulation 1143/2014

Genesis, adoption and implementation: an assessment

SUMMARY: 4.1. Introduction – 4.2. The long genesis of the proposal for a regulation on invasive alien species (a. The "preparatory phase": 1998–2008; b. The "pre-legislative phase": 2008–2013) – 4.3. The Commission proposal and the inter-institutional debate (a. Details of the Commission proposal for a regulation on invasive alien species; b. The inter-institutional debate) – 4.4. The amended regulation and its adoption by the European Parliament and the Council – 4.5. A concluding assessment of the effectiveness of regulation 1143/2014 under a SWOT analysis perspective

4.1 Introduction

As already pointed out in Chapter 3, the first recognition by European institutions of the need for a comprehensive approach to the question of invasive alien species dates back to the Communication on a European Biodiversity Strategy issued by the Commission in 1998 (European Commission, 1998). Since 1998 – and until 2008 – the intention to establish a general regulatory framework on biological invasions was expressed in non-binding documents whose main value under a legal standpoint has to be identified in a *voluntas de legiferando* from European institutions. Since 2008, on the contrary, a long and complex debate has been initiated by an ad hoc communication by the European Commission on the development of a comprehensive regulatory response to biological invasions. Such a "triggering event" has split the flow of discussion in two main phases: the "preparatory phase", which lasted from 1998 to 2008, and a "pre-legislative phase", concluded in September 2013 by the proposal by the Commission of a regulation on invasive alien species.

In this respect, the chapter will present an in-depth analysis of the proposal forwarded by the Commission to the European co-legislators and a comprehensive review of the inter-institutional debate which has finally led to the adoption of the act by the European Parliament and the Council in October 2014. Conclusively, the last section of this work will try to assess the main strengths and weaknesses of the regulation, together with the most important opportunities and threats deriving from its adoption, in respect of the uncontrolled introduction and spread of invasive alien species into the European Union's territory.

4.2 The long genesis of the proposal for a regulation on invasive alien species

a The "preparatory phase": 1998–2008

As for the preparatory phase, the Communication issued by the European Commission in 1998 identified in biological invasions a cause for potentially irreversible "imbalances and changes" to the different European ecosystems. In fact, it stressed how the application of the precautionary principle was a fundamental tool in preventing those "detrimental effects", with an auxiliary role for other measures aimed at controlling, managing and – if possible – removing the risks which follow a successful introduction. In 2001 the Commission approved detailed action plans, with particular regard to sectors exposed to threats coming from exotic living organisms (i.e. natural resources, agriculture, fisheries and economic development). Contained in a communication from the Commission to the Council and the European Parliament, these action plans recognised in the proliferation of invasive alien species an issue to be addressed through "specific protection measures" whose scope had forcefully to overcome traditional conservative approaches (European Commission, 2001a). Pending the approval of new legal regimes, however, the non-binding action plan emphasised the need that "existing and planned environmental legislation and instruments are used to their full potential" in order to achieve the objectives set out in the 1998 biodiversity strategy. In relation to agriculture, the spread of non-indigenous forms of fauna and flora was presented as one of the main side effects of farming activities, but the document did not go any further in suggesting some type of intervention. Meanwhile, the report on the economic development saw in the spread of alien species a consequence of "policy, market and governance failures; demographic and climatic conditions; lack of knowledge and limited institutional capacity" and, at the same time, a cause of major biodiversity loss in the territories of the Union (European Commission 2001b). With particular regard to the action plan for natural resources, the communication recommended the continued implementation of import controls envisaged in the CITES regulation and the vigilance over the introduction into the Community of organisms harmful to plant or plant products, together with the enforcement of the relevant provisions contained in the *Birds* and *Habitats* directives. Actions to be taken in that particular field included the constant updating of – and exchange of information on – the list of alien species that are known to pose an ecological threat to native flora and fauna and habitats and ecosystems, and the promotion at the external level of international guidelines in the framework of the CBD (European Commission, 2001c). The action plan for fisheries was even more detailed in the light of the serious threats deriving from the introduction of non-indigenous species into the aquatic environment, such as the significant alteration in water quality and the overall food chain, with devastating impacts on fish, birds, seals and cetaceans (European Commission, 2001d). According to the European Commission, the phenomenon was even more alarming in the context of the increasing development of aquaculture and of its impacts on aquatic ecosystems through the introduction of "disease organisms, including viruses, bacteria, fungi and parasites" or "non-indigenous or possibly genetically modified organisms". The communication also stressed the importance of complying with the most relevant international standards, such as the FAO Code of Conduct for responsible fisheries, or the rules set in ICES Code of Practice on the Introduction and Transfer of Marine Organisms.

At the outset of the 21st century, invasive species were a priority on the European environmental policy agenda. Besides the political commitment contained in the abovementioned action plans, in fact, the Sixth Environmental Action Programme – adopted through the co-decision procedure by the European Parliament and the Council in 2002 – provided for a legally binding basis for the development of a comprehensive action in the field of biological invasions. In this strategic document, the question of alien species was emphasised from the preamble, as the 21st "whereas" acknowledges that "action is necessary to counteract pressures arising notably from pollution, the introduction of non-native species, potential risks from releasing genetically modified organisms and the way in which the land and sea are exploited". On the basis of the aims set in Article 2 – and particularly of the commitment to protect, conserve, restore and develop the functioning of natural systems, natural habitats, wild flora and fauna – Article 6 specified as a relevant priority the halting of biodiversity decline through, inter alia, prevention and/or mitigation of the impacts of invasive alien species and genotypes. Notwithstanding this binding and official "statement of intentions" by European institutions, the 2006 Biodiversity Action Plan had to acknowledge that "while support has been given to some localised eradication programmes via LIFE funding, the Community has still to develop a comprehensive strategy to address this issue", as many gaps remained with regard to prevention and control of invasive alien species (European Commission, 2006).

Those remarks marked a significant watershed in the path to an all-encompassing legal framework for biological invasions. At first, they served as a basis for the request made by the Environment Council to the European Commission to "assess gaps in the current legal, policy and economic framework for the prevention of introduction and for the control and eradication of invasive alien species". In addition, they contributed in preparing, in cooperation with Member States, "an EU strategy and an effective early warning system, taking into account bio-geographical regions" (Environment Council, 2006) in accordance with other international provisions (such as the relevant CBD Guiding Principles and the Bern Convention Strategy) and with "the efforts made by relevant Conventions and Organisations such as the IPPC and the EPPO" (Environment Council, 2006). The same auspice was then formulated by the European Parliament, as it urged "the development of a comprehensive Community response to the problem of invasive species, including an early warning system, and filling gaps in the legislative framework, including the development of an EU Strategy on invasive species" (European Parliament, 2007).

b The "pre-legislative phase": 2008–2013

For this reason, in 2008, the Commission – after having sought the views of relevant stakeholders and the general public – issued a new communication to the European Parliament and to the Council with specific regard to invasive alien species (European Commission, 2008a). In the annexed Impact Assessment, four main options were singled out as possible courses of action in order to counteract the negative impact of invasive alien species on European ecosystems, societies and economies. Option A suggested a "business-as-usual" approach, maintaining that no change was needed and that it was therefore possible to continue with the ongoing implementation of existing instruments; option B proposed the maximisation of existing legislation, combined with the development and implementation of voluntary codes of conduct, early warning and information systems, centralised inventories of invasive species, and establishment of a network for the exchange of best practices in terms of eradication and management; option B+ advocated for amending existing legislation in order to widen its scope to the coverage of all aspects related to biological invasions; finally, option C called for a comprehensive, dedicated EU legal instrument, coupled with maximal use of the basic tools described in option B, aimed at preventing intentional and unintentional introductions and at setting up early warning, eradication, containment and control systems (European Commission, 2008b). As the continuation of the ongoing fragmented and non-comprehensive system was not taken into consideration, and as options C and B+ were mutually exclusive, the real choice was between a "voluntary" maximisation of existing legislation by national authorities and the private sector (option B) and the development of a brand-new regulatory system (option C). However, the proliferation of voluntary measures both at the state and industry levels – though occasionally successful – was not considered to be a sufficient tool for the maximisation of the existing legislative framework, particularly in consideration of the expected increase in the introduction and diffusion of invasive alien species and the consequent pressures on biodiversity. For these reasons, option C – focused on the adoption of a dedicated, comprehensive framework aimed at decreasing the threat of new introductions on the one hand, and on coordinating measures for effective eradication and control on the other – had been chosen as "the most appropriate way to address the problem and meet the policy objectives". Furthermore, the conclusion of the report highlighted the need to strengthen Community and national efforts for the implementation of existing legislation as the best way to facilitate and prepare the elaboration of the new legislative framework, the cornerstones of which were identified in the internationally accepted three-tier approach – based on prevention, early warning and eradication, and mitigation and containment – elaborated in the framework of the CBD through the 2002 Guiding Principles on invasive alien species. The Commission suggested integrating this approach with some general principles on which an agreement existed with Member States: the precautionary and subsidiarity principles, public participation, cooperation and exchange of information, inter-state solidarity, and provision of administrative and legal sanctions to strengthen policy enforcement. Since the publication of this "strategy paper" the process of adoption of comprehensive legislation in the field of biological invasions became the object of a thorough discussion within European institutions, with endorsements of the Commission's work by the Council, the Committee of the Regions, and the European Economic and Social Council (EESC, 2009). In particular, in the conclusions of its June 2009 meeting the Council of the Ministers of Environment stressed the need for a strategic and comprehensive approach, taking into account the guiding principles enshrined in relevant CBD decisions – as well as the European Strategy on Invasive Alien Species under the Bern Convention – in order to fill existing gaps in EU legislation. Accordingly, any legislative action should have been based on the pillars of prevention, early detection, warning and rapid response, as well as on the monitoring, control and long-term containment and, as far as possible, restoration of biodiversity affected by non-native species.

Since 2008, in sum, the European institutions started the pre-legislative process of gathering data and information on the phenomenon, consulting relevant stakeholders and commissioning reports from experts and environmental organisations. In this sense, the Institute for European Environmental Policy produced a particularly relevant study containing recommendations on policy options to minimise the negative impacts of biological invasions in the territories of the European Union (Shine et al., 2009). This policy paper developed its reflections by beginning with an analysis of the environmental, social and economic impacts of over 100 invasive alien species covering all major ecosystems – ranging from terrestrial areas to inland and marine habitats – and all the most important *taxa*, including plants, animals, fungi and bacteria (Kettunen et al., 2009). As a large part of the negative consequences of biological invasions were spread in a cross-sectorial and cross-border way, and in consideration of the significant costs of policy inaction, the paper suggested the strengthening of the policy response at the EU-wide level (Shine et al., 2009). In fact, once again the gaps of the ongoing regulatory response at the EU level were assessed, emphasising, inter alia, that existing procedures, capacity and funding were focused on preventing entry and spread of selected categories (such as plant pests and animal diseases and pathogens), while the only explicit requirement to operate strict border controls "for invasiveness risks to biodiversity" on commodities entering into the European territories of Member States, or crossing increasingly non-existent internal borders, regarded aquaculture (in force of regulation 709/2007). Furthermore, the report required European institutions and Member States to put in place coordinate mechanisms of prevention, rapid response and management, with particular regard to newly detected species; on the other hand, a firmer reaction in terms of environmental liability was suggested in order to apply criminal legislation to damaging activities related to the intentional spread of invasive alien species. In 2010, the same think-tank produced a follow-up paper which stressed in its conclusions the need of abandoning the idea of approaching biological invasions on a "business-as-usual" basis or to limit the modifications to the maximisation of existing instruments, as such a choice – though pragmatic – would not be able to deliver the full range of necessary legislative changes (Shine et al., 2009). More specifically, the report analysed the type of legislative tool through which a more comprehensive policy on biological invasions had to be enacted without ipso facto ignoring the complementary need to implement existing instruments. The report identified regulations – the strictest legislative tool in the hands of European institutions specifying both the objectives of Member States' action and the means by which those aims have to be achieved – as an optimal solution in order to address several components of an all-encompassing strategy (such as risk assessment, regulation of voluntary movements, trade, monitoring of specific habitats and/or facilities, and compliance). At the same time, it also stressed the substantial downside of a difficult adaptation to diverse species or pathways and the lack of elasticity with regard to country-specific situations. As far as the instrument of the directive was concerned, it would have conversely provided for a greater amount of flexibility by means of setting minimum standards – leaving to Member States the regulatory action for particular bio-geographic situations – while at the same time establishing common goals, terminology and principles. However, the necessity of a state intervention to transfuse the directive into national legislation was deemed as a potential source of delays in a field in which rapid and uniform action is fundamental.

With such a detailed background of studies and a vast array of policy options under consideration, in May 2011 the Commission announced that it would have issued a legal act aimed at filling "policy gaps in combating invasive non-native species by developing a dedicated legislative instrument by 2012" (European Commission, 2011). The need for a new strategy – including a dedicated and comprehensive legislative instrument on invasive alien species – was reiterated by the Environment Council conclusions in December 2011 and by the European Parliament with a resolution approved on April 2012.

4.3 The Commission proposal and the inter-institutional debate

Following almost a year of delay with respect to the fixed timeline, on 9 September 2013 the Commission issued a proposal for a regulation of the European Parliament and of the Council on the prevention and management of the introduction and spread of invasive alien species. In the first instance, the proposal provided for a contextualisation of the phenomenon of invasive alien species within the territories of the European Union and gave the rationale for an intervention at the supranational level. Over 12,000 alien species were already present in the EU, out of which 10 to 15% were deemed to be invasive and posing a threat to the environmental, economic and social welfare of the Union. Therefore, the Commission found that action at the European level was necessary and justified under Article 192, first paragraph of the Treaty on the Functioning of the European Union (TFEU), aimed at implementing the overall objectives of the common environmental policy. Furthermore, given the cross-border nature of the issue, the Commission underlined the importance of two of the founding principles of the Union: on the one hand, the application of the principle of subsidiarity (Article 5, third paragraph, TEU) – according to which an action of the Union is necessary in so far as Member States cannot act in a manner that is sufficient to address and/or resolve the issue – ensured that actions already taken at the national level could effectively produce their effects without being undermined by the simultaneous lack of action by neighbouring countries thanks to the regulatory intervention of the Union. On the other, the solidarity principle justified an action at the Union level even if the damages deriving from biological invasions were unevenly distributed across Member States, since the involvement of European institutions and the efforts of all national authorities from all 28 countries could simultaneously protect the immediate interests of the most affected states and the long-term benefits to the Union as a whole. At the same time, however, a clause inserted in the preamble tempered this reference to the principle of solidarity by stressing the need to give priority to those "species of Union concern" contained in an ad hoc list prepared by the Commission "within one year of the entry into force of this legislation", and constantly revised and kept up-to-date. As for species not listed as invasive alien species of Union concern, the proposal allowed Member States to adopt "more stringent measures" such as the issue of permits for the release of these living organisms in the environment.

In its operative part, the proposed regulation was roughly divided into five chapters: the first part dealt with general provisions such as the subject matter, the scope and the basic obligations of the proposal and the tools for identifying the invasive alien species of Union concern; the second chapter set out the preventive measures aimed at avoiding any "unwanted" introduction or release into the European environment of invasive alien species; the third part presented ad hoc tools to ensure the early detection and rapid eradication of those exotic biomes which succeeded in spreading into a given ecosystem; the fourth chapter dealt with those management measures needed to tackle those situations in which prevention and eradication failed and the invasive species became established; the conclusive provisions were, in turn, dedicated to the obligations to implement, enforce, review and report pending upon Member States.

a Details of the Commission proposal for a regulation on invasive alien species

Article 1 clarified the subject matter of the regulation, addressed to prevent, minimise and mitigate the adverse effects deriving from both intentional and unintentional introductions of invasive species on biodiversity and ecosystem services. In this sense, the three-tier approach – (prevention, early warning and rapid response and management) contained in the Guiding Principles on Invasive Species adopted by the Conference of Parties to the CBD in 2002 – appeared since the beginning as the lodestar of the new European strategy on biological invasions. Article 2 detailed this rather general aim, limiting the scope of application of the regulation to "all invasive species in the Union as defined by Article 3(2)". Such an approach excluded all of those species which change their natural range without any implication of human agency; genetically modified organisms as defined in Article 2 of directive 2001/18/EC; and all those animal diseases, plant pests and micro-organisms manufactured or imported for use in plant protection or biocidal products whose introduction was already regulated in specific EU provisions. Article 3 provided interesting differentiations between "alien species", "invasive alien species", and "species of Union concern". In a "continuous climb" in terms of the seriousness of the threat, an "alien species" – defined as "any live specimens of species, subspecies or lower taxon of animals, plants, fungi or micro-organisms introduced outside its natural past or present distribution" – became "invasive" when its "introduction or spread has been found, through risk assessment, to threaten biodiversity and ecosystem services, and that may also have a negative impact on human health or the economy" and was raised to be a "Union concern" when its "negative impact has been deemed such as to require concerted action at the level of the Union pursuant to Article 4(2)". The following Article, in fact, entrusted the Commission with the task of adopting and updating a list of invasive alien species of Union concern on the basis of three main criteria: the "alien-ness" of the species "to the territory of the Union excluding the outermost regions"; the "invasiveness", intended as the capability of establishing a "viable population and spreading in the environment under current or foreseeable climate change conditions anywhere in the Union excluding the outermost regions"; and the degree of hazardousness, pursuant to a procedure of risk assessment, triggering the necessity of an action at the Union level for the prevention of establishment and spread. After having given to Member States the right to submit to the Commission requests for the inclusion of invasive species in this European list, Article 4 was closed by a provision establishing a cap on the number of species of Union concern, fixed to 50 species (including "any species which may be added as a result of the emergency measures"). The procedure of risk assessment was better described in Article 5, paragraph 1 of the proposal, containing those factual elements capable of making an alien species an invasive biome of Union concern: taxonomic identity, history, native range, potential range, reproduction and spread patterns, potential pathways of intentional or unintentional entry and/or diffusion, risk of establishment in consideration of current and foreseeable climate conditions, current distribution, negative impact on native species or habitats, adverse effects on human health and the economy, estimate of expected costs of inaction, and potential uses and benefits of the use of the concerned species. In conducing the assessment, the Commission had to be empowered with the authority to emanate "delegated acts" both in reference to the identification of the admissible scientific evidences referred to in Article 4(2) and to the provision of accurate descriptions of the standards of hazardousness set out in Article 5(1). Article 6 detailing particular procedures for the outermost regions of the Union closed the general provisions.

In relation to preventive measures, Article 7 introduced a general ban on a series of activities in relation to invasive alien biomes listed as "species of Union concern" according to Article 4(2). Those species could not be intentionally brought into – or transited through – the Union territory; permitted to reproduce; transported (except for transportation of species to facilities for eradication); placed on the market; used or exchanged; kept or grown (including in contained holding); or released into the environment. Furthermore, a less specific obligation to "prevent the unintentional introduction of invasive alien species of Union concern" was contained in the second paragraph of the same Article. However, Article 8 allowed for derogations from the bans referred to the introduction, reproduction, transport, use or exchange and keeping or growing of invasive alien species of Union concern in case of permits issued by Member States for research and ex-situ conservation in presence of certain conditions: the invasive alien species of Union concern had to be kept in and handled in closed facilities; the activity had to be carried out by personnel possessing specific scientific and technical qualifications; transport to and from the closed facility had to be authorised by the competent authority under conditions that exclude escape; in case of invasive alien species that are animals, they had to be marked where possible; the risk of escape or spread or removal had to be effectively managed; and a continuous surveillance and a contingency plan to cater for possible escape or spread, including an eradication plan, had to be drawn up. If Article 8 dealt with the issue of exceptions, Article 9 disciplined emergency situations, as it focused on the activities to be performed by Member States in cases of evidence concerning the presence in – or imminent danger of entry into – its territory of an invasive alien species which was not in the list of species of Union concern but was identified to be likely to meet the criteria set out in Article 4(2) on the basis of preliminary scientific evidence and of a risk assessment pursuant to Article 5(1). These emergency measures, which needed to be notified to the Commission and to the other Member States, had the role of "transitional hallway" until the Commission issued an implementing act on the basis of the bans set out in Article 7(1). Article 10, in turn, established restrictions to the intentional release of invasive alien species of "member state concern", whose hazardous effects – even if not fully ascertained – were significant in the national territory on the basis of scientific evidence and after due communication to the Commission and other Member States. Nonetheless, Member States were vested with the power to issue authorisation for certain intentional releases provided that there were no alternative indigenous species that could be used to obtain similar benefits, which had in turn to be "exceptionally high" in comparison to the risks of damage and complemented by opportune mitigation measures and adequate surveillance. The last measures dealing with prevention were contained in Article 11, which obliged Member States to carry out a comprehensive analysis of the pathways of unintentional introduction and spread of invasive alien species and identified those which required priority because of the volume of species or extent of the damage.

With regard to early detection and rapid eradication, Chapter III of the proposal bound Member States to set up rigid border controls and a dynamic surveillance system in order to detect the appearance in the environment of the Member States of any invasive alien species, and provided for a period of three months from the early detection to put in place a rapid eradication. As for border controls, Article 12 contained the duty for Member States to set up, within 12 months from the entry into force of the regulation, functioning systems of border controls in order to prevent the intentional introduction into the Union of species of Union concern, so as to allow the introduction of goods that were not on the list referred to in Article 4(1) or for whom a permit under Article 8 had been issued. In all other cases, the authorities designated for border controls would also have the responsibility to seize and confiscate the species. In case of failure of border controls, Article 12 called on Member States to establish and use surveillance systems in order to support early detection and rapid notification of the entry or presence of invasive alien species of Union concern. According to Article 15, within three months from detection and notification Member States should have applied eradication measures "aimed at the complete and permanent removal of the populations of the invasive alien species concerned", with due regard to human health and environmental protection, and ensuring that targeted animals were spared any avoidable pain or distress, and informing the Commission and other Member States on their content. In some cases – such as those situations in which the eradication was unavailable, hazardous for human health or technically unfeasible, or where the costs of an eradication campaign would be exceptionally high and disproportionate to the benefits of eradication – and in the presence of sound scientific evidence, Member States could submit to the Commission an application for a derogation from the obligation to apply eradication measures. Pending the decision of the Commission on the approval or rejection of such derogative measures, states were bound to a "standstill" clause according to which they were obliged to avoid further spread of the species.

In Chapter IV of the draft regulation, the Commission introduced uniform norms for management and measures aimed at minimising the impact of established invasive alien species on biodiversity, ecosystem services, human health and the economy through physical, chemical or biological control, and at restoring at the highest possible level the damaged ecosystems. As far as management measures were concerned, Article 17 established for Member States an obligation to put in place effective control for those invasive alien species of Union concern found to be widely spread on their territories "so that their impact on biodiversity and ecosystem services, human health and the economy are minimised". Based on a careful analysis of costs and benefits, the measures should have consisted of physical, chemical or biological actions aimed at the effective "eradication, population control or containment" of non-native species, with due regard for human health and the environment on the one hand, and for the avoidance of distress or suffering to targeted animals on the other. Complementarily to management, Member States were called on to take, under Article 18, proportionate restoration measures to assist "the recovery of an ecosystem that has been degraded, damaged, or destroyed" by an invasive alien species in a way to increase the ability of the ecosystem to resist, absorb, accommodate to and recover from the effects of disturbance and to ensure the prevention of new invasions.

Finally, Chapter V set out general rules in relation to reporting and enforcement measures. As far as reporting was concerned, Article 19 established that after three years from the date of entry into force of the regulation, and after that date every four years, Member States should transmit to the Commission updated information on the surveillance system and border controls; on the distribution of invasive species of Union and Member State concern present in their territories; on the action plan for prevention, eradication and management; and, on the format of permits referred to in Article 8. The same reporting obligations on the same array of topics were placed upon the Commission, which should have submitted a report to the European Parliament and to the Council within five years from the adoption of the regulation. Furthermore, according to Article 20, the Commission should have gradually established an information support mechanism aimed at facilitating the implementation by Member States. Article 21 contained a reference to the involvement of the public in all phases of control, eradication and management, while Article 22 made reference to the creation of an ad hoc Committee whose main task would have been to assist the Commission in effectively enforcing the regulation. Article 23 further detailed the modalities through which Member States delegated to the Commission the power to conduce a risk assessment for the identification of the species to include in the list of Union concern, specifying that this delegation could have been revoked at any time following a deliberation by the European Parliament or the Council; in addition, the fifth paragraph specified that those institutions had the power to object to the entry into force of delegated acts adopted pursuant to Article 5(2). Conclusively, the draft regulation provided some norms dealing with administrative and legal enforcement. Article 24 entailed the obligation for Member States to lay down rules on "effective, proportionate and dissuasive" administrative measures and sanctions applicable to any breach of the rules contained in the regulation. Article 25 then stated that "competent authorities shall have the power to impose administrative measures and sanctions on any natural or legal person who does not comply with this regulation", setting minimum standards (i.e. cease of the misconduct and desistence from repetition; confiscation of the non-compliant invasive alien species of Union concern at issue; a temporary ban on an activity; a permanent withdrawal of the authorisation of an activity; administrative pecuniary sanctions; an order requiring the natural or legal person to take remedial measures) and relevant circumstances (including the gravity and duration of the breach; the degree of involvement of the person responsible for the invasion; the profit deriving from the breach; the environmental, social and economic damage caused by the breach; the level of cooperation with the competent authority; and previous breaches by the person responsible). Another final disposition, contained in Article 26, dealt with transitional measures for non-commercial owners of companion animals, who were authorised to keep the invasive species until the end of their natural life under the condition that the specimens were kept before their inclusion in the list of species of Union concern and that all measures were put in place to ensure that reproduction or escape was not possible. In relation to commercial stocks, Article 27 allowed owners of commercial stocks of specimens of invasive species of Union concern acquired before their inclusion in the list to keep and transport those biomes – in order to sell or hand them over – for a transitional period of two years to the research or ex-situ conservation institutions referred to in Article 8.

b The inter-institutional debate

Having its legal basis in Article 192 of the Treaty on the Functioning of the European Union (TFEU), the proposed regulation on the prevention and management of the introduction and spread of invasive alien species was adopted through the ordinary legislative procedure (Articles 289 and 294 TFEU). The European Parliament and the Council thus received the text of the draft regulation on the same day it had been issued by the Commission, on 9 September 2013. The same act was also sent to the Committee of the Regions and to the European Economic and Social Committee to receive their mandatory consultative opinion on the matter. In addition, the proposal was sent to national parliaments for the control of the application and respect of the principles of subsidiarity and proportionality: in a general picture of acceptance, the only "dissenting opinion" was delivered by the Austrian Bundesrat, which ruled for an incompatibility of the proposed regulation with the principle of subsidiarity.[1] Facing this almost unanimous agreement on the proposal, the draft regulation was discussed in the occasion of a meeting of the Environment Council in December 2013. Besides deciding the lines of policy discussion in its preparatory bodies, the Council, under request of the Lithuanian presidency, focused on two main aspects, and namely on the decision by the Commission to put a cap on the list of invasive alien species of Union concern and on the way to prioritise them on the one hand, and on the possibility to cooperatively act at the level of biogeographic regions on the other. In January 2014, the European Economic and Social Committee (EESC) delivered an opinion on the draft regulation on the basis of the work of the Section for Agriculture, Rural Development and the Environment. Welcoming the Commission communication and supporting the desire to adopt a comprehensive legal instrument, the EESC expressed its doubts on limiting the list of species of Union concern to 50 elements while emphasising the need of a greater involvement of relevant stakeholders and civil society, particularly in the preventive phase. Conversely, the other consulted organ, the Committee of the Regions, decided not to deliver an opinion on the matter.

In February 2014, the Committee on Environment, Public Health and Food Safety of the European Parliament (ENVI) issued a report on the proposed regulation, which essentially confirmed the three-tier approach contained in the version drafted by the Commission with its accent on prevention, prioritisation and coordination. Those three principles, in fact, were deemed particularly effective in guaranteeing the reduction of invasive alien species introduction in the Union, the concentration of technical and financial resources on the worst and most dangerous "invaders", and the harmonisation of the response at the EU level. At the same time, the report emphasised some areas in which amendments seemed nonetheless of primary importance: at first, the proposed cap to a 3% of the estimated 1500 invasive alien species as "species of Union concern" – contained in the draft regulation – was considered to be a "serious shortcoming of the proposal", as a consequence of its arbitrary nature. Further, the impact assessment which accompanied the proposal from the Commission affirmed that "it is impossible to know in advance how many and what invasions will need to be tackled and how many species will be included in the list of invasive alien species of Union concern". As an alternative, the report by the ENVI suggested to adopt a flexible, responsive and easily adaptable mechanism. Secondly, the report sustained the necessity to attach the list of invasive alien species of Union concern to the basic act as an annex – and not to adopt it as a self-standing implementing act – because of the importance of such a list in the overall aim of the new legal approach to biological invasions. Thirdly, the report raised the question of the existence of certain species that are native in some parts of Europe and invasive in other parts of the Union. By abolishing the distinction between species that are exotic tout court and species which are non-native only in some regions or territories of the Union, in fact, cooperation between states would have increased and the prevention and management of the impacts of biological invasions would have significantly gained effectiveness. Furthermore, the report of the ENVI proposed that Member States that are already taking some action to tackle biological invasions should have been allowed to maintain – or, in case of voluntary actions by other Member States, to put in place – more stringent measures in order to ensure a more effective implementation and cater for some flexibility in relation to potential resource constraints at the Union level. The observations from the Rapporteur continued with a consideration of the need to strengthen public participation systems in order to allow relevant stakeholders and NGOs to express their opinions and concerns, with the final aim of increasing the accountability of the decision-making process. Finally, the report by the Committee for the Environment, Public Health and Food Safety of the European Parliament suggested inserting in the draft of the regulation a provision for the establishment of an ad hoc scientific body whose task would have been to support the Commission and Member States in the decision-making process. Those amendments were discussed in March 2014 with the Hellenic Presidency of the Council in the framework of the Permanent Representatives Committee (COREPER) in order to reach an agreement on a compromise text to be approved in first reading by the Parliament in April. This compromise opened a "fast track" towards the adoption of the regulation, as the main instances of the two institutions had been settled and agreed upon since the beginning: the cap to the number of species of Union concern was abolished in favour of an open list to be kept regularly updated and reviewed at least every six years. Furthermore, the Council obtained the insertion of a reference to cross-border cooperation, with an emphasis on the role of bio-geographical regions, while the Parliament obtained the inclusion of its suggestions for the establishment of a dedicated scientific forum of experts, as well as the inclusion of a list of species of Member State concern and a reference to cooperation for those species native to some regions of the Union but invasive in others.

4.4 The amendments to the proposal and the adoption of the regulation

On 16 April 2014, the European Parliament approved in its plenary session a legislative resolution on the proposal for a regulation on the prevention and management of the introduction and spread of invasive alien species. In its 10th recital, the Preamble confirmed the usefulness of a list of invasive species of Union concern, but abolished the reference to the initial capping to the top 3% of invasive alien species to develop and update the list with a "gradual and phased-in approach", with a focus on those biomes whose inclusion would have given serious and cost-effective advantages in terms of prevention, minimisation and mitigation of adverse impacts. The draft legislation approved by the Parliament also added a recital in which the Commission is invited to "take into consideration the socio-economic aspects, the implementation cost for member states and the cost of non-action" when proposing the list and consequential measures, "in order to avoid disproportionate or excessive costs for any member state and safeguard the added value of Union action through this regulation". In particular, the Commission should pay special attention to "species that are widely used and provide significant social and economic benefits in a member state, without compromising the objectives of this regulation". Furthermore, in the Preamble reference is made to the importance of regional cooperation between Member States concerned with "locally invasive" species: in cases in which prevention or management could be better achieved at the Union level, it could be possible that such organisms are listed as "species of Union concern". In relation to the derogatory regime for research and ex-situ conservation, the legislative proposal made by the Parliament added the exceptional power for the Commission to authorise – for compelling causes of public interest – the extension of derogations to other activities, and particularly to the commercial sector. As far as eradication and management measures were concerned, important innovations brought on in the wake of the work of the Rapporteur and on the basis of the indications of the Council were the consideration for animal welfare, for the bio-geographic and climatic conditions of Member States, and for the relevance of cross-border cooperation between neighbouring countries. The amended version of the draft regulation also referred to the importance of the participation of the scientific community through a dedicated forum in order to "provide an adequate knowledge base to address the problems raised by invasive alien species". As for enforcement and compliance with the regulation, Member States were invited to take into account when imposing sanctions not only the nature and gravity of the infringement, but also the principles of the "polluter pays" and of recovery of the costs; moreover, Member States were authorised under the regulation to "impose obligations on holders or users of alien species as well as owners and tenants of lands concerned". Indeed, the last recital of the Preamble reiterated the right for Member States to "maintain or adopt rules on invasive alien species of Union concern that are more stringent than those laid down in this regulation", or to apply the measures set out in the regulation for species of Union concern to organisms of Member State concern, provided that those actions are compatible with the TFEU and duly notified to the Commission in accordance with Union law.

With reference to the operative part of the regulation, Article 1 clarified the spatial ambit of application of the regulation, which spread its effects "within the Union". Article 3, in turn, added to the proposal of the Commission the definition of "invasive alien species of member state concern", intended as "invasive alien species other than invasive alien species of Union concern, for which a Member State considers on the basis of scientific evidence that the adverse impact from their release and spread, even where not fully ascertained, is of significance for its territory, or part of it, and requires action at the level of that Member State". At the same time, the new Article 3 modified the definitions of "eradication", "management" and "population control", so as to take into account considerations for animal welfare. If these revisions seem to be "cosmetic" in nature, Article 4 regarding the definition and identification of species to be included in the list of "invasive alien species of Union concern" underwent a major re-structuring: in particular, the appositely added second paragraph obliged the Commission to make a "comprehensive review of the list at the latest every six years", and to update it with the addition or removal of species on the basis of the criteria laid down in paragraph 3 (Article 4.2 of the Commission's proposal). This paragraph added to the evaluation of the spread of the species on the territory of the Union a precise reference to the possibility that these species "have significant adverse effects on biodiversity or the related ecosystem services, and may also have an adverse impact on human health or the economy", combined with a consideration on the potential effects of the inclusion of the species at issue in the list in the light of the effective prevention, minimisation and mitigation of their adverse effects. In spite of the capping to 50 species, paragraph 5 of the re-written Article 4 stated that "the list referred to . . . shall make reference, where relevant, to the goods with which the species are generally associated and their Combined Nomenclature codes", thus recognising the need to link official controls to the increasing flow of international trade. Furthermore, paragraph 6 added a burden to the Commission in adopting and updating the list of invasive species of Union concern, as it has to pay "due consideration to the implementation cost for the member states, the cost of non-action, the cost-effectiveness and socio-economic aspects". Under this paragraph, priority should thus be assigned to those species that "are not yet present in the Union or are at an early stage of invasion and are most likely to have significant adverse impacts" or "are already established in the Union and have the most significant adverse impacts". Article 4 was then concluded with a reference to the principle of subsidiarity, as according to paragraph 7 the Commission should justify the inclusion of an alien species in the list of species of Union concern by explaining how the objectives of the regulation are better achieved by measures at the Union level. Under Article 5, a relevant improvement regarded the role of Member States and of the Commission in carrying out the risk assessment for inclusion of new organisms in the open list of species of Union concern. In Article 6, then, the amended text of the regulation details in a more thorough way the discipline for the outermost regions.

As for preventive measures, Article 7 remained unvaried. Article 8, in turn, introduced the possibility to include in the permit system those species whose use or products are useful to "advance human health". Furthermore, Member States saw their right to withdraw the permit recognised – temporarily or permanently, and on the basis of scientific evidences or in full respect of the precautionary principle – in case of unforeseen events producing hazardous effects on biodiversity or ecosystem services. On the other hand, Member States who issue a permit should make available as soon as appropriate – even online – some important details with regard to the exception: the scientific and common name of the species, the number or volume of specimens, and the purpose and – where applicable – the Combined Nomenclature code of the goods on which they are present.[2] Article 9 represented an addition with respect to the initial proposal, and contained provisions regarding the authorisations regime: in fact, in exceptional cases – and for reasons of "compelling public interest" – Member States were allowed, following an authorisation by the Commission and observing certain pre-conditions listed in paragraph 4 of the same Article, to issue permits to carry out activities other than research or ex-situ conservation. Articles 11 and 12 of the legislative proposal forwarded by the European Parliament deeply innovated the initial draft written by the Commission insofar as they introduced the questions of invasive alien species of regional concern on the one hand, and of invasive alien species of Member State concern on the other. Article 11 authorises states to identify, from their national lists, species – whether native or non-native to the Union – requiring enhanced regional cooperation through a "facilitating" intervention by the Commission. As for the list of invasive species of Member

State concern, national authorities were authorised to put in place measures of prevention, eradication and management as far as these acts are compatible with the TFEU and are notified to the Commission.

With reference to early detection and eradication measures, the first relevant amendment regarded the extension of the surveillance system set out in Article 14 to marine waters as defined in Article 3(1) of Directive 2008/56/EC. The details of border controls were set out in Article 15: according to paragraph 1, Member States should have in place "fully functioning structures to perform the official controls necessary to prevent the intentional introduction into the Union of invasive species of Union concern" in order to apply a strict control regime to the categories of goods falling within the Combined Nomenclature codes, pursuant to Article 4(5). In particular, paragraph 2 entrusted to competent authorities the role of performing risk-based controls – such as documentary, identity and (if necessary) physical checks – on imported goods in order to verify that they were not listed as species of Union concern or that they were covered by a valid permit as referred to in Article 8. Similar controls were also extended, under paragraph 4 of Article 15, to those goods "under customs procedures of release for free circulation, transit, customs warehousing, inward processing, processing under customs control and temporary admission". In case of non-compliance with the regulation, customs authorities could suspend the placing under a customs procedure or detain the goods, accordingly to national legislation in force, with the costs of verification and/or non-compliance at the expense of the natural or legal persons within the Union who brought the goods into the Union. As for the derogatory regime to the obligation to apply eradication measures – as provided for in Article 17 – Article 18 prescribed that the only possible justification relied on the submission by the concerned Member States of robust scientific evidences supporting the inaction.

Article 19 opened the chapter dedicated to the management of already widely spread species. Partially amending paragraph 2 with respect to the initial proposal by the Commission, the European Parliament allowed – under strict justification and provided that any further spread is avoided – the commercial use of already established invasive alien species as part of the programme of control. Furthermore, Article 20 limited the incidence of restoration measures to those cases in which a cost-benefit analysis demonstrated that the costs of the measures were not disproportionate to the benefits of restoration.

The draft legislation approved in first reading by the Parliament then added an entire chapter focused on horizontal provisions to the proposed regulation issued by the Commission. In particular, Article 21 faced the issue of cost recovery by referring to the "polluter pays" principle: in this sense, Member States should aim at "recovering the costs of the measures needed to prevent, minimise or mitigate the adverse impact of the invasive alien species, including environmental and resources costs as well as the restoration cost". Article 22 contained dispositions on the cooperation and coordination between Member States – in particular within the same marine or biogeographical regions, or in case of common river basins or borders – both in relation to species of Union and Member State concern. Furthermore, as of Article 23, Member States "may maintain or lay down more stringent national measures with the aim of preventing the introduction, establishment and spread of invasive alien species", provided such measures are compatible with the TFEU and are notified to the Commission.

Finally, the European Parliament introduced important modifications with regard to the final dispositions of the regulation. According to Article 24, by June 2019 Member States should submit to the Commission an update report regarding, inter alia, the presence and distribution of invasive alien species of Union or regional concern on their territories; information about the species considered of Member State concern; the action plans and actual measures adopted for early detection and eradication; and the number and purpose of the permits granted in compliance with Article 8. In its third paragraph, Article 24 imposed on the Commission a duty to assess, through a report submitted to the European Parliament and to the Council, the application of the regulation by 1 June 2021 with reference to the list of species of Union concern, the action plans for eradication, the surveillance system, customs controls and management obligations. The European Parliament provided the Commission with two auxiliary bodies for the fulfilment of its tasks: a Committee established under regulation 182/2011 (Article 27, already present in the initial draft by the Commission in the then Article 22); and as per Article 28, a Scientific Forum formed by experts appointed by Member States to provide advice on any question related to the application of the regulation and, in particular, with regard to Articles 5, 10 and 18. Furthermore, the European Parliament fully amended the proposal of the Commission with reference to enforcement and sanctions, as the new Article 30 included a list of "penalties" applicable to infringement of the provisions in the regulation. Though Member States are entrusted with the task of laying down such penalties, the assembly stressed the need that they shall be "effective, proportionate and dissuasive" and suggested the inclusion, inter alia, of fines, seizure of non-compliant invasive alien species of Union concern and immediate suspension or withdrawal of a permit granted in accordance with Article 8. However, the re-drafted version has eliminated any reference to the elements to be taken into account in the determination of the penalties or to the actual addressee of sanctions, as the distinction between natural and legal persons disappeared.

On July 2014, the Commission approved the amendments introduced by the European Parliament to the draft regulation so that the final word on the adoption of the instrument rested with the Council. On 29 September 2009, the Italian presidency communicated the adoption – without discussion – of the regulation on the prevention and management of the introduction and spread of invasive alien species, which was been published in the *Official Journal of the European Union* on 4 November 2014 and entered into force on 1 January 2015.

4.5 The effectiveness of regulation 1143/2014 under a SWOT analysis perspective

Regulation 1143/2014 stands as the "first piece of legislation on biodiversity in more than 20 years" (Genovesi et al., 2015), and shares many of its main provisions with the guidelines provided by the Conference of Parties to the Convention on Biological Diversity. In particular, the new legislative intervention by Brussels authorities can give an irreplaceable contribution to the transition of the three-tier approach based on prevention, eradication and containment from the nuanced territories of soft law to far more solid legal basis, at least within the boundaries of the European Union. To put this in perspective, the development of this new regulatory regime can have consequences on the formation of a praxis and on the consolidation of an *opinio iuris* on the need to fight the adverse effects of biological invasions at the supranational level.

However, a prima facie analysis of the freshly adopted legislation offers a valuable opportunity to highlight its key strengths, while at the same time opening some room for critical remarks.

From the first point of view, the general merits of the regulation are the comprehensiveness of the scope and the recognition of the role of human agency in the process of introduction of alien species in the Union territory.

There are some elements deserving particular attention if analysed under the lenses of the three-tier approach. If the decision to set aside the initial cap to 50 species in the list of "invasive species of Union concern" has led to a mutually beneficial rapprochement between policy-makers and the scientific community which vocally opposed the close-list approach, it has primarily permitted Member States to significantly widen the possibility to carry out adequate preventive measures (including more accurate border control and the enactment of a ban on import, trade, breeding, transport, use and release into the environment). Furthermore – and with an unprecedented normative force at the supranational level – state authorities not only have the duty to react to already occurring invasions, but also the duty to identify and assess the main pathways of introduction for the species listed as of "Union concern" and to put in place action plans aimed at preventing any voluntary displacement or unwanted dispersal of those organisms (Genovesi et al., 2015). It is also interesting to note how the establishment of a surveillance system may overcome the significant absence of early warning measures in many Member States aimed at detecting and responding to non-widespread invasions (Davies, 2016).

Secondly, during the eradication phase, the just recognition of the right to pursue the goal with the most effective methods has been tempered by the complementary provision aimed at avoiding to the greatest possible extent animal pain or suffering, thus giving formal recognition and practical application to Article 13 of the Treaty on the Functioning of the European Union (TFEU). More generally, the text of the regulation calls for better and deeper coordination and cooperation between Member States, particularly in those cases regarding species of "regional" concern.

On the negative side, a first significant shortcoming of the regulation has already emerged: in July 2016, in fact, the Commission has approved an implementing regulation adopting the first list of 37 species of "Union concern" – well below the initial 50-species cap – on the basis of rather restrictive risk-assessment criteria.[3] Already foreshadowed by some experts (inter alia Beninde et al., 2015), the final list is fully in line with the results of an enquiry conducted by a group of experts and funded by the European Commission on the basis of risk-assessment protocols already used by other organisations (such as the European and Mediterranean Plant Protection Organization and the Great Britain Non-Native Species Risk Assessment). These experts concluded that there were 25 plant species, 12 vertebrate species and 13 invertebrate species likely complying with the requirements of the regulation (Roy et al., 2014). In December 2015 the European Parliament also expressed its doubts, considering how the inclusion of the species in the list was not based on scientific but "rather on political criteria", thus failing to "address the problem of invasive alien species in a comprehensive manner, so as to protect native biodiversity and ecosystem services, as well as to minimise and mitigate the human health or economic impacts that these species could have".[4] Notwithstanding the criticism by the assembly, the Commission decided to adopt the list as "based on a systematic and robust scientific analysis [and not] on the basis of political criteria".[5]

Other critical remarks came from several environmental NGOs, which considered that the inclusion of such a small number of species in the list was a way for the Commission to fall short of the political commitment and legal responsibility necessary to address a global environmental problem of significant magnitude. According to those relevant stakeholders, the proposed list failed to tackle some of the most problematic, widely spread and harmful species – even so far as to include species with high impact on biodiversity that are absent or in the early stages of invasion. Conversely, in October 2016, the Asociación de la pesca y acuicultura del entorno de Doñana y del Bajo Guadalquívir filed a claim before the General Court against the European Commission, submitting that as regards the species *Procambarus clarkii* the requirements laid down in Article 4 of Regulation 1143/2014 were not met and a risk assessment under the terms set out in Article 5(1) was not carried out. Consequently, the claimant asked for the annulment of the implementing regulation or, as an alternative, to annul the inclusion of the species.

As a consequence of the significant controversy raised by the enacted list, the Commission started a second round of risk-assessment evaluations and, on 12 July 2017, adopted implementing regulation 2017/1263 updating the list of invasive species of Union concern.[6]

Another critical remark referred to the list regarded the adequateness of the year interval in the synchronisation of the list and in the production of monitoring reports with reference to the effectiveness of the preventative measures, as such a timeframe risks losing touch with accumulating scientific knowledge on the one hand, and with exponential expansion of invasive alien species – such as in the case of *Xylella fastidiosa* – on the other (Lockwood et al., 2007; Casado, 2013; Hochkirch et al., 2013).

Transiting from the technical to the political, the regulation has caused much controversy since its adoption. On the one hand, some Member States have stressed the "invasiveness" of the regulation itself on their national socio-economic structure with reference to the possible inclusion of economically profitable non-native species on the "black list" of invasive species of Union concern; on the other, environmental organisations are alarmed by the possible shortcomings in terms of effective and uniform implementation of the regulation as a consequence of the compromised version which allows for many derogations and exemptions from the strict duty to prevent, eradicate and manage, which had been initially infused to the Commission proposal. Indeed, if the regulation has been adopted by the Council without discussion, the vote has been far from unanimous. As an example, Romania decided to abstain from the adoption of the regulation considering the final text not "fully in line with the principles of subsidiarity and proportionality", particularly with respect to the question of invasive species of regional concern. Even supporting the facilitating role of the Commission in coordinating regional cooperation against biological invasions, Romania considered the adoption of implementing acts by the Commission for species of regional concern as in conflict with the principle of subsidiarity. In turn, representatives from other Member States emphasised the need to bear in mind social and economic factors in the implementation of the regulation. In this sense, Hungary underlined in a relevant statement how special attention should be given to those species that are "widely used and provide significant socio-economic benefits for a member state". Making the case of the false acacia (*Robinia pseudoacacia*), the Hungarian delegation expressed the opinion that the species should not be included in the Union list, but rather managed at the national level. The same position was taken in a joint declaration by Denmark and Finland. Though both states welcomed the introduction of a regulation in the field of biological invasions, they nevertheless emphasised how socio-economic impacts of such a phenomenon – together with the implementation costs of the regulation – are an "integral part of the analysis and procedure" regarding the inclusion of certain specimens in the list of species of Union concern under Article 4. For this reason, and almost repeating the wording of the Hungarian representative, Denmark and Finland asked that the American mink would not be included in the list of species of Union concern. These political and economic struggles may also be crucial to understand and explain the last weak link of the regulation: if confronted with other biosecurity legislation existing outside Europe, the regulation suffers from poor allocation of resources as it has no proper and dedicated funding (Bretsché, 2015). At the same time, this "financial crunch" can be partially justified if read in conjunction with the current economic situation: it would have been almost impossible to explain to citizens-electors how short-term prosperity had to be traded for long-term goals such as environmental conservation.

In the absence of substantial resources – and in order to maximise results – the European Union and its Member States should seize two parallel opportunities: on the one hand, they should start a campaign among citizens with the final aim of raising awareness on such a crucial topic with a profound impact on everyday life as biological invasion. On the other, they should put in place meaningful and fruitful cooperation with other international organisations or third countries (such as the United States, Canada, Australia and New Zealand) which have already attributed fundamental importance to the goal of stemming the tide of invasive alien species. From this point of view, privileged interlocutors should be the Secretariat of the Convention on Biological Diversity and the Council of Europe, under whose auspices was concluded in 1997 the Bern Convention on the conservation of European wildlife and natural habitats (Trouwbortst, 2015).

In trying to give a conclusive opinion on the regulation adopted by the European Parliament and the Council in September 2014, it would be fair to avoid ideological and extremist interpretations. Even if its limits are evident, it is nevertheless true that the new regulation not only covers a lot of ground in a vast array of previously unaddressed areas – such as the question of species native to a particular region of the Union but invasive in others; the involvement of scientists and stakeholders in the implementing process; and the consideration for animal welfare in all stages of prevention,

Table 4.1 SWOT matrix for EU regulation 1143/2014

Strengths	*Weaknesses*
– Comprehensiveness of the agreement – Consideration for animal welfare – Recognition of the role of human agency in the introduction of invasive alien species (Article 3 *sub* 7) – Stress placed on prevention rather than eradication – Derogatory procedure centralised in the hands of a *super partes* institution (Commission) – Involvement of stakeholders, public opinion and scientific community	– Restrictive criteria for the inclusion of species in the list of "Union concern" – Significant space for derogations – Compromise between ecological and economic instances – Scarce economic resources – Lack of elements for ascertaining the real addressee of penalties and sanctions
Opportunities	*Threats*
– Room for even more stringent measures at the national level – Possibility for the European Union to work as a role model for other international organisations – Interplay with other relevant agreements (CBD, Bern Convention)	– Resistances from Member States – Pressures from affected interest groups – General socio-economic situation (short-term prosperity versus long-term preservation)

Source: Author's elaboration

eradication and management – but it also works as a legislative basis for even more stringent provisions at the national level. Furthermore, in relation to the derogations for socio-economic reasons which emerged during the negotiation phase and were introduced in the amended version of the proposal by the European Parliament, it is important not to indulge in an extremist interpretation. Indeed, the criteria for obtaining exemptions to the Union-wide general bans are quite stringent and include requirements for contingency and eradication plans in case of escapes or spread. More than simply placing an "environmental hat" on the regulation, it would be important to maintain a high level of vigilance on its implementation and, in particular, on the primary role of ecological and biodiversity considerations over socio-economic factors on the process of risk assessment centralised in the hands of the Commission at first, and on the implementation and enforcement by Member States later (Tollington et al., 2015). In the words of the Institute for European Environmental Policy (IEEP), "the final regulation text can still be considered as a reasonable compromise, providing a long-awaited legislative framework for addressing invasive alien species at the European Union level".

Notes

1 See Reasoned opinion of the European Affairs Committee of the Federal Council of 8 October 2013 pursuant to Article 23g(1) of the Austrian Constitution in conjunction with Article 6 of the Protocol n.2 on the application of the principles of subsidiarity and proportionality on the proposal for a regulation of the European Parliament and the Council on the prevention and management of the introduction and spread of invasive alien species. The Committee concluded that "the project under consideration is incompatible with the principle of subsidiarity" with particular reference to Article 10 of the proposal, introducing rules applicable to invasive alien species of member state concern. This norm is deemed to be excessive in relation to the principle of subsidiarity, as "in a case of national or regional spread, the eradication or containment of the alien invasive species can be better attained by the member states concerned".

2 Pursuant to the provisions contained in Article 8(6), the European Commission issued on 4 February 2016 an implementing regulation (Commission implementing regulation 2016/145) adopting the format of the document serving as evidence for the permit issued by the competent authorities of Member States allowing establishments to carry out certain activities concerning invasive alien species of Union concern pursuant to Regulation 1143/2014 of the European Parliament and of the Council.

3 European Commission (2016), Commission Implementing Regulation 2016/1141 of 13 July 2016 adopting a list of invasive alien species of Union concern pursuant to Regulation (EU) No 1143/2014 of the European Parliament and of the Council. In the list issued by the Commission, 37 species were identified as meeting all criteria set out in Article 4(3) of regulation 1143/2014: *Baccharis halimifolia* L, *Cabomba caroliniana* Gray, *Callosciurus erythraeus* Pallas, *Corvus splendens* Viellot, *Eichhornia crassipes* (Martius) Solms, *Eriocheir sinensis* H. Milne Edwards, *Heracleum persicum* Fischer, *Heracleum sosnowskyi* Mandenova, *Herpestes javanicus* É. Geoffroy Saint-Hilaire, *Hydrocotyle ranunculoides* L. f., *Lagarosiphon major* (Ridley) Moss, *Lithobates (Rana) catesbeianus* Shaw, *Ludwigia grandiflora* (Michx.) Greuter & Burdet, *Ludwigia peploides* (Kunth) P.H. Raven, *Lysichiton americanus* Hultén and St. John, *Muntiacus reevesi* Ogilby, *Myocastor coypus* Molina,

Myriophyllum aquaticum (Vell.) Verdc., *Nasua nasua* Linnaeus, *Orconectes limosus* Rafinesque, *Orconectes virilis* Hagen, *Oxyura jamaicensis* Gmelin, *Pacifastacus leniusculus* Dana, *Parthenium hysterophorus* L., *Perccottus glenii* Dybowski, *Persicaria perfoliata* (L.) H. Gross (*Polygonum perfoliatum* L.), *Procambarus clarkii* Girard, *Procambarus fallax* (Hagen) f. *virginalis*, *Procyon lotor* Linnaeus, *Pseudorasbora parva* Temminck & Schlegel, *Pueraria montana* (Lour.) Merr. *var. lobata* (Willd.) (*Pueraria lobata* (Willd.) Ohwi), *Sciurus carolinensis* Gmelin, *Sciurus niger* Linnaeus, *Tamias sibiricus* Laxmann, *Threskiornis aethiopicus* Latham, *Trachemys scripta* Schoepff, *Vespa velutina nigrithorax* de Buysson.

4 European Parliament (2015), Resolution on the draft Commission Implementing Regulation adopting a list of invasive alien species of Union concern pursuant to Regulation (EU) No 1143/2014 of the European Parliament and of the Council, 16 December 2015.

5 European Commission (2016), Follow up to the European Parliament resolution on the draft Commission Implementing Regulation adopting a list of invasive alien species of Union concern pursuant to Regulation (EU) No 1143/2014 of the European Parliament and of the Council, adopted by the Commission on 2 February 2016.

6 The Commission has concluded, on the basis of the available evidence and the risk assessments carried out pursuant to Article 5(1) of Regulation (EU) No 1143/2014, that all criteria set out in Article 4(3) of that Regulation are also met for the following invasive alien species: *Alopochen aegyptiacus* Linnaeus, 1766; *Alternanthera philoxeroides* (Mart.) Griseb.; *Asclepias syriaca* L.; *Elodea nuttallii* (Planch.) St. John; *Gunnera tinctoria* (Molina) Mirbel; *Heracleum mantegazzianum* Sommier & Levier; *Impatiens glandulifera* Royle; *Microstegium vimineum*(Trin.) A. Camus; *Myriophyllum heterophyllum* Michaux; *Nyctereutes procyonoides* Gray, 1834; *Ondatra zibethicus* Linnaeus, 1766; *Pennisetum setaceum* (Forssk.) Chiov.

Bibliography

Beninde, J., Fischer, M.L., Hochkhirch, A. and Zink, A. (2015), Ambitious advances in the legislation of the European Union on invasive alien species in *Conserv Lett* 8(3): 199–205.

Bretsché, T. (2015), Le règlement (UE) n° 1143/2014 relatif à la prévention et à la gestion de l'introduction et de la propagation des espèces exotiques envahissantes du 22 octobre 2014: un nouvel instrument communautaire au service de la protection de la biodiversité in *Revenue Juridique De L'Environnement* 4: 631–648.

Casado, S. (2013), The importance of being listed: birds, lists and the history of conservation in *Ardeola* 60: 397–401.

Davies, P.G.G. (2016), Alien invasive species: Is the EU's strategy fit for purpose? in Bowman, N., Davies, P. and Goodwin, E. (eds.), *Research handbook on biodiversity and law*, Edward Elgar, Cheltenham, 184–218.

Environment Council. (2006), *Council conclusions on halting the loss of biodiversity* COM(2006)216, 18 December.

European Commission. (1998), *Communication from the Commission to the European Parliament and the Council on a EC strategy on biological diversity*, COM(1998)42, 4 February 1998, Brussels, Belgium.

European Commission. (2001a), *Communication from the Commission to the Council and the European Parliament – Biodiversity action plans in the areas of conservation of natural resources, agriculture, fisheries, and development and economic co-operation*, COM(2001)162/01, 27 March 2001, Brussels, Belgium.

European Commission. (2001b), *Communication from the Commission to the Council and the European Parliament – Biodiversity action plan for economic and development co-operation*, COM(2001)162/05, 27 March 2001, Brussels, Belgium.

European Commission. (2001c), *Communication from the Commission to the Council and the European Parliament – Biodiversity action plan for the conservation of natural resources*, COM(2001)162/02, 27 March 2001, Brussels, Belgium.

European Commission. (2001d), *Communication from the Commission to the Council and the European Parliament – Biodiversity action plan for fisheries*, COM(2001) 162/02, 27 March 2001, Brussels, Belgium.

European Commission. (2006), *Communication from the Commission to the Council and the European Parliament – Halting the loss of biodiversity by 2010 – and beyond – sustaining ecosystem services for human well-being*, COM(2006)607.

European Commission. (2008a), *Communication from the Commission to the Council, the European Parliament, the European Economic and Social Committee and the Committee of the Regions – Towards an EU strategy on invasive species*, COM(2008) 789, 3 December 2008, Brussels, Belgium.

European Commission. (2008b), *Impact assessment, annex to the communication "Towards an EU strategy on invasive alien species*, 3 December 2008, Brussels, Belgium.

European Commission. (2011), *Communication from the Commission to the European Parliament, the Council, the Economic and Social Committee and the Committee of the Regions – "Our life insurance, our natural capital: An EU biodiversity strategy to 2020*, COM(2011)244.

European Economic and Social Committee. (EESC, 2009), *Opinion of the European Economic and Social Committee on the Communication from the Commission "Towards an EU strategy on invasive alien species"*, 11 June 2009, Brussels, Belgium.

European Parliament. (2007), *Report on halting the loss of biodiversity by 2010*, Committee on the Environment, Public Health and Food Safety, European Parliament, 28 March 2007, Strasbourg, France.

Genovesi, P., Carboneras, C., Vilà, M. and Walton, P. (2015), EU adopts innovative legislation on invasive species: A step towards a global response to biological invasions? in *Biol Inv* 17: 1307–1311.

Hochkirch, A., Schmitt, T., Beninde, J. J., Hiery, M., Kinitz, T., Kirschey, J., Matenaar, D., Rohde, K., Stoefen, A., Wagner, N., Zink, A., Lotters, S., Veith, M. and Proeless, A. (2013), Europe needs a new vision for Natura 2000 network in *Conserv Lett* 6: 462–467.

Kettunen, M., Genovesi, P., Gollasch, S., Pagad, S., Starfinger, U., Ten Brink, P. and Shine, C. (2009), *Technical support to EU strategy on invasive species (IAS): Assessment of the impacts of IAS in Europe and the EU* – Final report for the European Commission, Institute for European Environmental Policy (IEEP), Brussels, Belgium.

Lockwood, J.L., Hoopes, M.F. and Marchetti, M.P. (eds., 2007), *Invasion ecology*, Blackwell Publishing Ltd, Oxford, UK.

Roy, H., Schonrogge, K., Dean, H., Peyton, J., Branquart, E., Vanderhoeven, S., Copp, G., Stebbing, P., Rabirsch, W., Essl, F., Schindler, S., Brunel, S., Kettunen, M., Mazza, L., Nieto, A., Kemp, J., Genovesi, P., Scalera, R. and Stewart, A. (2014), *Invasive alien species: Framework for the identification of invasive alien species of EU concern*. Report to the EC, project ENV.B.2/ETU/2013/0026.

Shine, C., Kettunen, M., Ten Brink, P., Genovesi, P. and Gollasch, S. (2009), *Technical support to EU strategy on invasive species (IAS): Recommendations on policy options to control the negative impacts of IAS on biodiversity in Europe and the EU* – Final report for the European Commission, Institute for European Environmental Policy (IEEP), Brussels, Belgium.

Tollington, S., Turbé, A., Rabitsch, W., Groombridge, J.J., Scalera, R., Essl, F. and Shwartz, A. (2015), Making the EU legislation on invasive species a conservation success in *Conserv Lett.* Available at http://onlinelibrary.wiley.com/doi/10.1111/conl.12214/epdf

Trouwborst, A. (2015), EU regulation 1143/2014 and the Bern Convention: Allied forces in the war on invasive alien species in Europe in *EEEL Review* 4: 83–99.

Conclusions

The first chapter of this work has clarified that, as a consequence of their nature, which overhauls national borders and disciplinary aspects, biological invasions cannot be effectively dealt with at the state level or under particular sectorial approaches. Rather, the issue should be solved at the international level, and in specie through a multi-dimensional approach including identification, assessment, control and management. On the other hand, this international cooperation should not repeat the mistake made by many national regulators, which in the trade-off between economic growth and environmental protection – in those cases in which exotic species were used in agriculture or forestry or aquaculture (to cite three of the most exposed sectors to biological invasions) – have favoured the first aspect. In this sense, a paradigmatic shift leading to environmentally friendly solutions should be realised by taking advantage of the ongoing specialisation of the international legal framework.

In this particular respect, the second chapter has identified in the progressive specialisation of the supranational legal order the regulatory tool through which an effective response to biological invasions has been attempted. Indeed, in the last decades international environmental law has emerged as an autonomous body of legal norms that found their origin in the combination of pressures by ecologist non-governmental organisations and fragmentation of the once granitic *ius gentium*. Although innovative, the supranational regulation of environmental concerns at the universal level has been characterised by gaps, overlaps and inconsistencies that have negatively impacted on the success of the attempts put in place by states to give a unitary response to the pressing dangers provoked by invasive alien species on native ecosystems, human beings and socio-economic stability. In fact, the quantitative proliferation and qualitative evolution of legal instruments at the universal level has not been followed by results in terms of effectiveness. However, the reasons for such a regulatory fiasco cannot be simplistically reduced to the individuation of mechanical causes. The lack of a shared glossary and the limited geographical and functional coverage represent significant shortcomings. The impact of economic considerations over law-making procedures and the prevalence of instruments dedicated to those species which are more dangerous for economically profitable activities are a source of ineffectiveness. Finally, the lack of binding value of the large majority of the existing legal tools in relation to the control of pathways and vectors of introduction, and the absence of operative coherency or concrete indicators for practical implementations, are causes of major concern. Yet, this work has explored more rooted – or, to put it better, structural – causes of the current ineffectiveness, identifying them in the difficult compatibility between the state-centric system established at the time of the Peace of Westphalia and the eminently trans-territorial nature of biological invasions. In fact, the response to the transboundary challenges posed by exotic species clashes in many critical points with the indissoluble link between territory and the exercise of state sovereignty set up in 1648. Furthermore, the Westphalian system was characterised by a certain degree of anthropocentricity, while the fight against invasive species, to be successful, needs an "ethical cleansing" aimed at dehumanising the legal framework in the name of a superior good, that is, the conservation of the environment.

With a view to this epochal transition from a system based on states and men to a reality in which territories are not only cartographic expressions of state sovereignty and the balance of regulation is shifted towards nature and environment conservation, new actors should take on the responsibilities of governance. The second chapter has clarified the role of regional organisations in the development of closer institutional linkages among neighbouring countries on the basis of shared values, principles and legal traditions. Through the creation of a new "space of governability" transcending national borders and regulations, regional organisations offer an optimal scale of intervention against transbondary issues such as biological invasions.

The third chapter presented the European Union as the only contemporary example of a regional organisation which has moved beyond mere cooperation in the environmental sector to reach a degree of integration marked by legal pervasiveness and specialised regulation. This has happened through the progressive communitarisation of environmental concerns, since the approval of the first Environmental Action Programme (1973), and their inclusion within the treaty provisions at the time of the conclusion of the Single European Act (1987). Since then, and increasingly until the final formulation in the Lisbon Treaty (2007), environmental protection has become one of the cornerstones, as well as a fundamental objective, of the European Union. In fact, one of the most important tasks of the organisation has become, according to Article 191 of the Treaty on the Functioning of the European Union, the achievement of "a high level of protection taking into account the diversity of situations in the various regions of the Union" on the basis of three principles which constitute the core of the emerging customary international environmental law: prevention, precaution, "polluter pays". Furthermore, in the European context, other relevant principles regard the rectification at the source of environmental damage, and the respect of paramount norms of the organisation such as subsidiarity and proportionality. These principles and objectives have been embodied in a vast array of regulatory provisions which have followed a pattern going from sectorial interventions, mainly enacted on the basis of some ecological emergency (such as in the case of Council Directive 82/501/CEE, better known as "Seveso directive") or following societal pressures on the quality of air and water, to progressively more comprehensive pieces of legislation challenging inter-sectorial issues.

With particular regard to invasive alien species, the action of Brussels institutions against "unwanted introductions" had already begun at the end of the 1970s, when Council Directive 79/409/EEC established a general duty for Member States to put in place adequate measures aimed at protecting all species of wild birds in Europe by designing as special protection areas (SPAs) their living habitats, together with a specific obligation for Member States – contained in Article 11 – to "see that any introduction of species of birds which do not occur naturally in the wild state in the European territory . . . does not prejudice the local flora and fauna". In 1992, Council Directive 92/43/EEC (also known as the *Habitats* directive) generalised the obligation to protect and preserve nature by including all kinds of habitats and all species of wild fauna and flora within a network of special areas of conservation (SACs). Specifically, Article 22 called on Member States to ensure that "the deliberate introduction into the wild of any species which is not native to their territory is regulated so as not to prejudice natural habitats within their natural range or the wild native fauna and flora".

These provisions, integrated during the 1990s and 2000s by specific legislation enacted to cover individual pathways or species (such as Council Regulation 338/97/EC on trade of wild flora and fauna, Council Directive 2000/29/EC on plant health, the 2000 Water Framework Directive, the 2007 Animal Health Strategy and Action Plan, Council Regulation 708/2007/EC concerning use of alien and locally absent species in aquaculture, and the Marine Strategy Framework Directive 2008/56/EC), have had some limited impact on context-related situations, but the overall issue has remained almost untouched, and Europe is increasingly vulnerable to the threats posed by invasive alien species. In fact, until an ad hoc regulation was proposed the legislative framework was characterised by a rather piecemeal approach, in a scenario marked by poor implementation, incoherent and non-homogeneous application and lack of coverage for significant aspects such as pathogens and parasites threatening biodiversity, exotic species kept in captivity or in managed environments, and the absence of coordinated border controls.

Given these shortcomings, the regulation for the prevention and management of the introduction and spread of invasive alien species – approved by the European Parliament and the Council in October 2014 and entered into force on 1 January 2015 – has been conclusively analysed in the fourth chapter as a possible comprehensive solution and as a demonstration that the regional level can be the optimal scale of environmental governance with particular reference to biological invasions. In its final text the regulation maintains its operative background, based on the three-tier approach (prevention, early detection and eradication, mitigation and control) first elaborated in the framework of the Sixth Conference of Parties to the Convention on Biological Diversity in 2002. Furthermore, it enhances the quality of the protection ensured by the European legal framework because of the agreement between the co-legislators to abolish the initial – a-scientific – limitation to the top 3% of exotic biomes as part of the list of "species of Union concern" and to introduce dedicated references to animal welfare, bio-geographic and climatic conditions, and the relevance of cross-border cooperation. Nonetheless, the final version contains some elements of perplexity when assuming a fully environmental perspective. Social and economic considerations have been included as a basis for action with paramount regard to the analysis of the cost-benefit analysis of the implementation for Member States and to the management of those "species that are widely used and provide significant social and economic benefits" so as to "avoid disproportionate or excessive costs for any member state". In addition, economic activities can benefit from wide spaces for derogation from the provisions of the regulation.

Even if the concluding remarks of the fourth chapter stressed the need not to overstate the impact of these derogations on the effectiveness of the regulation – as the last word firmly rests with the Commission – it nevertheless seems interesting to look at other examples of regulatory approaches to biological invasions in the world. In particular, the new piece of legislation enacted by the European Union has many points of contact with the Biosecurity Act approved by the New Zealand Parliament in 1993.

The choice of a case that – for geo-political and socio-economic reasons – seems to be so antipodal with respect to the European Union is explained by the role of New Zealand as a forerunner in the protection of native flora and fauna from threats coming from invasive alien species. In fact, the colonisation of New Zealand by European settlers in the mid-1800s has led to the disruption of the particularly vulnerable island ecosystems. As early as the 1860s, a system of quarantine stations for the inspection of incoming passengers and animals was built on islands close to New Zealand's major harbours. However, together with this remedy, pressures by economic operators led to the opening of a continuously expanding loophole, since the rigour of the controls was attenuated for those species that were regarded as useful to settlers. This trend has increased in the 20th century, with particular regard to the agricultural sector, as the primary industry is one of the major sources of wealth of the country.

The New Zealand Biosecurity Act was only approved in 1993, meaning that simple biological control gave way to a more comprehensive approach encompassing economic, social, cultural and environmental aspects. Intended as "the exclusion, eradication or effective management of risks posed by pests and diseases to the economy, environment and human health", biosecurity became a matter of first importance both at the central and local levels of government, as well as significantly influencing New Zealand's external relations and international trade. The Ministry for Agriculture and Forestry and an ad hoc group of inspectors were given special powers of control in order to protect the native habitat and avoid threats coming from exotic pests and diseases. However, through the review of the legislation in 2003 and increasingly after the new biosecurity strategy issued in 2007, the first aim of the regulatory intervention became "trade, as well as marketing New Zealand as product for tourism" and "economic growth, opportunities and prosperity". As argued in 2006 by Jay and Morad, the institutional arrangements created by the legislation of the Biosecurity Act allowed for faster and more efficient conduct of trade, but not for effective control of environmental hazards.

Bearing in mind the New Zealand experience and its shift towards economic objectives as the years passed by, it would be vital for the effectiveness of the European Union's intervention against biological invasions that the derogations to the regulation on invasive alien species for socio-economic – or whatever non-environmentally related – reasons are limited to the role of exception, and that the Commission actively and carefully oversees the implementation of the new piece of legislation by Member States. Only in this way will the "biosecurity dilemma" receive a new answer able to embody the paradigmatic shift according priority to environmental protection over economic interests, which would not even exist without a healthy ecosystem capable of sustaining human life and, therefore, human activities.

Regulation (EU) No 1143/2014 of the European Parliament and of the Council of 22 October 2014 on the prevention and management of the introduction and spread of invasive alien species

THE EUROPEAN PARLIAMENT AND THE COUNCIL OF THE EUROPEAN UNION,

Having regard to the Treaty on the Functioning of the European Union, and in particular Article 192(1) thereof,
Having regard to the proposal from the European Commission,
After transmission of the draft legislative act to the national parliaments,
Having regard to the opinion of the European Economic and Social Committee[1],
After consulting the Committee of the Regions,
Acting in accordance with the ordinary legislative procedure[2],

Whereas:

(1) The appearance of alien species, whether of animals, plants, fungi or micro-organisms, in new locations is not always a cause for concern. However, a significant subset of alien species can become invasive and have serious adverse impact on biodiversity and related ecosystem services, as well as have other social and economic impact, which should be prevented. Some 12 000 species in the environment of the Union and in other European countries are alien, of which roughly 10 to 15% are estimated to be invasive.

(2) Invasive alien species represent one of the main threats to biodiversity and related ecosystem services, especially in geographically and evolutionarily isolated ecosystems, such as small islands. The risks such species pose may intensify due to increased global trade, transport, tourism and climate change.

(3) The threat to biodiversity and related ecosystem services that invasive alien species pose takes different forms, including severe impacts on native species and the structure and functioning of ecosystems through the alteration of habitats, predation, competition, the transmission of diseases, the replacement of native species throughout a significant proportion of range and through genetic effects by hybridisation. Furthermore, invasive alien species can also have a significant adverse impact on

human health and the economy. Only live specimens, and parts that can reproduce, represent a threat to biodiversity and related ecosystem services, human health or the economy, and therefore, only those should be subject to the restrictions under this Regulation.

(4) The Union, as a party to the Convention on Biological Diversity, approved by Council Decision 93/626/EEC[3], is bound by Article 8(h) of that Convention, according to which the Parties shall, as far as possible and as appropriate, 'prevent the introduction of, control or eradicate those alien species which threaten ecosystems, habitats or species'.

(5) The Union, as a Party to the Convention on the Conservation of European Wildlife and Natural Habitats, approved by Council Decision 82/72/EEC[4], has undertaken to take all appropriate measures to ensure the conservation of the habitats of the wild flora and fauna species.

(6) To support the achievement of the objectives of Directives 2000/60/EC[5], 2008/56/EC[6] and 2009/147/EC[7]of the European Parliament and of the Council and Council Directive 92/43/EEC[8], this Regulation should establish rules to prevent, minimise and mitigate the adverse effects of invasive alien species on biodiversity and related ecosystem services, and on human health and safety as well as to reduce their social and economic impact.

(7) Some species migrate naturally in response to environmental changes. They should not be considered as alien species in their new environment and should be excluded from the scope of this Regulation. This Regulation should focus only on species introduced into the Union as a consequence of human intervention.

(8) There are currently over 40 Union legislative acts on animal health which include provisions on animal diseases. Moreover, Council Directive 2000/29/EC[9] includes provisions on organisms which are harmful to plants or plant products, and Directive 2001/18/EC of the European Parliament and of the Council[10] sets out the regime applicable to genetically modified organisms. Therefore, any new rules on invasive alien species should be aligned with and not overlap with those legislative acts of the Union and should not apply to the organisms targeted by those legislative acts.

(9) Regulations (EC) No 1107/2009[11] and (EU) No 528/2012[12] of the European Parliament and of the Council and Council Regulation (EC) No 708/2007[13] provide for rules concerning the authorisation for the use of certain alien species for particular purposes. The use of certain species has already been authorised under those regimes at the time of entry into force of this Regulation. To ensure a coherent legal framework, species used for those purposes should thus be excluded from the scope of this Regulation.

(10) As invasive alien species are numerous, it is important to ensure that priority is given to addressing the subset of invasive alien species considered to be of Union concern. A list of such invasive alien species

considered to be of Union concern ("the Union list") should therefore be established and regularly updated. An invasive alien species should be considered to be of Union concern if the damage that it causes in affected Member States is so significant that it justifies the adoption of dedicated measures applicable across the Union, including in the Member States that are not yet affected or are even unlikely to be affected. To ensure that the identification of invasive alien species of Union concern remains proportionate, the Union list should be established and updated gradually and be focused on species whose inclusion on the Union list would effectively prevent, minimise or mitigate the adverse impact of those species in a cost efficient manner. As species within the same taxonomic group often have similar ecological requirements and may pose similar risks, the inclusion of taxonomic groups of species on the Union list should be allowed, where appropriate.

(11) The criteria for inclusion on the Union list are the core instrument of application of this Regulation. To ensure the effective use of resources, those criteria should ensure that among the potential invasive alien species currently known, those that have the most significant adverse impact will be listed. The Commission should submit to the committee established by this Regulation a proposal for a Union list based on those criteria within one year of the entry into force of this Regulation. When proposing the Union list, the Commission should inform that committee on how it took those criteria into account. The criteria should include a risk assessment pursuant to the applicable provisions under the relevant Agreements of the World Trade Organisation (WTO) on placing trade restrictions on species.

(12) To avoid disproportionate or excessive costs for any Member State and to safeguard the added value of Union action through this Regulation, when proposing the Union list and consequential measures, the Commission should take into consideration the implementation cost for Member States, the cost of inaction, the cost-effectiveness and the socio-economic aspects. In this context, in selecting the invasive alien species to be included on the Union list, special attention should be given to species that are widely used and provide significant social and economic benefits in a Member State, without compromising the objectives of this Regulation.

(13) To ensure compliance with the rules under the relevant Agreements of the WTO and the coherent application of this Regulation, common criteria should be established to carry out the risk assessment. Where appropriate, those criteria should be based on existing national and international standards and should encompass different aspects of the characteristics of the species, the risk and modes of introduction into the Union, the adverse social, economic and biodiversity impact of the species, the potential benefits of uses and the costs of mitigation to weigh them against the adverse impact, as well as on an assessment of the potential costs of environmental, social and economic damage

demonstrating the significance for the Union, so as to further justify action. In order to develop the system progressively and build upon the experience gained, the overall approach should be assessed by 1 June 2021.

(14) Some invasive alien species are included in Annex B to Council Regulation (EC) No 338/97[14], and their importation into the Union is prohibited because their invasive character has been recognised and their introduction into the Union has an adverse impact on native species. Those species are: *Callosciurus erythraeus, Sciurus carolinensis, Oxyura jamaicensis, Lithobates (Rana) catesbeianus, Sciurus niger, Chrysemys picta and Trachemys scripta elegans.* To ensure a coherent legal framework and uniform rules on invasive alien species at Union level, the listing of those invasive alien species as invasive alien species of Union concern should be considered as a matter of priority.

(15) Prevention is generally more environmentally desirable and cost-effective than reaction after the fact, and should be prioritised. Therefore, priority should be given to the listing of invasive alien species that are not yet present in the Union or are at an early stage of invasion and of invasive alien species that are likely to have the most significant adverse impact. As new invasive alien species can be introduced continuously into the Union and alien species present are spreading and expanding their range, it is necessary to ensure that the Union list is constantly reviewed and kept up-to-date.

(16) Regional cooperation should be explored between Member States concerned with the same species that are not able to establish a viable population in a large part of the Union. Where the objectives of this Regulation are better achieved by measures at Union level, those species could also be included on the Union list.

(17) In pursuing the objectives of this Regulation, it is appropriate to take account of the specific situation of the outermost regions, and in particular their remoteness, insularity and the uniqueness of their respective biodiversities. Therefore, the requirements under this Regulation to take restrictive and preventive measures relating to invasive alien species of Union concern should be adapted to the specificities of the outermost regions, as defined by the Treaty on the Functioning of the European Union (TFEU), taking into account European Council Decisions 2010/718/EU[15]and 2012/419/EU[16].

(18) The risks and concerns associated with invasive alien species represent a cross-border challenge affecting the whole of the Union. It is therefore essential to adopt a ban at Union level on intentionally or negligently bringing into the Union, reproducing, growing, transporting, buying, selling, using, exchanging, keeping and releasing invasive alien species of Union concern in order to ensure that early and consistent action is taken across the Union to avoid distortions of the internal market and to prevent situations where action taken in one Member State is undermined by inaction in another Member State.

(19) With a view to enabling scientific research and ex-situ conservation activities, it is necessary to provide specific rules for the invasive alien species of Union concern subject to those activities. Those activities should be carried out in closed establishments where the organisms are in contained holding and with all the necessary measures taken to avoid the escape or unlawful release of invasive alien species of Union concern. Where authorised by the Commission in duly motivated exceptional cases of compelling public interest it should be possible for those rules to apply also to certain other activities, including commercial activities. In implementing those rules, particular attention should be paid to avoiding any adverse impact on protected species and habitats, in accordance with relevant Union law.

(20) There may be cases where alien species not yet recognised as invasive alien species of Union concern appear at the Union borders or are detected in the territory of the Union. Member States should therefore be granted the possibility to adopt certain emergency measures on the basis of available scientific evidence. Such emergency measures would allow immediate reaction against invasive alien species which could pose risks related to their introduction, establishment and spread in those countries, while Member States assess the actual risks posed by them, in line with the applicable provisions of the relevant Agreements of the WTO, in particular with a view to having those species recognised as invasive alien species of Union concern. There is a need to couple national emergency measures with the possibility of adopting emergency measures at Union level to comply with the provisions of the relevant Agreements of the WTO. Furthermore, emergency measures at Union level would equip the Union with a mechanism to act swiftly in case of presence or imminent danger of entry of a new invasive alien species in accordance with the precautionary principle.

(21) A large proportion of invasive alien species are introduced unintentionally into the Union. It is therefore crucial to manage the pathways of unintentional introduction more effectively. Action in this area should be gradual, given the relatively limited experience in this field. Action should include voluntary measures, such as the actions proposed by the International Maritime Organisation's Guidelines for the Control and Management of Ships' Biofouling, and mandatory measures. Action should build on the experience gained in the Union and in Member States in managing certain pathways, including measures established through the International Convention for the Control and Management of Ships Ballast Water and Sediments adopted in 2004. Accordingly, the Commission should take all appropriate steps to encourage Member States to ratify that Convention.

(22) To develop an adequate knowledge base to address the problems raised by invasive alien species, it is important that Member States undertake research, monitoring and surveillance of such species. As surveillance systems offer the most appropriate means for early detection of new

invasive alien species and for the determination of the distribution of already established species, those systems should include both targeted and general surveys and benefit from the involvement of different sectors and stakeholders, including regional and local communities. Surveillance systems should imply paying continuous attention to any new invasive alien species anywhere in the Union and aim to provide an effective and complete picture at Union level. In the interest of efficiency and cost-effectiveness, existing systems of customs control, surveillance and monitoring already established by Union law should be applied, in particular those set out in Directives 92/43/EEC, 2000/60/EC, 2008/56/EC and 2009/147/EC.

(23) Official controls on animals and plants should be carried out to prevent the intentional introduction of invasive alien species. Live animals and plants should only enter the Union through border control entities in accordance with Regulation (EC) No 882/2004 of the European Parliament and of the Council[17], and Council Directives 91/496/EEC[18] and 97/78/EC[19] or points of entry in accordance with Directive 2000/29/EC. To ensure efficiency gains and avoid creating parallel systems of customs controls, competent authorities should verify whether those species are invasive alien species of Union concern at the first border control entity or point of entry.

(24) After the introduction of an invasive alien species, early detection and rapid eradication measures are crucial to prevent their establishment and spread. The most effective and cost efficient response is often to eradicate the population as soon as possible while the number of specimens is still limited. In the event that eradication is not feasible or the costs of eradication outweigh the environmental, social and economic benefits in the long term, containment and control measures should be applied. Management measures should be proportional to the impact on the environment and take due consideration of the biogeographic and climatic conditions of the Member State concerned.

(25) Management measures should avoid any adverse impact on the environment as well as on human health. Eradicating and managing some animal invasive alien species, while necessary in some cases, may induce pain, distress, fear or other forms of suffering to the animals, even when using the best available technical means. For that reason, Member States and any operator involved in the eradication, control or containment of invasive alien species should take the necessary measures to spare avoidable pain, distress and suffering of animals during the process, taking into account as far as possible the best practices in the field, for example the Guiding Principles on Animal Welfare developed by the World Organisation for Animal Health. Non-lethal methods should be considered and any action taken should minimise the impact on non-targeted species.

(26) Invasive alien species generally cause damage to ecosystems and reduce the resilience of those ecosystems. Therefore proportionate restoration

measures should be undertaken to strengthen the ecosystems' resilience towards invasions, to repair the damage caused and to enhance the conservation status of species and their habitats in accordance with Directives 92/43/EEC and 2009/147/EC, the ecological status of inland surface waters, transitional waters, coastal waters and groundwater in accordance with Directive 2000/60/EC, and the environmental status of marine waters in accordance with Directive 2008/56/EC. The costs of such restoration measures should be recovered in accordance with the polluter pays principle.

(27) Cross-border cooperation, particularly with neighbouring countries, and coordination between Member States, particularly within the same biogeographical region of the Union, should be fostered to contribute to the effective application of this Regulation.

(28) A system to address invasive alien species should be underpinned by a centralised information system collating the existing information on alien species in the Union and allowing access to information on the presence of species, their spread, their ecology, invasion history and all other information necessary to underpin policy and management decisions and allowing also the exchange of best practices.

(29) Directive 2003/35/EC of the European Parliament and of the Council[20] has established a framework for public consultation in environment related decisions. In defining action in the field of invasive alien species, effective public participation should enable the public to express, and the decision-maker to take account of, opinions and concerns which may be relevant to those decisions. That should increase the accountability and transparency of the decision-making process and contribute to public awareness of environmental issues and support for the decisions taken.

(30) The participation of the scientific community is important to provide an adequate knowledge base to address the problems raised by invasive alien species. A dedicated scientific forum should be set up to provide advice on the scientific aspects related to the application of this Regulation, in particular as regards establishing and updating the Union list, risk assessments, emergency measures and rapid eradication measures.

(31) In order to ensure uniform conditions for the implementation of this Regulation, implementing powers should be conferred on the Commission in respect of the adoption and updating of the Union list, the format of the documents serving as evidence for permits, the adoption of emergency measures at Union level, the requirement to apply certain provisions in the Member States concerned in the case of enhanced regional cooperation, the rejection of the Member States' decisions not to apply eradication measures and the technical formats for reporting to the Commission. Those powers should be exercised in accordance with Regulation (EU) No 182/2011 of the European Parliament and of the Council[21].

(32) In order to take into account the latest scientific developments in the environmental field, the power to adopt acts in accordance with Article 290 TFEU should be delegated to the Commission in respect of determining how it may be concluded that invasive alien species are capable of establishing viable populations and of spreading, as well as for setting out the common elements for the development of risk assessments. It is of particular importance that the Commission carry out appropriate consultations during its preparatory work, including at expert level. The Commission, when preparing and drawing up delegated acts, should ensure a simultaneous, timely and appropriate transmission of relevant documents to the European Parliament and to the Council.

(33) To guarantee compliance with this Regulation, it is important that Member States impose effective, proportionate and dissuasive sanctions for infringements, taking into account the nature and gravity of the infringement, the principle of recovery of the costs and the polluter pays principle.

(34) Through measures taken under this Regulation, Member States may impose obligations on holders or users of alien species as well as owners and tenants of the land concerned.

(35) To enable non-commercial owners to keep their companion animals that belong to species included on the Union list until the end of the animal's natural life, it is necessary to provide transitional measures, on condition that all measures are put in place to avoid reproduction or escape.

(36) To enable commercial operators, who may have legitimate expectations, for instance those who have received an authorisation in accordance with Regulation (EC) No 708/2007, to exhaust their stock of invasive alien species of Union concern following the entry into force of this Regulation, it is justified to allow them two years to slaughter, humanely cull, sell or, where relevant, hand over the specimens to research or ex-situ conservation establishments.

(37) Since the objectives of this Regulation, namely to prevent, minimise and mitigate the adverse impact on biodiversity of the introduction and spread of invasive alien species within the Union, cannot be sufficiently achieved by the Member States but can rather, by reason of its scale and effects, be better achieved at Union level, the Union may adopt measures, in accordance with the principle of subsidiarity as set out in Article 5 of the Treaty on European Union. In accordance with the principle of proportionality, as set out in that Article, this Regulation does not go beyond what is necessary in order to achieve those objectives.

(38) It should be possible for Member States to maintain or adopt rules on invasive alien species of Union concern that are more stringent than those laid down in this Regulation and to apply provisions such as those set out in this Regulation for invasive alien species of Union concern to invasive alien species of Member State concern. Any such measures should be compatible with the TFEU and be notified to the Commission in accordance with Union law,

HAVE ADOPTED THIS REGULATION:

Chapter I General provisions

Article 1

Subject matter

This Regulation sets out rules to prevent, minimise and mitigate the adverse impact on biodiversity of the introduction and spread within the Union, both intentional and unintentional, of invasive alien species.

Article 2

Scope

1 This Regulation applies to all invasive alien species.
2 This Regulation does not apply to:

(a) species changing their natural range without human intervention, in response to changing ecological conditions and climate change;
(b) genetically modified organisms as defined in point 2 of Article 2 of Directive 2001/18/EC;
(c) pathogens that cause animal diseases; for the purpose of this Regulation, animal disease means the occurrence of infections and infestations in animals, caused by one or more pathogens transmissible to animals or to humans;
(d) harmful organisms listed in Annex I or Annex II to Directive 2000/29/EC, and harmful organisms for which measures have been adopted in accordance with Article 16(3) of that Directive;
(e) species listed in Annex IV to Regulation (EC) No 708/2007 when used in aquaculture;
(f) micro-organisms manufactured or imported for use in plant protection products already authorised or for which an assessment is ongoing under Regulation (EC) No 1107/2009; or
(g) micro-organisms manufactured or imported for use in biocidal products already authorised or for which an assessment is ongoing under Regulation (EU) No 528/2012.

Article 3

Definitions

For the purposes of this Regulation, the following definitions apply:

(1) 'alien species' means any live specimen of a species, subspecies or lower taxon of animals, plants, fungi or micro-organisms introduced outside

its natural range; it includes any part, gametes, seeds, eggs or propagules of such species, as well as any hybrids, varieties or breeds that might survive and subsequently reproduce;

(2) 'invasive alien species' means an alien species whose introduction or spread has been found to threaten or adversely impact upon biodiversity and related ecosystem services;

(3) 'invasive alien species of Union concern' means an invasive alien species whose adverse impact has been deemed such as to require concerted action at Union level pursuant to Article 4(3);

(4) 'invasive alien species of Member State concern' means an invasive alien species other than an invasive alien species of Union concern, for which a Member State considers on the basis of scientific evidence that the adverse impact of its release and spread, even where not fully ascertained, is of significance for its territory, or part of it, and requires action at the level of that Member State;

(5) 'biodiversity' means the variability among living organisms from all sources, including terrestrial, marine and other aquatic ecosystems and the ecological complexes of which they are part; this includes diversity within species, between species and of ecosystems;

(6) 'ecosystem services' means the direct and indirect contributions of ecosystems to human wellbeing;

(7) 'introduction' means the movement, as a consequence of human intervention, of a species outside its natural range;

(8) 'research' means descriptive or experimental work, undertaken under regulated conditions to obtain new scientific findings or to develop new products, including the initial phases of identification, characterisation and isolation of genetic features, other than those features which make a species invasive, of invasive alien species only insofar as essential to enable the breeding of those features into non-invasive species;

(9) 'contained holding' means keeping an organism in closed facilities from which escape or spread is not possible;

(10) 'ex-situ conservation' means the conservation of components of biological diversity outside their natural habitat;

(11) 'pathways' means the routes and mechanisms of the introduction and spread of invasive alien species;

(12) 'early detection' means the confirmation of the presence of a specimen or specimens of an invasive alien species in the environment before it has become widely spread;

(13) 'eradication' means the complete and permanent removal of a population of invasive alien species by lethal or non-lethal means;

(14) 'population control' means any lethal or non-lethal action applied to a population of invasive alien species, while also minimising the impact on non-targeted species and their habitats, with the aim of keeping the number of individuals as low as possible, so that, while not being able to eradicate the species, its invasive capacity and adverse impact on biodiversity, the related ecosystem services, on human health or the economy, are minimised;

(15) 'containment' means any action aimed at creating barriers which minimises the risk of a population of an invasive alien species dispersing and spreading beyond the invaded area;
(16) 'widely spread' means an invasive alien species whose population has gone beyond the naturalisation stage, in which a population is self-sustaining, and has spread to colonise a large part of the potential range where it can survive and reproduce;
(17) 'management' means any lethal or non-lethal action aimed at the eradication, population control or containment of a population of an invasive alien species, while also minimising the impact on non-targeted species and their habitats.

Article 4

List of invasive alien species of Union concern

1 The Commission shall adopt, by means of implementing acts, a list of invasive alien species of Union concern ('the Union list'), on the basis of the criteria laid down in paragraph 3 of this Article. Those implementing acts shall be adopted in accordance with the examination procedure referred to in Article 27(2). The draft implementing acts shall be submitted to the Committee referred to in Article 27(1) by 2 January 2016.

2 The Commission shall undertake a comprehensive review of the Union list at least every six years and shall, in the meantime, update it, as appropriate, in accordance with the procedure referred to in paragraph 1 with:

(a) the addition of new invasive alien species;
(b) the removal of listed species if they no longer meet one or more of the criteria laid down in paragraph 3.

3 Invasive alien species shall only be included on the Union list if they meet all of the following criteria:

(a) they are found, based on available scientific evidence, to be alien to the territory of the Union excluding the outermost regions;
(b) they are found, based on available scientific evidence, to be capable of establishing a viable population and spreading in the environment under current conditions and in foreseeable climate change conditions in one biogeographical region shared by more than two Member States or one marine subregion excluding their outermost regions;
(c) they are, based on available scientific evidence, likely to have a significant adverse impact on biodiversity or the related ecosystem services, and may also have an adverse impact on human health or the economy;
(d) it is demonstrated by a risk assessment carried out pursuant to Article 5(1) that concerted action at Union level is required to prevent their introduction, establishment or spread;
(e) it is likely that the inclusion on the Union list will effectively prevent, minimise or mitigate their adverse impact.

4 Member States may submit to the Commission requests for the inclusion of invasive alien species on the Union list. Those requests shall include all of the following:

(a) the name of the species;
(b) a risk assessment carried out in accordance with Article 5(1);
(c) evidence that the criteria set out in paragraph 3 of this Article are met.

5 The Union list shall make reference, where relevant, to the goods with which the invasive alien species are generally associated and their Combined Nomenclature codes as provided by Council Regulation (EEC) No 2658/87[22], indicating the categories of goods that shall be subject to official controls pursuant to Article 15 of this Regulation.

6 When adopting or updating the Union list, the Commission shall apply the criteria set out in paragraph 3 with due consideration to the implementation cost for Member States, the cost of inaction, the cost-effectiveness and the socio-economic aspects. The Union list shall include as a priority those invasive alien species that:

(a) are not yet present in the Union or are at an early stage of invasion and are most likely to have a significant adverse impact;
(b) are already established in the Union and have the most significant adverse impact.

7 When proposing the Union list, the Commission shall also justify that the objectives of this Regulation are better achieved by measures at Union level.

Article 5

Risk assessment

1 For the purposes of Article 4, a risk assessment shall be carried out in relation to the current and potential range of invasive alien species, having regard to the following elements:

(a) a description of the species with its taxonomic identity, its history, and its natural and potential range;
(b) a description of its reproduction and spread patterns and dynamics including an assessment of whether the environmental conditions necessary for its reproduction and spread exist;
(c) a description of the potential pathways of introduction and spread of the species, both intentional and unintentional, including where relevant the commodities with which the species is generally associated;
(d) a thorough assessment of the risk of introduction, establishment and spread in relevant biogeographical regions in current conditions and in foreseeable climate change conditions;
(e) a description of the current distribution of the species, including whether the species is already present in the Union or in neighbouring countries, and a projection of its likely future distribution;

(f) a description of the adverse impact on biodiversity and related ecosystem services, including on native species, protected sites, endangered habitats, as well as on human health, safety, and the economy including an assessment of the potential future impact having regard to available scientific knowledge;
(g) an assessment of the potential costs of damage;
(h) a description of the known uses for the species and social and economic benefits deriving from those uses.

2 When proposing species for listing as invasive alien species of Union concern, the Commission shall carry out the risk assessment referred to in paragraph 1.

Whenever a Member State submits a request for the inclusion of a species on the Union list it shall be responsible for carrying out the risk assessment referred to in paragraph 1. Where necessary, the Commission may assist the Member States in the development of such risk assessments in so far as it relates to their European dimension.

3 The Commission shall be empowered to adopt delegated acts, in accordance with Article 29, to further specify the type of evidence acceptable for the purposes of point (b) of Article 4(3) and provide a detailed description of the application of points (a) to (h) of paragraph 1 of this Article. The detailed description shall include the methodology to be applied in the risk assessments, taking into account relevant national and international standards and the need to prioritise action against invasive alien species associated with, or that have the potential to cause, a significant adverse impact on biodiversity or related ecosystem services, as well as on human health or the economy, such adverse impact being considered as an aggravating factor. It is of particular importance that the Commission follow its usual practice and carry out consultations with experts, including Member States' experts, before adopting those delegated acts.

Article 6

Provisions for the outermost regions

1 Invasive alien species of Union concern shall not be subject to Article 7 or Articles 13 to 20 in the outermost regions.
2 By 2 January 2017, each Member State with outermost regions shall adopt for each of those regions a list of invasive alien species of concern, in consultation with those regions.
3 As regards the invasive alien species included on the lists referred to in paragraph 2 of this Article, Member States may, within the respective outermost regions, apply the measures as provided for in Articles 7 to 9, 13 to 17, 19 and 20, as appropriate. Those measures shall be compatible with the TFEU and be notified to the Commission in accordance with Union law.

4 Member States shall immediately notify the Commission and shall inform the other Member States of the lists referred to in paragraph 2 and of any update to those lists.

Chapter II Prevention

Article 7

Restrictions

1 Invasive alien species of Union concern shall not be intentionally:

(a) brought into the territory of the Union, including transit under customs supervision;
(b) kept, including in contained holding;
(c) bred, including in contained holding;
(d) transported to, from or within the Union, except for the transportation of species to facilities in the context of eradication;
(e) placed on the market;
(f) used or exchanged;
(g) permitted to reproduce, grown or cultivated, including in contained holding; or
(h) released into the environment.

2 Member States shall take all necessary steps to prevent the unintentional introduction or spread, including, where applicable, by gross negligence, of invasive alien species of Union concern.

Article 8

Permits

1 By way of derogation from the restrictions set out in points (a), (b), (c), (d), (f) and (g) of Article 7(1), and subject to paragraph 2 of this Article, Member States shall establish a permit system allowing establishments to carry out research on, or ex-situ conservation of, invasive alien species of Union concern. Where the use of products derived from invasive alien species of Union concern is unavoidable to advance human health, Member States may also include scientific production and subsequent medicinal use within their permit system.

2 Member States shall empower their competent authorities to issue the permits referred to in paragraph 1 for activities carried out in contained holding that fulfil all of the following conditions:

(a) the invasive alien species of Union concern is kept in and handled in contained holding in accordance with paragraph 3;
(b) the activity is to be carried out by appropriately qualified personnel as laid down by the competent authorities;

(c) transport to and from contained holding is carried out under conditions that exclude escape of the invasive alien species as established by the permit;
(d) in the case of invasive alien species of Union concern that are animals, they are marked or otherwise effectively identified where appropriate, using methods that do not cause avoidable pain, distress or suffering;
(e) the risk of escape or spread or removal is effectively managed, taking into account the identity, biology and means of dispersal of the species, the activity and the contained holding envisaged, the interaction with the environment and other relevant factors;
(f) a continuous surveillance system and a contingency plan covering possible escape or spread is drawn up by the applicant, including an eradication plan. The contingency plan shall be approved by the competent authority. If an escape or spread occurs, the contingency plan shall be implemented immediately and the permit may be withdrawn, temporarily or permanently.

The permit referred to in paragraph 1 shall be limited to a number of invasive alien species and specimens that does not exceed the capacity of the contained holding. It shall include the restrictions necessary to mitigate the risk of escape or spread of the species concerned. It shall accompany the invasive alien species to which it refers at all times when those species are kept, brought into and transported within the Union.

3 Specimens shall be considered to be kept in contained holding if the following conditions are fulfilled:

(a) the specimens are physically isolated and they cannot escape or spread or be removed by unauthorised persons from the holdings where they are kept;
(b) cleaning, waste handling and maintenance protocols ensure that no specimens or reproducible parts can escape, spread or be removed by unauthorised persons;
(c) the removal of the specimens from the holdings, disposal or destruction or humane cull is done in such way as to exclude propagation or reproduction outside of the holdings.

4 When applying for a permit, the applicant shall provide all necessary evidence to allow the competent authority to assess whether the conditions set out in paragraphs 2 and 3 are fulfilled.

5 Member States shall empower their competent authorities to withdraw the permit at any point in time, temporarily or permanently, if unforeseen events with an adverse impact on biodiversity or related ecosystem services occur. Any withdrawal of a permit shall be justified on scientific grounds and, where scientific information is insufficient, on the grounds of the precautionary principle and having due regard to national administrative rules.

6 The Commission shall adopt, by means of implementing acts, the format of the document serving as evidence for the permit issued by the competent authorities of a Member State. Those implementing acts shall be adopted in accordance with the examination procedure referred to in Article 27(2). Member States shall use that format for a document accompanying the permit.

7 For all permits issued in accordance with paragraph 1 of this Article, Member States, shall, without delay, make publicly available on the internet at least the following:

(a) the scientific and common names of the invasive alien species of Union concern for which the permit has been issued;
(b) the number or the volume of specimens concerned;
(c) the purpose for which the permit has been issued; and
(d) the codes of Combined Nomenclature as provided by Regulation (EEC) No 2658/87.

8 Member States shall ensure that inspections are carried out by their competent authorities to ensure that the establishments comply with the conditions set out in those permits issued.

Article 9

Authorisations

1 In exceptional cases, for reasons of compelling public interest, including those of a social or economic nature, Member States may issue permits allowing establishments to carry out activities other than those set out in Article 8(1) subject to authorisation by the Commission, in accordance with the procedure laid down in this Article and subject to the conditions set out in Article 8(2) and (3).

2 The Commission shall set up and operate an electronic authorisation system and shall decide on applications for authorisation within 60 days of receipt of an application.

3 Applications for authorisation shall be submitted by Member States using the system referred to in paragraph 2.

4 An application for an authorisation shall include the following:

(a) details of the establishment or groups of establishments including their name and address;
(b) the scientific and common names of the invasive alien species of Union concern for which an authorisation is requested;
(c) the codes of Combined Nomenclature as provided by Regulation (EEC) No 2658/87;
(d) the number or the volume of specimens concerned;
(e) the reasons for the requested authorisation;

(f) a detailed description of the envisaged measures to ensure that escape or spread are not possible from contained holding facilities in which the invasive alien species of Union concern is to be kept in and handled, as well as of the measures to ensure that any transport of the species that may be necessary is carried out under conditions that exclude escape;
(g) an assessment of the risk of escape of the invasive alien species of Union concern for which an authorisation is requested, accompanied by a description of the risk mitigation measures to be put in place;
(h) a description of the surveillance system planned and of the contingency plan drawn to cater for possible escape or spread, including an eradication plan where necessary;
(i) a description of relevant national law applicable to those establishments.

5 Authorisations granted by the Commission shall be notified to the competent authority of the Member State concerned. An authorisation shall be specific to an individual establishment, irrespective of the application procedure followed in accordance with point (a) of paragraph 4, and shall include the information referred to in paragraph 4 and the duration of the authorisation. An authorisation shall also include provisions regarding the supply to the establishment of additional or replacement specimens for use in the activity for which that authorisation is requested.

6 Following an authorisation by the Commission, the competent authority may issue the permit referred to in paragraph 1 of this Article in accordance with Article 8(4) to (8). The permit shall include all provisions specified in the authorisation issued by the Commission.

7 The Commission shall reject an application for an authorisation if any relevant obligations set out in this Regulation are not complied with.

8 The Commission shall, as soon as possible, inform the Member State concerned of any rejection of an application pursuant to paragraph 7 and shall specify the reason for the rejection.

Article 10

Emergency measures

1 Where a Member State has evidence concerning the presence in, or imminent risk of introduction into its territory of an invasive alien species, which is not included on the Union list but which the competent authorities have found, on the basis of preliminary scientific evidence, to be likely to meet the criteria set out in Article 4(3), it may immediately take emergency measures, consisting of any of the restrictions set out in Article 7(1).

2 The Member State introducing emergency measures in its national territory which include the application of points (a), (d) or (e) of Article 7(1)

shall immediately notify the Commission and all other Member States of the measures taken and the evidence justifying those measures.

3 The Member State concerned shall without delay carry out a risk assessment pursuant to Article 5 for the invasive alien species subject to the emergency measures, given the available technical and scientific information, and in any case within 24 months from the date of the adoption of the decision to introduce emergency measures, with a view to include that species on the Union list.

4 Where the Commission receives the notification referred to in paragraph 2 of this Article or has other evidence concerning the presence in or imminent risk of introduction into the Union of an invasive alien species which is not included on the Union list, but is likely to meet the criteria set out in Article 4(3), it shall, by means of implementing acts, conclude, on the basis of preliminary scientific evidence, whether the species is likely to meet those criteria and adopt emergency measures for the Union consisting of any of the restrictions set out in Article 7(1) for a limited time as regards the risks posed by that species, where it concludes that the criteria set out in Article 4(3) are likely to be fulfilled. Those implementing acts shall be adopted in accordance with the examination procedure referred to in Article 27(2).

5 Where the Commission adopts an implementing act referred to in paragraph 4, Member States shall repeal or amend, as appropriate, any emergency measures which they have taken.

6 Where the Commission includes the invasive alien species on the Union list, Member States shall also repeal or amend their emergency measures.

7 When, following the risk assessment carried out pursuant to paragraph 3 of this Article, the Commission does not include the invasive alien species on the Union list, Member States shall repeal their emergency measures taken pursuant to paragraph 1 of this Article and may include that species on a national list of invasive alien species of Member State concern, pursuant to Article 12(1), and consider enhanced regional cooperation in accordance with Article 11.

Article 11

Invasive alien species of regional concern and species native to the Union

1 Member States may identify, from their national list of invasive alien species of Member State concern established in accordance with Article 12, species native or non-native to the Union that require enhanced regional cooperation.

2 At the request of the Member States involved, the Commission shall act to facilitate the cooperation and coordination among those Member States involved, in accordance with Article 22(1). Where necessary, based on the impact of certain invasive alien species on biodiversity and related ecosystem services as well as on human health and the economy and

provided that it is thoroughly substantiated by a comprehensive analysis of the justification for an enhanced regional cooperation carried out by the requesting Member States, the Commission may require, by means of implementing acts, that the Member States concerned apply, *mutatis mutandis*, in their territory or part of it, Articles 13, 14 and 16, Article 17 notwithstanding Article 18, as well as apply Articles 19 and 20, as appropriate. Those implementing acts shall be adopted in accordance with the examination procedure referred to in Article 27(2).

3 Invasive alien species of regional concern which are native to a Member State shall not be subject to the provisions of Articles 13, 14, 16, 17, 19, 20 and 24 in the territory of that Member State. Member States to which those species are native, shall cooperate with the Member States concerned for the assessment of the pathways in accordance with Article 13 and, in consultation with the other Member States, may adopt relevant measures to avoid further spread of those species in accordance with the procedure referred to in Article 22(1).

Article 12

Invasive alien species of Member State concern

1 Member States may establish a national list of invasive alien species of Member State concern. For those invasive alien species, Member States may apply, in their territory, measures such as those provided for in Articles 7, 8, 13 to 17, 19 and 20, as appropriate. Those measures shall be compatible with the TFEU and be notified to the Commission in accordance with Union law.

2 Member States shall inform the Commission and the other Member States of the species they consider to be invasive alien species of Member State concern and of the measures applied in accordance with paragraph 1.

Article 13

Action plans on the pathways of invasive alien species

1 Member States shall, within 18 months of the adoption of the Union list carry out a comprehensive analysis of the pathways of unintentional introduction and spread of invasive alien species of Union concern at least in their territory, as well as in their marine waters as defined in point (1) of Article 3 of Directive 2008/56/EC, and identify the pathways which require priority action ('priority pathways') because of the volume of species or of the potential damage caused by the species entering the Union through those pathways.

2 Within three years of the adoption of the Union list, each Member State shall establish and implement one single action plan or a set of action plans to address the priority pathways it has identified pursuant to paragraph 1.

Action plans shall include timetables for action and shall describe the measures to be adopted and, as appropriate, voluntary actions and codes of good practice, to address the priority pathways and to prevent the unintentional introduction and spread of invasive alien species into or within the Union.

3 Member States shall ensure coordination with the aim of establishing one single action plan or a set of action plans coordinated at the appropriate regional level in accordance with Article 22(1). Where such regional action plans are not established, Member States shall establish and implement action plans for their territory and as far as possible coordinated at the appropriate regional level.

4 The action plans referred to in paragraph 2 of this Article shall include, in particular, measures based on an analysis of costs and benefits, in order to:

(a) raise awareness;
(b) minimise contamination of goods, commodities, vehicles and equipment by specimens of invasive alien species, including measures to tackle transportation of invasive alien species from third countries;
(c) ensure appropriate checks at the Union borders, other than the official controls pursuant to Article 15.

5 The action plans established in accordance with paragraph 2 shall be transmitted to the Commission without delay. Member States shall review their action plans and transmit them to the Commission at least every six years.

Chapter III Early detection and rapid eradication

Article 14

Surveillance system

1 Within 18 months of the adoption of the Union list, Member States shall establish a surveillance system of invasive alien species of Union concern, or include it in their existing system, which collects and records data on the occurrence in the environment of invasive alien species by survey, monitoring or other procedures to prevent the spread of invasive alien species into or within the Union.

2 The surveillance system referred to in paragraph 1 of this Article shall:

(a) cover the territory, including marine territorial waters, of the Member States to determine the presence and distribution of new as well as already established invasive alien species of Union concern;
(b) be sufficiently dynamic to detect rapidly the appearance in the environment of the territory or part of the territory of a Member State of any invasive alien species of Union concern, whose presence was previously unknown;

(c) build upon, be compatible with, and avoid duplication of relevant provisions for assessment and monitoring laid down by Union law or under international agreements and make use of the information provided by the existing systems of surveillance and monitoring set out in Article 11 of Directive 92/43/EEC, Article 8 of Directive 2000/60/EC and Article 11 of Directive 2008/56/EC;
(d) take into account the relevant transboundary impact and transboundary features, to the extent possible.

Article 15

Official controls

1 By 2 January 2016, Member States shall have in place fully functioning structures to carry out the official controls necessary to prevent the intentional introduction into the Union of invasive alien species of Union concern. Those official controls shall apply to the categories of goods falling within the Combined Nomenclature codes to which a reference is made in the Union list, pursuant to Article 4(5).

2 Competent authorities shall carry out the appropriate risk-based controls to the goods mentioned in paragraph 1 of this Article verifying that:

(a) they are not on the Union list; or
(b) they are covered by a valid permit as referred to in Article 8.

3 The controls referred to in paragraph 2 of this Article, consisting of documentary, identity and where necessary, physical checks, shall take place when goods referred to in paragraph 1 of this Article are brought into the Union. Where Union law on official controls already provides for specific official controls at border entities in accordance with Regulation (EC) No 882/2004 and Directives 91/496/EEC and 97/78/EC or at points of entry in accordance with Directive 2000/29/EC, for categories of goods referred to in paragraph 1 of this Article, Member States shall confer the responsibility of carrying out the controls referred to in paragraph 2 of this Article to the competent authorities tasked with those controls in accordance with Article 4 of Regulation (EC) No 882/2004 or with point (g) of Article 2(1) of Directive 2000/29/EC.

4 The handling in free zones or free warehouses and the placing of goods referred to in paragraph 1 under the customs procedures of release for free circulation, transit, customs warehousing, inward processing, processing under customs control and temporary admission shall be subject to the declaration to the customs authorities of:

(a) the relevant entry document duly completed by the competent authorities referred to in paragraph 3 of this Article attesting that the conditions referred to in paragraph 2 of this Article are met, in cases where the controls have been carried out at border entities in accordance with Regulation (EC) No 882/2004 and Directives 91/496/EEC and 97/78/EC or at points of entry in accordance with point (j) of Article 2(1) of Directive 2000/29/EC. The customs procedure indicated therein shall be followed; or

(b) where goods are not subject to official controls according to Union law, other documentary evidence that the controls have been carried out with satisfactory results and the subsequent entry document.

Those documents may also be submitted electronically.

5 If the controls establish non-compliance with this Regulation:

(a) customs authorities shall suspend the placing under a customs procedure or detain the goods;
(b) competent authorities referred to in paragraph 3 shall detain the goods.

Where goods are detained, they shall be entrusted to the competent authority in charge of applying this Regulation. That authority shall act in accordance with national legislation. Member States may delegate specific functions to other authorities.

6 Costs incurred while the verification is carried out and those arising from any non-compliance shall be at the expense of the natural or legal person within the Union who brought the goods into the Union, except where the Member State concerned determines otherwise.

7 Member States shall put in place procedures to ensure the exchange of relevant information and the efficient and effective coordination and cooperation between all authorities involved for the verification referred to in paragraph 2.

8 Based on best practices, the Commission, together with all Member States, shall develop guidelines and training programmes to facilitate the identification and detection of invasive alien species of Union concern and the performance of efficient and effective controls.

9 Where permits have been issued in accordance with Article 8, reference to a valid permit covering the declared goods shall be made in the customs declaration or relevant notifications to the border entity.

Article 16

Early detection notifications

1 Member States shall use the surveillance system established in accordance with Article 14 and the information collected at official controls provided for by Article 15 to confirm early detection of the introduction or presence of invasive alien species of Union concern.

2 Member States shall without delay notify the Commission, in writing, of the early detection of the introduction or presence of invasive alien

species of Union concern and inform the other Member States, in particular of:

(a) the appearance on their territory or part of their territory of any species included on the Union list whose presence was previously unknown in their territory or in part of their territory;
(b) the re-appearance on their territory or part of their territory of any species included on the Union list after it has been reported as eradicated.

Article 17

Rapid eradication at an early stage of invasion

1 After early detection and within three months after the transmission of the early detection notification referred to in Article 16, Member States shall apply eradication measures and notify those measures to the Commission and inform the other Member States.
2 When applying eradication measures, Member States shall ensure that the methods used are effective in achieving the complete and permanent removal of the population of the invasive alien species concerned, with due regard to human health and the environment, especially non-targeted species and their habitats, and ensuring that animals are spared any avoidable pain, distress or suffering.
3 Member States shall monitor the effectiveness of the eradication. Member States may use the surveillance system provided for in Article 14 to this effect. The monitoring shall also assess the impact on non-targeted species, as appropriate.
4 Member States shall inform the Commission of the effectiveness of the measures taken and notify the Commission when a population of an invasive alien species of Union concern has been eradicated. They shall also provide that information to other Member States.

Article 18

Derogations from the obligation of rapid eradication

1 A Member State may, based on robust scientific evidence, decide, within two months of the detection of an invasive alien species referred to in Article 16, not to apply eradication measures if at least one of the following conditions is met:

(a) eradication is demonstrated to be technically unfeasible because the eradication methods available cannot be applied in the environment where the invasive alien species is established;
(b) a cost-benefit analysis demonstrates on the basis of the available data with reasonable certainty that the costs will, in the long

term, be exceptionally high and disproportionate to the benefits of eradication;

(c) eradication methods are not available or are available but have very serious adverse impact on human health, the environment or other species.

The Member State concerned shall without delay notify the Commission of its decision in writing. The notification shall be accompanied by all the evidence referred to in points (a), (b) and (c) of the first subparagraph.

2 The Commission may decide, by means of implementing acts, to reject the decision notified in accordance with the second subparagraph of paragraph 1 where the conditions set out therein are not met.

3 Those implementing acts shall be adopted in accordance with the examination procedure referred to in Article 27(2). The draft implementing acts shall be submitted to the Committee referred to in Article 27(1) within two months of receipt of the Member State's notification.

4 Member States shall ensure that containment measures are in place to avoid further spread of the invasive alien species to other Member States when, pursuant to paragraph 1, no eradication measures are applied.

5 Where the Commission rejects a decision notified in accordance with the second subparagraph of paragraph 1 of this Article, the Member State concerned shall apply the eradication measures referred to in Article 17 without delay.

6 Where the Commission does not reject a decision notified in accordance with the second subparagraph of paragraph 1 of this Article, the invasive alien species shall be subject to the management measures referred to in Article 19.

Chapter IV Management of invasive alien species that are widely spread

Article 19

Management measures

1 Within 18 months of an invasive alien species being included on the Union list, Member States shall have in place effective management measures for those invasive alien species of Union concern which the Member States have found to be widely spread on their territory, so that their impact on biodiversity, the related ecosystem services, and, where applicable, on human health or the economy are minimised.

Those management measures shall be proportionate to the impact on the environment and appropriate to the specific circumstances of the

Member States, be based on an analysis of costs and benefits and also include, as far as is feasible, the restoration measures referred to in Article 20. They shall be prioritised based on the risk evaluation and their cost effectiveness.

2 The management measures shall consist of lethal or non-lethal physical, chemical or biological actions aimed at the eradication, population control or containment of a population of an invasive alien species. Where appropriate, management measures shall include actions applied to the receiving ecosystem aimed at increasing its resilience to current and future invasions. The commercial use of already established invasive alien species may be temporarily allowed as part of the management measures aimed at their eradication, population control or containment, under strict justification and provided that all appropriate controls are in place to avoid any further spread.

3 When applying management measures and selecting methods to be used, Member States shall have due regard to human health and the environment, especially non-targeted species and their habitats, and shall ensure that, when animals are targeted, they are spared any avoidable pain, distress or suffering, without compromising the effectiveness of the management measures.

4 The surveillance system provided for in Article 14 shall be designed and used to monitor the effectiveness of eradication, population control or containment measures in minimising the impact on biodiversity, the related ecosystems services and, where applicable, on human health or the economy. The monitoring shall also assess the impact on non-targeted species, as appropriate.

5 Where there is a significant risk that an invasive alien species of Union concern will spread to another Member State, the Member States in which that species is present shall immediately notify the other Member States and the Commission. Where appropriate, the Member States concerned shall establish jointly agreed management measures. Where third countries may also be affected by the spread, the Member State affected shall endeavour to inform the third countries concerned.

Article 20

Restoration of the damaged ecosystems

1 Member States shall carry out appropriate restoration measures to assist the recovery of an ecosystem that has been degraded, damaged, or destroyed by invasive alien species of Union concern unless a cost-benefit analysis demonstrates, on the basis of the available data and with reasonable certainty, that the costs of those measures will be high and disproportionate to the benefits of restoration.

2 The restoration measures referred to in paragraph 1 shall include at least the following:

(a) measures to increase the ability of an ecosystem exposed to disturbance caused by the presence of invasive alien species of Union concern to resist, absorb, accommodate to and recover from the effects of disturbance;
(b) measures to support the prevention of reinvasion following an eradication campaign.

Chapter V Horizontal provisions

Article 21

Costs recovery

In accordance with the polluter pays principle and without prejudice to Directive 2004/35/EC of the European Parliament and of the Council[23], Member States shall aim to recover the costs of the measures needed to prevent, minimise or mitigate the adverse impact of invasive alien species, including environmental and resources costs as well as the restoration cost.

Article 22

Cooperation and coordination

1 Member States shall, when complying with their obligations under this Regulation, make every effort to ensure close coordination with all Member States concerned and, where practical and appropriate, use existing structures arising from regional or international agreements. In particular, Member States concerned shall endeavour to ensure coordination with other Member States that share:

(a) the same marine subregions in accordance with Article 4(2) of Directive 2008/56/EC, regarding marine species;
(b) the same biogeographical region in accordance with point (iii) of point (c) of Article 1 of Directive 92/43/EEC, regarding non-marine species;
(c) the same borders;
(d) the same river basin in accordance with point (13) of Article 2 of Directive 2000/60/EC, regarding fresh water species; or
(e) any other common concern.

At the request of the Member States involved, the Commission shall act to facilitate the coordination.

2 Member States shall, when complying with their obligations under this Regulation, endeavour to cooperate with third countries, as appropriate,

including by using existing structures arising from regional or international agreements, for the purpose of meeting the objectives of this Regulation.

3 Member States may also apply provisions, such as those referred to in paragraph 1 of this Article, to ensure coordination and cooperation with other relevant Member States as regards invasive alien species of Member State concern identified in national lists adopted in accordance with Article 12(1). Member States may also establish mechanisms for cooperation at the appropriate level for those invasive alien species. Such mechanisms may include exchange of information and data, action plans on pathways and exchange of best practice on management, control and eradication of invasive alien species, early warning systems and programmes related to public awareness or education.

Article 23

More stringent national rules

Member States may maintain or lay down more stringent national rules with the aim of preventing the introduction, establishment and spread of invasive alien species. Those measures shall be compatible with the TFEU and be notified to the Commission in accordance with Union law.

Chapter VI Final provisions

Article 24

Reporting and review

1 By 1 June 2019, and every six years thereafter, Member States shall update and transmit to the Commission the following:

(a) a description, or an updated version thereof, of the surveillance system pursuant to Article 14 and of the official control system on alien species entering the Union pursuant to Article 15;
(b) the distribution of the invasive alien species of Union concern or regional concern in accordance with Article 11(2) present in their territory, including information regarding migratory or reproductive patterns;
(c) information about the species considered as invasive alien species of Member State concern pursuant to Article 12(2);
(d) the action plans referred to in Article 13(2);
(e) aggregated information covering the entire national territory on the eradication measures taken in accordance with Article 17, the management measures undertaken in accordance with Article 19, their effectiveness, and their impact on non-targeted species;

(f) the number of the permits referred to in Article 8 and the purpose for which they were issued;
(g) measures taken to inform the public about the presence of an invasive alien species and any actions that citizens have been requested to take;
(h) the inspections required under Article 8(8); and
(i) information on the cost of action undertaken to comply with this Regulation, when available.

2 By 5 November 2015, Member States shall notify the Commission and inform the other Member States of the competent authorities in charge of applying this Regulation.

3 By 1 June 2021, the Commission shall review the application of this Regulation including the Union list, the action plans referred to in Article 13(2), the surveillance system, customs controls, eradication obligation and management obligations, and submit a report to the European Parliament and to the Council, which may be accompanied by legislative proposals for the amendment of this Regulation, including changes to the Union list. That review shall also examine the effectiveness of the implementing provisions on invasive alien species of regional concern, the need for and the feasibility of, including species native to the Union in the Union list and whether further harmonisation is needed to increase the effectiveness of the action plans and measures undertaken by the Member States.

4 The Commission shall, by means of implementing acts, specify the technical formats for reporting in order to simplify and streamline reporting obligations for the Member States in relation to the information pursuant to paragraph 1 of this Article. Those implementing acts shall be adopted in accordance with the examination procedure referred to in Article 27(2).

Article 25

Information support system

1 The Commission shall progressively establish an information support system necessary to facilitate the application of this Regulation.

2 By 2 January 2016 that system shall include a data support mechanism interconnecting existing data systems on invasive alien species, paying particular attention to information on the invasive alien species of Union concern, so as to facilitate the reporting pursuant to Article 24.

The data support mechanism referred to in the first subparagraph shall become a tool to assist the Commission and the Member States in handling the relevant notifications required by Article 16(2).

3 By 2 January 2019, the data support mechanism referred to in paragraph 2 shall become a mechanism for exchanging information on other aspects of the application of this Regulation.

It may also include information on invasive alien species of Member State concern, and on pathways, risk assessment, management and eradication measures, when available.

Article 26

Public participation

Where action plans are being established pursuant to Article 13 of this Regulation and where management measures are put in place pursuant to Article 19 of this Regulation, Member States shall ensure that the public is given early and effective opportunities to participate in their preparation, modification or review, using the arrangements already determined by the Member States in accordance with the second subparagraph of Article 2(3) of Directive 2003/35/EC.

Article 27

Committee

1 The Commission shall be assisted by a committee. That committee shall be a committee within the meaning of Regulation (EU) No 182/2011 and may be assisted in its tasks by the scientific forum referred to in Article 28.
2 Where reference is made to this paragraph, Article 5 of Regulation (EU) No 182/2011 shall apply.
3 Where the committee delivers no opinion, the Commission shall not adopt the draft implementing act and the third subparagraph of Article 5(4) of Regulation (EU) No 182/2011 shall apply.

Article 28

Scientific forum

The Commission shall ensure the participation of representatives of the scientific community appointed by the Member States in providing advice on any scientific question related to the application of this Regulation, in particular as regards Articles 4, 5, 10 and 18. Those representatives shall meet in a scientific forum. The rules of procedure of that forum shall be established by the Commission.

Article 29

Exercise of the delegation

1 The power to adopt delegated acts is conferred on the Commission subject to the conditions laid down in this Article.

2 The power to adopt delegated acts referred to in Article 5(3) shall be conferred on the Commission for a period of five years from 1 January 2015. The Commission shall draw up a report in respect of the delegation of power not later than nine months before the end of the five-year period. The delegation of power shall be tacitly extended for periods of an identical duration unless the European Parliament or the Council opposes such extension not later than three months before the end of each period.

3 The delegation of power referred to in Article 5(3) may be revoked at any time by the European Parliament or by the Council. A decision to revoke shall put an end to the delegation of the power specified in that decision. It shall take effect the day following the publication of the decision in the *Official Journal of the European Union* or at a later date specified therein. It shall not affect the validity of any delegated act already in force.

4 As soon as it adopts a delegated act, the Commission shall notify it simultaneously to the European Parliament and to the Council.

5 A delegated act adopted pursuant to Article 5(3) shall enter into force only if no objection has been expressed either by the European Parliament or the Council within a period of two months of notification of that act to the European Parliament and the Council or if, before the expiry period, the European Parliament and the Council have both informed the Commission that they will not object. That period shall be extended by two months at the initiative of the European Parliament or of the Council.

Article 30

Penalties

1 Member States shall lay down the provisions on penalties applicable to infringements of this Regulation. Member States shall take all the necessary measures to ensure that they are applied.

2 The penalties provided for shall be effective, proportionate and dissuasive.

3 The penalties provided may include, inter alia:

(a) fines;
(b) seizure of the non-compliant invasive alien species of Union concern;
(c) immediate suspension or withdrawal of a permit issued in accordance with Article 8.

4 By 2 January 2016, Member States shall communicate to the Commission the provisions referred to in paragraph 1, and any subsequent amendments without delay.

Article 31

Transitional provisions for non-commercial owners

1 By way of derogation from points (b) and (d) of Article 7(1), owners of companion animals not kept for commercial purposes that belong to the

invasive alien species included on the Union list shall be allowed to keep them until the end of the animals' natural life, provided the following conditions are met:

(a) the animals were kept before their inclusion on the Union list;
(b) the animals are kept in contained holding and all appropriate measures are put in place to ensure that reproduction or escape are not possible.

2 Competent authorities shall take all reasonable steps to inform non-commercial owners of the risks posed by keeping the animals referred to in paragraph 1 and of the measures to be taken to minimise the risk of reproducing and escaping through awareness-raising and education programmes organised by Member States.
3 Non-commercial owners who cannot ensure that the conditions set out in paragraph 1 are met, shall not be permitted to keep the animals concerned. Member States may offer them the possibility of having their animals taken from them. Where this occurs, due regard to animal welfare shall be given.
4 The animals referred to in paragraph 3 of this Article may be kept by the establishments referred to in Article 8 or in facilities established by Member States for that purpose.

Article 32

Transitional provisions for commercial stocks

1 Keepers of a commercial stock of specimens of invasive alien species acquired before their inclusion on the Union list shall be allowed up to two years after inclusion of the species on that list to keep and transport live specimens or reproducible parts of those species in order to sell or transfer them to the research or ex-situ conservation establishments and for the purposes of medicinal activities referred to in Article 8, provided that the specimens are kept and transported in contained holding and all appropriate measures are put in place to ensure that reproduction or escape are not possible; or in order to slaughter or humanely cull those specimens to exhaust their stock.
2 The sale or transfer of live specimens to non-commercial users shall be allowed for one year after inclusion of the species on the Union list provided that the specimens are kept and transported in contained holding and all appropriate measures are put in place to ensure that reproduction or escape are not possible.
3 Where a permit has been issued in accordance with Article 6 of Regulation (EC) No 708/2007 for an aquaculture species that is subsequently included on the Union list, and the duration of the permit exceeds the period referred to in paragraph 1 of this Article, the Member State shall withdraw the permit in accordance with Article 12 of Regulation (EC) No 708/2007 by the end of the period referred to in paragraph 1 of this Article.

Article 33

Entry into force

This Regulation shall enter into force on 1 January 2015.

This Regulation shall be binding in its entirety and directly applicable in all Member States.

Done at Strasbourg, 22 October 2014.

For the European Parliament
The President
M. SCHULZ
For the Council
The President
B. DELLA VEDOVA

Notes

1 *OJ C 177, 11.6.2014, p. 84.*
2 Position of the European Parliament of 16 April 2014 (not yet published in the Official Journal) and decision of the Council of 29 September 2014.
3 Council Decision 93/626/EEC of 25 October 1993 concerning the conclusion of the Convention on Biological Diversity (*OJ L 309, 13.12.1993, p. 1*).
4 Council Decision 82/72/EEC of 3 December 1981 concerning the conclusion of the Convention on the conservation of European wildlife and natural habitats (*OJ L 38, 10.2.1982, p. 1*).
5 Directive 2000/60/EC of the European Parliament and of the Council of 23 October 2000 establishing a framework for Community action in the field of water policy (*OJ L 327, 22.12.2000, p. 1*).
6 Directive 2008/56/EC of the European Parliament and of the Council of 17 June 2008 establishing a framework for community action in the field of marine environmental policy (Marine Strategy Framework Directive) (*OJ L 164, 25.6.2008, p. 19*).
7 Directive 2009/147/EC of the European Parliament and of the Council of 30 November 2009 on the conservation of wild birds (*OJ L 20, 26.1.2010, p. 7*).
8 Council Directive 92/43/EEC of 21 May 1992 on the conservation of natural habitats and of wild fauna and flora (*OJ L 206, 22.7.1992, p. 7*).
9 Council Directive 2000/29/EC of 8 May 2000 on protective measures against the introduction into the Community of organisms harmful to plants or plant products and against their spread within the Community (*OJ L 169, 10.7.2000, p. 1*).
10 Directive 2001/18/EC of the European Parliament and of the Council of 12 March 2001 on the deliberate release into the environment of genetically modified organisms and repealing Council Directive 90/220/EEC (*OJ L 106, 17.4.2001, p. 1*).
11 Regulation (EC) No 1107/2009 of the European Parliament and of the Council of 21 October 2009 concerning the placing of plant protection products on the market and repealing Council Directives 79/117/EEC and 91/414/EEC (*OJ L 309, 24.11.2009, p. 1*).
12 Regulation (EU) No 528/2012 of the European Parliament and of the Council of 22 May 2012 concerning the making available on the market and use of biocidal products (*OJ L 167, 27.6.2012, p. 1*).

13 Council Regulation (EC) No 708/2007 of 11 June 2007 concerning use of alien and locally absent species in aquaculture (*OJ L 168, 28.6.2007, p. 1*).

14 Council Regulation (EC) No 338/97 of 9 December 1996 on the protection of species of wild fauna and flora by regulating trade therein (*OJ L 61, 3.3.1997, p. 1*).

15 European Council Decision 2010/718/EU of 29 October 2010 amending the status with regard to the European Union of the island of Saint-Barthélemy (*OJ L 325, 9.12.2010, p. 4*).

16 European Council Decision 2012/419/EU of 11 July 2012 amending the status of Mayotte with regard to the European Union (*OJ L 204, 31.7.2012, p. 131*).

17 Regulation (EC) No 882/2004 of the European Parliament and of the Council of 29 April 2004 on official controls performed to ensure the verification of compliance with feed and food law, animal health and animal welfare rules (*OJ L 165, 30.4.2004, p. 1*).

18 Council Directive 91/496/EEC of 15 July 1991 laying down the principles governing the organization of veterinary checks on animals entering the Community from third countries and amending Directives 89/662/EEC, 90/425/EEC and 90/675/EEC (*OJ L 268, 24.9.1991, p. 56*).

19 Council Directive 97/78/EC of 18 December 1997 laying down the principles governing the organisation of veterinary checks on products entering the Community from third countries (*OJ L 24, 30.1.1998, p. 9*).

20 Directive 2003/35/EC of the European Parliament and of the Council of 26 May 2003 providing for public participation in respect of the drawing up of certain plans and programmes relating to the environment and amending with regard to public participation and access to justice Council Directives 85/337/EEC and 96/61/EC (*OJ L 156, 25.6.2003, p. 17*).

21 Regulation (EU) No 182/2011 of the European Parliament and of the Council of 16 February 2011 laying down the rules and general principles concerning mechanisms for control by the Member States of the Commission's exercise of implementing powers (*OJ L 55, 28.2.2011, p. 13*).

22 Council Regulation (EEC) No 2658/87 of 23 July 1987 on the tariff and statistical nomenclature and on the Common Customs Tariff (*OJ L 256, 7.9.1987, p. 1*).

23 Directive 2004/35/EC of the European Parliament and of the Council of 21 April 2004 on environmental liability with regard to the prevention and remedying of environmental damage (*OJ L 143, 30.4.2004, p. 56*).

Index

www.ingramcontent.com/pod-product-compliance
Ingram Content Group UK Ltd.
Pitfield, Milton Keynes, MK11 3LW, UK
UKHW011015180926
475701UK00004B/757
* 9 7 8 0 3 6 7 8 8 6 7 4 5 *